D0849340

The Corpus of
Clandestine Literature
in France, 1769–1789

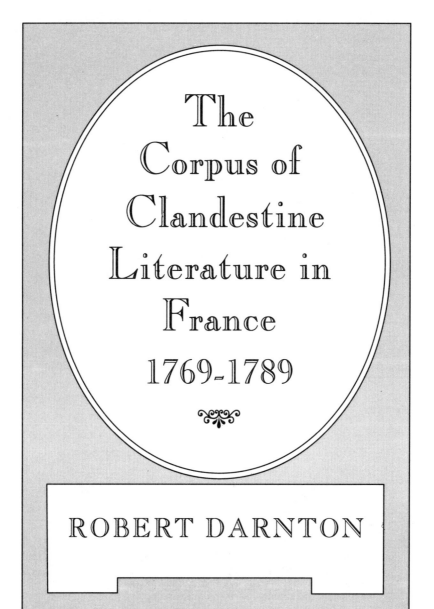

The Corpus of Clandestine Literature in France

1769-1789

ROBERT DARNTON

W. W. Norton & Company   New York London

The text of this book is composed in Garamond with the display set in Caslon Open Face and Cochin Italic. Composition and manufacturing by The Maple-Vail Book Manufacturing Group.
Book design by Charlotte Staub

Library of Congress Cataloging-in-Publication Data

Darnton, Robert.
    The corpus of clandestine literature in France, 1769–1789 / Robert
Darton.
      p.   cm.
    Companion volume to the author's The forbidden bestsellers of pre-
revolutionary france.
    1. French literature—18th century—History and criticism.
2. Underground literature—Publishing—France—History—18th
century. 3. Underground literature—France—History and criticism.
4. Literature publishing—France—History—18th century. I. Title.
PQ265.D367 1995
840.9'005—dc20   94-24179
    ISBN 0-393-03745-2

W. W. Norton & Company, Inc., 500 Fifth Avenue, New York, N.Y. 10110
W. W. Norton & Company Ltd., 10 Coptic Street, London WC1A 1PU

1 2 3 4 5 6 7 8 9 0

Contents

I.

A BASIC CHECKLIST   1

Introduction 3

Bibliographic Sources 9

720 Forbidden Books 11

II.

STATISTICS OF DEMAND   189

Best-Sellers 191

Best-Selling Authors 198

Genres 201

III.

PROFILES OF THE TRADE   209

IV.

CLANDESTINE CATALOGUES   229

Publishers in Geneva, Lausanne, and Bern 231

A Clandestine Catalogue of the STN 235

V.

POLICE RAIDS   249

VI.

CONFISCATIONS IN THE PARIS CUSTOMS   255

The Corpus of
Clandestine Literature
in France,
1769–1789,

is the companion volume
to Robert Darnton's

The
Forbidden Best-Sellers of
Pre-Revolutionary
France,

also published by
W. W. Norton & Company

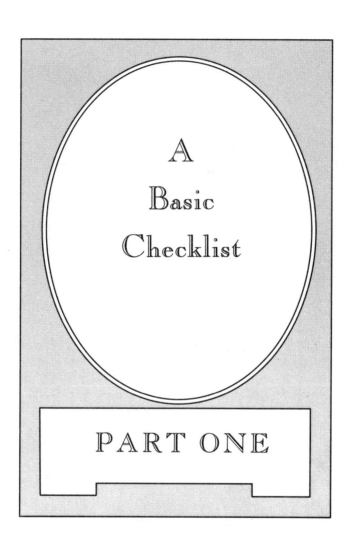

A

Basic

Checklist

PART ONE

Introduction

THE FOLLOWING LIST provides a guide to the literature that circulated outside the law in France from 1769 to 1789. Although it does not cover every book sold "under the cloak" *(sous le manteau)* during those years, it offers a fairly complete view of the entire corpus of illegal literature, 720 works in all; and it indicates the relative importance of the demand for most of those books, the 457 ordered on a large scale by booksellers who drew their stock from the Société typographique de Neuchâtel, (STN).

In order to complete the picture that can be sketched from the archives of the STN and to correct for any bias inherent in those documents, information has been culled from three other sources: publishers' catalogues of their illegal stock (1772–80); inventories of books seized in police raids on bookshops (1773–83); and registers of books confiscated in the Paris Customs (1771–89). Each of these sources has peculiar strengths and weaknesses, and none is exhaustive in itself. When taken together, however, they provide an overview of the whole range of forbidden books in pre-Revolutionary France.

Nearly all the titles generated by the manuscript sources have been identified, but it has not been possible to examine a first edition of each work and to trace the metamorphoses of the text through subsequent editions. Therefore the list should not be taken as a descriptive bibliography. For the same reason and in the interest of consistency, spelling and punctuation, including the use

3

of ampersands and other eighteenth-century typographical peculiarities, have been made to conform to modern usage. The places and dates of publication appear as on the originals, despite the use of obvious false addresses such as "Rome" and "Philadelphie," because in many cases—"Londres," "Cologne"—one cannot know for sure whether the address is false or not.

Most of this information—and further details about attributions of authorship, sources of translations, variations in titles, and probable dates of first editions—comes from the works cited under Bibliographic Sources (pp. 9–10). Unfortunately, the bibliographies vary in reliability and precision, and they sometimes contradict one another. To conduct a physical examination of all the editions of all the illegal books would have taken many years or even lifetimes. I have had to settle for the best information available from the standard sources. They generally agree on the place and date of the first editions, but provide wildly different accounts of subsequent editions. By comparing and combining their entries, however, one can make at least some minimal estimates of the number of editions of a given book before 1789; and those estimates can be helpful in assessing the demand registered in the papers of the STN. So the title for each book is followed by some modest information about the editions.

Attributions of authorship pose additional problems, because most illegal works appeared anonymously or even with malicious false fronts: thus d'Holbach, or someone in his circle, presented *Théologie portative* as "par M. l'abbé Bernier, licencié en théologie," and the title page of *Les Questions de Zapata* attributed Voltaire's impieties to one of France's most orthodox theologians, "le sieur Tamponet, docteur de Sorbonne." I have put the names of the probable authors of anonymous works in square brackets, followed by question marks in doubtful or disputed cases.

The books are listed alphabetically by title. Each entry includes information grouped under a standard set of rubrics, which occur in the same sequence.

Rubric A shows the demand for the book among the customers of the STN—that is, the sampling of booksellers whose orders have been compiled from the accounts and the commercial correspondence in the archives at Neuchâtel. The first number after each bookseller's name represents the total number of copies he ordered; the second number, set off by parentheses, represents the number of orders that he placed. One can therefore measure the demand for a book in two ways, studying the repetition of orders as a check against the statistics of copies per title. I also have plotted the size and incidence of orders over time, so that the demand for each book can be studied week by week. That information proved to be too bulky to be included here, but I have included enough data on the geographical origins of the orders for one to trace diffusion patterns of works and genres and to reconstruct the trade of individual booksellers. Because the STN succeeded in filling the vast majority of the orders it received, the statistics show supply as well as demand. Although they do not cover sales at the retail level, they indicate what illegal books went into bookshops everywhere in France. Booksellers were generally cautious in their ordering. As they could not return unsold copies, they usually ordered in small quantities, often after arranging sales in advance with their clients. The STN statistics therefore provide a fairly accurate picture of the books that actually reached readers throughout the kingdom during the twenty years before the Revolution.

In order to make the picture as complete as possible and to bring out the different shades within it, the booksellers have been arranged in groups, which always appear in the same sequence: first, the twelve "major" provincial dealers of the sample, i.e., those who ordered in sufficient volume for one to see a clear pattern in their trade; then the eighteen booksellers who, taken as a group, indicate the general pattern of the trade in Lorraine; next, seven Parisian and five Lyonnais booksellers who represent the trade in their cities; and four *colporteurs* (book peddlers) who ordered enough books to indicate the character of peddling in the Loire Valley. The statistics from these five subcategories have been aggregated to form a subtotal that represents the STN's trade with its regular customers. The statistics from the other subcategory, seventeen of the STN's "minor" customers, have been compiled separately, because the STN did not trade enough with them for one to have a clear view of their individual businesses. When taken together, however, they provide a general indication of the demand for the book in other parts of the kingdom. The total for each book indicates its importance within the sample as a whole—

and the sample, I believe, is large enough and diverse enough to represent the entire body of illegal literature in pre-Revolutionary France. It can be summarized as follows:

Major and minor dealers combined:
    Total number of books ordered   28,212
    Total number of orders   3,266

Major dealers:
    Total number of books ordered   24,435
    Total number of orders   2,635

Minor dealers:
    Total number of books ordered   3,777
    Total number of orders   631

Twenty-three (5 percent) of the 457 works ordered from the STN have not been identified, either because they are so obscure that they do not appear in any bibliography or because the phrasing in the manuscript source is so inaccurate or ambiguous that it cannot be reliably connected with a known work. None of the unidentified books was much in demand. All of them are preceded on the list by an asterisk.

Rubrics B,C, and D correspond to the three other sources that were studied in order to widen the sample and to test the representativeness of the STN material. They generated 263 additional titles.

Rubric B covers 261 works that appear in the clandestine catalogues of forbidden books produced by six different publishers. The existence of such catalogues had not been suspected before they turned up in the papers of the STN. And because they contain valuable information about the price, format, and illustrations of particular editions, their bibliographical remarks have been transcribed as they appear in the original texts.

Rubric C covers 300 works that were listed in accounts of raids on bookshops by the police. I have found nine such lists from the period of 1769–89 in various Parisian archives and have added to them an inventory of forbidden books kept in the *pilon* (pulping room) of the Bastille. A systematic survey of provincial archives would probably turn up many more documents of this sort, although they are difficult to exploit because they sometimes contain an admixture of legal and illegal works. Having combed through a great many lists, I believe the ten I selected provide an adequate sample of this kind of material. The name of the bookseller in whose shop the work was confiscated appears after each title.

Rubric D covers 280 works that were confiscated in the Parisian Customs. Fortunately, the syndics of the booksellers' guild and the *inspecteurs de la librairie* distinguished the forbidden books from books that were merely pirated or *non permis* (not strictly legal but inoffensive in the eyes of the authorities) in the registers they kept. The incidence of customs confiscations therefore provides a final indication of what works circulated most widely in the clandestine book trade. In each case the year of the confiscation is given; and if the book was confiscated several times in the same year, the number of confiscations appears in parentheses.

The books ordered from the STN form the core of this list, and with a few exceptions they also represent the main ingredients within the general body of forbidden books. That conclusion is supported by the way in which the STN did business—it tried to make money by satisfying demand, not to push one kind of literature at the expense of another—and also by the statistics, which overlap in a significant pattern:

A. Orders with the STN: 457 titles (the STN list).
B. Publishers' catalogues: 261 titles, of which 175 (67 percent) are on the STN list.
C. Police confiscations: 300 titles, of which 179 (60 percent) are on the STN list.
D. Customs confiscations: 280 titles, of which 167 (60 percent) are on the STN list.

Each of these four sources has provided the material for a separate list, which was used to calculate statistics and then conflated in the following master list of 720 titles. Of them, 66 (9 percent) could not be identified. They seem to have been peripheral works, which were not much in demand.

The list can be read in several ways. In order to estimate the importance of best-sellers, authors, and genres, one should begin with the statistics published at the end of this volume and then work through all the entries. By compiling information from the relevant rubrics, one can study the stocking, pricing, and policing of illegal literature. And by analyzing all the information on a particular book, one can form a general idea of its place within the corpus as a whole.

For example, *L'Arrétin,* the forty-third book on the list, looks like a best-seller according to several different standards of measurement, even though it and its author, Henri-Joseph Du Laurens (?), have been nearly forgotten today. The major and minor dealers who traded with the STN ordered a great many copies (512, the seventh highest in the samples from the STN's accounts), and ordered them repeatedly (29 times, sixteenth in the statistics of the most frequent orders). The text reappeared in at least thirteen editions and under two new titles. It figures on four of the six catalogues of forbidden books, at prices varying from 1 livre, 4 sous to 6 livres. It shows up on six of the ten lists of books confiscated in police raids, making it one of the five most confiscated books in the sample. And it was seized four times, from 1776 to 1784, in the Paris Customs—a weaker showing, although only 32 books were seized more often. By contrast, *L'Avocat national,* the fiftieth book of the list, appears only one time in one source, the police confiscations. It had a place in the body of illegal literature, but a very minor place. The list therefore provides several ways of situating works within the corpus as a whole. In order to study the dimensions of the entire corpus, the reader should consult the statistics based on the list, which are published in the sections that follow it.

Bibliographic Sources

Barbier, Antoine-Alexandre. *Dictionnaire des ouvrages anonymes, troisième édition, revue et augmentée par MM. Olivier Barbier, René et Paul Billard.* 4 vols. Paris, 1872–79; reprint, Paris, 1964.

Bengesco, Georges. *Voltaire. Bibliographie de ses œuvres.* 4 vols. Paris: Emile Perrin, 1882–85.

Bibliothèque Nationale, Paris. *Catalogue d'ouvrages anonymes* (index cards, unpublished). *Catalogue général des livres imprimés de la Bibliothèque Nationale. Auteurs.* 228 vols. Paris: Imprimerie Nationale, 1897–1979.

Brenner, Clarence D. *A Bibliographical List of Plays in the French Language 1700–1789.* Berkeley, Calif.: University of California Press, 1947.

British Library, London. *General Catalogue of Printed Books.* 263 vols. London: Trustees of the British Museum, 1965–66, and Supplements.

Caillet, Albert-Louis. *Manuel bibliographique des sciences psychiques ou occultes.* 4 vols. Paris: Lucien Dorbon, 1913.

Catalogue de l'histoire de France. Vol. II. Paris: Didot, 1855.

Cioranescu, Alexandre. *Bibliographie de la littérature française du dix-huitième siècle.* 3 vols. Paris: Centre National de la Recherche Scientifique, 1969.

Conlon, Pierre M. *Le Siecle des lumieres: bibliographie chronologique.* Geneva: Librairie Droz, 1983– .

Dawson, Robert L. *Additions to the Bibliographies of French Prose Fiction 1618–1806.* Oxford: The Voltaire Foundation (Studies on Voltaire and the Eighteenth Century, 236), 1985.

Fesch, Paul. *Bibliographie de la Franc-Maçonnerie et des sociétés secrètes.* George Deny, ed. 1910; reprint, Brussels: George A. Deny, 1976.

[Gay, Jules.] *Bibliographie des ouvrages relatifs à l'amour, aux femmes, au mariage et des livres facétieux, pantagruéliques, scatalogiques, satyriques, etc., par M. le C. d'I***.* 4th ed. 4 vols. J. Lemonnyer, ed. Paris: Lemonnyer, 1894–1900.

Index of Prohibited Books, Revised and Edited by Order of His Holiness Pope Pius XI. Rome: Vatican Polyglot Press, 1930.

Jones, S. Paul. *A List of French Prose Fiction from 1700 to 1750.* New York: H. W. Wilson, 1939.

Martin, Angus, Vivienne G. Mylne, and Richard Frautschi. *Bibliographie du genre romanesque français, 1751–1800.* London: Mansell, 1977.

The National Union Catalogue. Pre-1956 Imprints. 754 vols. London: Mansell, 1968–81.

Peignot, Etienne Gabriel. *Dictionnaire critique, littéraire et bibliographique des principaux livres condamnés au feu, supprimés ou censurés.* 2 vols. Paris: Renouard, 1806.

Pia, Pascal. *Les Livres de l'Enfer du XVIème siècle à nos jours.* 2 vols. Paris: C. Coulet et A. Faire, 1978.

Quérard, Joseph-Marie. *La France littéraire.* 12 vols. Paris: Didot, 1827.

————. *Les Supercheries littéraires dévoilées.* 5 vols. Paris: Didot, 1847–53.

Sénelier, Jean. *Bibliographie générale des œuvres de Jean-Jacques Rousseau.* Paris: Centre National de la Recherche Scientifique, 1949.

Vercruysse, Jeroom. *Bibliographie descriptive des écrits du baron d'Holbach.* Paris: Lettres modernes, 1971.

Weil, Françoise. *L'Interdiction du roman et de la librairie, 1728–1750.* Paris: Aux Amateurs des Livres, 1986.

Weller, Emil. *Die falschen und fingierten Druckorte.* 2 vols. Leipzig: Wilhelm Engelmann, 1864.

720 Forbidden Books

1. *A.B.C. (1'), dialogue curieux, traduit de l'anglais de M. Huet.*
   [François-Marie Arouet de Voltaire.] London, 1762 (actually
   1768, according to Cioranescu and Bengesco). At least 4
   other editions by 1776.
   A. STN
   Major Dealers: Malherbe, Loudun 6 (1);
   Letourmy, Orléans 10 (2); Blouet,
   Rennes 2 (1).
   Lorraine: Bergue, Thionville 6 (1).   51   (9)
   Lyon: Flandin 12 (1); Barret 6 (1).
   Paris: Prévost 6 (1); Barré 3 (1).

   Minor Dealers: Malassis, Nantes 4 (1):
   Billault, Tours 3 (1); Caldesaigues,   11   (3)
   Marseille 4 (1).
   _____
   Total: 62   (12)
   B. Catalogues: 2 of 6 lists: (Grasset: "10 s."; Décombaz).

2. *Abrégé de l'histoire ecclésiastique de Fleury, traduit de l'anglais.*
   2 vols. [trans. by Frederick II?] Bern, 1766. At least 1 other
   edition by 1767.
   B. Catalogues: 1 of 6 lists: (Bern: "3 1.").
   C. Police Confiscations: 3 of 10 lists: Stockdorf, Pilon, Prot.

3. *Abrégé du code de la nature.* [Paul-Henri-Dietrich Thiry, baron

d'Holbach?] London, 1770. (Vercruysse cites as a re-edition of last chapter of d'Holbach's *Système de la nature*.)

A. STN

Paris: Barré 3 (1); Prévost 6 (1).	}	9	(2)
Minor Dealers: Billault, Tours 13 (1); Caldesaigues, Marseille 3 (1)	}	16	(2)
	Total:	25	(4)

B. Catalogues: 1 of 6 lists: (Cailler: "par Mirabeau").

4. *Abus (les) dans les cérémonies et dans les mœurs développés par M. L***, auteur du Compère Mathieu, trouvés en manuscrit dans son portefeuille après sa mort.* [Henri-Joseph Du Laurens.] Geneva, 1767. At least 2 other editions by 1788.

A. STN

Major Dealers: Pavie, La Rochelle 12 (1).	}	12	(1)
	Total:	12	(1)

5. *Académie (l') des dames, ou les entretiens galants d'Aloysia.* 2 vols. Trans. by Nicolas Chorier. n.p. (1680). (trans. from *Aloisiae Sigeae Tolentanae Satyra sotadica*, c. 1658.) At least 7 other 18th-century editions by 1788; also as *Aloysia . . .* and as *Le Meursius Français . . .*

A. STN

Major Dealers: Bergeret, Bordeaux 4 (1); Malherbe, Loudun 52 (1); Pavie, La Rochelle 8 (1); Robert et Gauthier, Bourg-en-Bresse 20 (3). *Lorraine:* Bertrand, Thionville 21 (4); Matthieu, Nancy 2 (1). *Lyon:* Baritel 6 (1). *Colporteurs:* Gilles 29 (2); "Troisième" 6 (1).	}	148	(15)
Minor Dealers: Chevrier, Poitiers 1 (1); Habert, Bar-sur-Aube 4 (1); Malassis, Nantes 15 (1)	}	20	(3)
	Total:	168	(18)

B. Catalogues: 3 of 6 lists: (Décombaz: "revue, corrigée & augmentée, 8°. 2 vol. fig. 1775, 12 l."; Chappuis et Didier: "gr. 8°. belle éd. de Holl. ornée de 37 estampes. 13 l." and "2 vol. 12°. fig., 3 l."; Bern: "24 l.").

    C. Police Confiscations: 6 of 10 lists: Pilon, Manoury, Moureau, Prot, Paris, Versailles.

    D. Customs Confiscations: 6 instances: 1771 (2), 1776, 1778, 1781, 1784.

6. *Adieux (les) du duc de Bourgogne et de l'abbé Fénelon, son précepteur, ou dialogue sur les différentes sortes de gouvernements.* [Dieudonné Thiébault.] Douay, 1772. At least 1 other edition by 1788.

    B. Catalogues: 1 of 6 lists: (Bern: "3 1.").

7. *Admirables Secrets (les) d'Albert le Grand, contenant plusieurs traités sur la conception des femmes et les vertus des herbes, des pierres précieuses, etc.* Cologne, 1706. At least 8 other editions by 1785.

    A. STN

Major Dealers: Letourmy, Orléans 3 (1); Malherbe, Loudun 10 (1).		
Lorraine: Chénoux, Lunéville 6 (1); Bertrand, Thionville 2 (1).	27	(5)
Paris: Prévost 6 (1)		
Minor Dealers; Bonnard, Auxerre 9 (2)	9	(2)
Total:	36	(7)

    B. Catalogues: 1 of 6 lists: (Cailler).

8. *Adoption (l'), ou la maçonnerie des dames en trois grades.* [Guillemain de Saint-Victor?] The Hague and Geneva, 1000 700 75 (1775). At least 2 other editions by 1785.

    A. STN

Major Dealers: Charmet, Besançon 18 (2); Letourmy, Orléans 3 (1); Malherbe, Loudun 4 (1); Manoury, Caen 12 (1); Mossy, Marseille 6 (1); Pavie, La Rochelle 69 (4).		
Lorraine: Choppin, Bar-le-Duc 2 (1); Bernard, Lunéville 1 (1); Matthieu, Nancy 2 (1).	131	(16)
Lyon: Cellier 2 (1).		
Paris: Barré 6 (1); Prévost 6 (1).		
Minor Dealers: Billault, Tours 2 (1); Caldesaigues, Marseille 3 (1); Cazin,		

continued

Reims 6 (1); Chevrier, Poitiers 13
(1); Sombert, Châlons-sur-Marne 6
(1)

30   (5)

Total: 161   (21)

9. *Adorateurs (les), ou les louanges de Dieu. Ouvrage unique de M. Imhof, traduit du latin.* [François-Marie Arouet de Voltaire.] Berlin, 1769.
   B. Catalogues: 1 of 6 lists: (Bern: "4 l.").
   C. Police Confiscations: 1 of 10 lists: Pilon.

10. *Affaire des cent—un tableau.* n.p., n.d. (c. 1759).
    D. Customs Confiscations: 1 instance: 1779.

11. *Agrippa. La Philosophie occulte de Henri-Corneille Agrippa, divisée en trois livres et traduite du latin.* 2 vols. [trans. by A. Le Vasseur.] The Hague, 1727. (trans. from works by Heinrich Cornelius Agrippa.)
    B. Catalogues: 1 of 6 lists: (Décombaz: "8°. 2 vol. La Haye, 1555, 18 l.").

12. *Alcoran (l') des Cordeliers, tant en latin qu'en français, ou recueil des plus notables bourdes et blasphèmes impudents de ceux qui ont osé comparer S. François à Jésus-Christ, tiré du grand livre des conformités, jadis composé par frère Barthélemy de Pise, Cordelier en son vivant.* 2 vols. Trans. by Conrad Badius. Amsterdam, 1734. (trans. from a work by Barthélemy Abbizzi de Pise, 1556.)
    A. STN
       Major Dealers: Mauvelain, Troyes 8 (3).

       Total: 8   (3)
       8   (3)

13. *Alcoran des princes destinés au trône.* [Stephano Zannowich or Stjefan Zanovic?] St. Petersburg, 1783.
    D. Customs Confiscations: 1 instance: 1784.

Aloysia. See #5, *Académie (l') des dames. . .*[1]

14. **Ami des hommes.* (Probably *Ami des hommes, ou traité de la*

---

[1] Titles as they appear in sources are cross-referenced to their more common title.

*An asterisk before a title indicates that the work has not been definitively identified.

population. 5 vols. [Victor Riqueti, marquis de Mirabeau, and François Quesnay.] Avignon, 1756–60.)
  D. Customs Confiscations: 1 instance: 1775.

15. *Ami (l') des lois.* [Martin de Marivaux.] Paris, 1775.
  A. STN
      Major Dealers: Letourmy, Orléans 25
        (1); Pavie, La Rochelle 48 (2). } 73 (3)
                              Total: 73 (3)

16. *Amour (l') décent et délicat, ou le beau de la galanterie.* [Claude-Prosper Jolyot de Crébillon, fils.] A la tendresse, chez les Amants, 1760. At least 2 other editions by 1768.
  C. Police Confiscations: 1 of 10 lists: Prot.

17. *Amours (les) d'Anne d'Autriche, épouse de Louis XIII, avec Monsieur le C. de R., le véritable père de Louis XIV, aujourd'hui roi de France, où l'on voit au long comment on s'y prit pour donner un héritier à la couronne, les ressorts qu'on fit jouer pour cela et enfin tout le dénouement de cette comédie.* [Pierre Le Noble?] Cologne, 1692. At least 4 other editions by 1768.
  B. Catalogues: 1 of 6 lists: (Bern: "4 1.").

18. *Amours (les) de Charlot et Toinette, pièce dérobée à V***.* Paris, 1779. At least 1 other edition by 1789.
  A. STN
      Major Dealers: Mauvelain, Troyes 6 (1) } 6 (1)
                              Total: 6 (1)

19. *Amours (les) de Mirtil.* [Claude-Louis-Michel de Sacy.] Constantinople, 1761. At least 1 other edition in 1761.
  B. Customs Confiscations: 1 instance: 1775.

20. *Amours (les) de Sainfroid, jésuite, et d'Eulalie, fille dévote.* The Hague, 1729. At least 3 other editions by 1760.
  B. Catalogues: 1 of 6 lists: (Bern: "3 1.").

21. *Amours (les) de Zéokinizul, roi des Kofirans, ouvrage traduit de l'arabe du voyageur Krinelbol.* [Laurent Angliviel de La Beaumelle?, or Claude-Prosper Jolyot de Crébillon, fils?] Amsterdam, 1746. At least 8 other editions by 1779.

15

A. STN
    Major Dealers: Mauvelain, Troyes 26 (2). }   26 (2)

                                 Total: 26 (2)

B. Catalogues: 1 of 6 lists: (Bern: "3 1.").
C. Police Confiscations: 1 of 10 lists: Desauges.
D. Customs Confiscations: 1 instance: 1779.

22. *Amours (les) et aventures du visir Vergennes.* (Probably a separate printing of the second part of a *libelle* published in London in 1783 under the title *Les Passe-temps d'Antoinette et les amours du vizir de Vergennes.*)
    A. STN
        Major Dealers: Mauvelain, Troyes 6 (1). }   6 (1)
                              Total: 6 (1)

23. *Amusement des gens du monde.* 2 vols. [Jean-Pierre-Louis de la Roche du Maine, marquis de Luchet.] n.p., 1785.
    D. Customs Confiscations: 1 instance: 1786.

24. *Amusements, gaietés et frivolités poétiques, par un bon Picard.* [Pierre-Antoine de La Place.] London, 1783.
    A. STN
        Lorraine: Audéart, Lunéville 2 (1) }   2 (1)
                              Total: 2 (1)

26. *Analyse de la la religion chrétienne, par du Marsais.* [César Chesneau du Marsais, ed. by François-Marie Arouet de Voltaire.] n.p., 1768 (first appeared in the *Recueil nécessaire* [1766], according to Bengesco).
    C. Police Confiscations: 1 of 10 lists: Stockdorf.

27. *Analyse de l'ouvrage du pape Benoît XIV sur les béatifications et les canonisations.* Nicolas Baudeau. Paris, 1759.
    C. Police Confiscations: 1 of 10 lists: Prot.

28. *Analyse raisonnée de Bayle, ou abrégé méthodique de ses ouvrages, particulièrement de son Dictionnaire historique et critique dont les remarques ont été fondues dans le texte pour former un corps agréable et instructif de lectures suivies.* 8 vols. [François-Marie de Marsy (vols. 1–4) and Jean-Baptiste-René Robinet (vols. 5–8).] London, 1755–70.

A. STN

Major Dealers: Charmet, Besançon 6
(1). ⎫
Colporteurs: Blaisot 6 (1). ⎬   12   (2)
Minor Dealers: Malassis, Nantes 1 (1). }   <u>1   (1)</u>
                      Total: 13   (3)

D. Customs Confiscations: 11 instances: 1771 (5), 1772, 1773 (2), 1774 (2), 1775.

29. *Anatomie de la messe où est montré par l'Ecriture Sainte que la messe est contraire à la parole de Dieu et éloignée du chemin de salut. Par Pierre Du Moulin.* Pierre Du Moulin. Geneva, 1636–39. At least 3 other editions by 1647.
D. Customs Confiscations: 1 instance: 1772.

30. *An (l') deux mille quatre cent quarante, rêve s'il en fût jamais.* [Louis-Sébastien Mercier.] Amsterdam, 1771 (actually 1770, according to Martin-Mylne-Frautschi). At least 24 other editions by 1787.
A. STN

Major Dealers: Bergeret, Bordeaux 74
(3); Blouet, Rennes 100 (3); Buchet,
Nîmes 2 (1); Charmet, Besançon 57
(6); Letourmy, Orléans 34 (4); Malherbe, Loudun 3 (2); Mauvelain,
Troyes 32 (15); Manoury, Caen 151
(4); Mossy, Marseille 44 (3); Pavie,
La Rochelle 38 (2); Robert et Gauthier, Bourg-en-Bresse 37 (4);
Rigaud, Pons, Montpellier 346 (16).
Lorraine: Carez, Toul 6 (1); Chénoux,
Lunéville 36 (2); Augé, Lunéville 8
(2); Choppin, Bar-le-Duc 7 (2); Gerlache, Metz 53 (4); Betrand, Thionville 18 (2); Bergue, Thionville 25
(1); Oberlin, Thionville 12 (2); Gay,
Lunéville 18 (2); Audéart, Lunéville
10 (3); Matthieu, Nancy 66 (6); Bonthoux, Nancy 23 (4).

continued

17

Lyon: Baritel 24 (1); Cellier 4 (1); Jacquenod 13 (1); Barret 12 (1). *Paris:* Desauges 25 (1); Barré 6 (1); Cugnet 6 (1); Prévost 6 (2). *Colporteurs:* Blaisot 14 (2); Planquais 14 (2); Gilles 12 (1).	1,336 (108)
Minor Dealers: Malassis, Nantes 3 (1); Petit, Reims 12 (4); Sens, Toulouse 12 (1); Bonnard, Auxerre 3 (1); Waroquier, Soissons 5 (3); Habert, Bar-sur-Aube 10 (1); Jarfaut, Melun 5 (2); Billault, Tours 1 (1); Lair, Blois 3 (1); Caldesaigues, Marseille 4 (1).	58 (16)

Total: 1,394 (124)

B. Catalogues: 2 of 5 lists: (Grasset; Décombaz: "8°. Londres, 1773, 2 1. 10 s."; Bern: "5 1.").

C. Police Confiscations: 4 of 10 lists: Stockdorf, Moureau, Prot, Paris.

D. Customs Confiscations: 6 instances: 1771, 1772, 1773, 1777, 1778 (2).

31. **Anecdotes amoureuses.* (Anonymous. Possibly part of a two-volume collection of gallant literature published in 1780 as *Lettres de la tendresse et d'amour,* which includes three other novels by Edmé Boursaut, Gabriel-Joseph de Lavergne de Guilleragues, and Charlotte-Antoinette de Bressay, marquise de Lezay-Marnézia. See Martin-Mylne-Frautschi.)

  D. Customs Confiscations: 1 instance: 1779.

32. *Anecdotes du XVIII Siècle.* [Guillaume Imbert de Bourdeaux.] 2 vols. London, 1783.

  A. STN

Major Dealers: Mauvelain, Troyes 31 (4).	31 (4)

Total: 31 (4)

  D. Customs Confiscations: 2 instances: 1784, 1785.

33. *Anecdotes ecclésiastiques, contenant la police et la discipline de l'Eglise chrétienne depuis son établissement jusqu'au XI siècle, les intrigues des évêques de Rome et leurs usurpations. Tirés de l'Histoire du royaume de Naples, de Giannone.* [Jacob Vernet.] Amsterdam, 1738. At least 1 other edition by 1758.

18

B. Catalogues: 1 of 6 lists: (Bern: "4 1.").
C. Police Confiscations: 2 of 10 lists: Stockdorf, Pilon.

34. *Anecdotes historiques sur les principaux personnages qui jouent maintenant un rôle en Angleterre.* n.p., 1784.
    D. Customs Confiscations: 1 instance: 1786.

35. *Anecdotes jésuitiques, ou le Philotanus moderne.* 3 vols. [Claude-François Lambert?, or Nicolas Jouin?] The Hague, 1740. At least 2 other editions by 1760.
    B. Catalogues: 1 of 6 lists: (Bern: "10 1.").
    C. Police Confiscations: 1 of 10 lists: Stockdorf.

36. *Anecdotes pour servir à l'histoire secrète des Ebugors.* A Medoso, 3333 (Amsterdam, 1733, according to Gay).
    B. Catalogues: 1 of 6 lists: (Bern: "30 s.").

37. *Anecdotes sur Mme la comtesse du Barry.* [Mathieu-François Pidansat de Mairobert?, or Charles Théveneau de Morande?] London, 1775. At least 4 other editions by 1778.
    A. STN

Major Dealers: Bergeret, Bordeaux 12 (1); Buchet, Nîmes 26 (1); Charmet, Besançon 107 (5); Letourmy, Orléans 56 (3); Malherbe, Loudun 338 (7) Mauvelain, Troyes 14 (4); Manoury, Caen 37 (2); Mossy, Marseille 13 (1); Pavie, La Rochelle 94 (4); Robert et Gauthier, Bourg-en-Bresse 27 (2); Rigaud, Pons, Montpellier 68 (2).
Lorraine: Choppin, Bar-le-Duc 3 (2).
Lyon: Cellier 12 (1).
Paris: Prévost 10 (3); Cugnet 4 (1); Desauges 100 (2).
Colporteurs: Gilles 25 (1). — 946 (42)

Minor Dealers: Petit, Reims 1 (1); Sombert, Châlons-sur-Marne 30 (2); Bonnard, Auxerre 4 (1); Laisney Beauvais 12 (1); Habert, Bar-sur-Aube 40 (1); Jarfaut, Melun 28 (3); Caldesaigues, Marseille 10 (1). — 125 (10)

Total: 1,071 (52)

19

C. Police Confiscations: 2 of 10 lists: Moureau, Prot.

D. Customs Confiscations: 3 instances: 1777, 1778, 1779.

38. *Angola, histoire indienne, ouvrage sans vraisemblance.* 2 vols. [Charles-Jacques-Louis-Auguste Rochette de La Morlière?] Agra, 1746. At least 14 other editions by 1786.

A. STN

Colporteurs: Planquais 6 (1).	}	6 (1)
	Total:	6 (1)

C. Police Confiscations: 2 of 10 lists: Jouy, et al., Paris.

D. Customs Confiscations: 4 instances: 1772, 1774, 1779, 1781.

39. *Anti-Bernier (l') ou nouveau dictionnaire de théologie, par l'auteur des P.A.* . . . . [François-Louis Allamand.] n.p., 1770.

C. Police Confiscations: 1 of 10 lists: Paris.

D. Customs Confiscations: 2 instances: 1771, 1771.

40. *Antiquité (l') dévoilée par ses usages, ou examen critique des principales opinions, cérémonies et institutions religieuses des différents peuples de la terre. Par feu M. Boulanger.* [Nicolas-Antoine Boulanger; ed. by Paul-Henri-Dietrich Thiry, baron d'Holbach.] Amsterdam, 1766. At least 7 other editions by 1778.

A. STN

Major Dealers: Buchet, Nîmes 6 (1); Pavie, La Rochelle 8 (2); Malherbe, Loudun 3 (2).		
Colporteurs: Planquais 1 (1).	}	18 (6)
Minor Dealers: Chevrier, Poitiers 1 (1). }		1 (1)
	Total:	19 (7)

B. Catalogues: 2 of 6 lists: (Décombaz: "12°. 3 vol. Amsterdam, 1772, 6 l."; Bern: "9 l.").

C. Police Confiscations: 3 of 10 lists: Stockdorf, Pilon, Desauges.

D. Customs Confiscations: 9 instances: 1771, 1772, 1775, 1776, 1779 (3), 1786, n.d.

41. *Antiquité (l') et perpétuité de la religion protestante démontrée en forme de manifeste par J.-B. R. à tous les franciscains vulgairement dits les cordeliers en France au sujet de l'excommunication qu'ils ont fulminée contre lui.* Jean-Baptiste Renoult. Amsterdam, 1703.

20

A. STN

Major Dealers: Buchet, Nîmes 162 (2);
Manoury, Caen 12 (1); Malherbe,
Loudun 6 (2).
} 180 (5)

Total: 180 (5)

42. *Apologie de la Bastille, pour servir de réponse aux Mémoires de M. Linguet sur la Bastille, avec des notes politiques, philosophiques et littéraires, lesquelles n'auront avec le texte que le moindre rapport possible. Par un homme en pleine campagne.* [Michel-Joseph-Antoine Servan.] Philadelphia, 1784.

A. STN

Major Dealers: Mauvelain, Troyes 6 (1).
Paris: Desauges 25 (1).
} 31 (2)

Total: 31 (2)

43. *Arrétin (l').* 2 vols. [Henri-Joseph Du Laurens.] Rome, 1763. At least 13 other editions by 1783; also as *L'Arétin, ou la débauche de l'esprit en fait de bon sens* and *L'Arrétin moderne.*

A. STN

Major Dealers: Blouet, Rennes 72 (3);
Charmet, Besançon 137 (4); Malherbe, Loudun 110 (6); Robert et
Gauthier, Bourg-en-Bresse 12 (1);
Letourmy, Orléans 36 (3).
Lorraine: Chénoux, Lunéville 6 (1); Bertrand, Thionville 6 (1); Bergue, Thionville 12 (1); Audéart, Lunéville
9 (2).
Lyon: Flandin 12 (1).
Colporteurs: Blaisot 6 (1); "Troisième"
6 (1).
} 424 (25)

Minor Dealers: Malassis, Nantes 66 (1);
Sens, Toulouse 12 (1); Sombert, Châlons-sur-Marne 6 (1); Caldesaigues,
Marseille 4 (1).
} 88 (4)

Total: 512 (29)

B. Catalogues: 4 of 6 lists: (Grasset; Décombaz: "12°. 2 part. Rome, 1774. 2 1."; Chappuis et Didier: "2 vol. 12°. nouv. édit. 1779, 1 1. 4 s."; Bern: "6 1.").

21

    C. Police Confiscations: 6 of 10 lists: Stockdorf, Pilon, Moureau, Prot, Paris, Versailles.

    D. Customs Confiscations: 4 instances: 1776, 1778, 1779, 1784.

44. *Art (l') d'aimer et le remède d'amour d'Ovide.* Trans. from *De Arte amandi et de remedio amoris.* First translation into French, c. 1510. Gay cites 18 editions in the 18th century.

    A. STN

Colporteurs: Planquais 2 (1). }   2 (1)

Total: 2 (1)

    D. Customs Confiscations: 2 instances: 1774, 1775.

45. *Art (l') de péter, essai théori-physique et méthodique, à l'usage des personnes constipées, des personnages graves et austères, des dames mélancoliques et de tous ceux qui sont esclaves du préjugé.* [trans. by Pierre-Thomas-Nicolas Hurtault.] (trans. from *De Peditu ejusque speciebus* [1619], by Dornavius.) En Westphalie, 1751. At least 2 others editions by 1776.

    D. Customs Confiscations: 2 instances: 1775, 1779.

46. *Asiatique (l') tolérant, traité à l'usage de Zéokinizul, roi des Kofirans, surnommé le Chéri, ouvrage traduit de l'arabe du voyageur Bekrinoll par M. de ***.* [Laurent Angliviel de la Beaumelle?] Paris, 1748. At least 2 other editions by 1755.

    A. STN

Major Dealers: Mauvelain, Troyes 26 (2). }   26 (2)

Total: 26 (2)

    B. Catalogues: 1 of 6 lists: (Décombaz: "8°. 1770, 15 s.").

Assassinats (les) juridiques du chevalier de la Barre et du général Lally. See #302, *Histoire du parlement de Paris . . .*

47. *Aux mânes de Louis XV et des grands hommes qui ont vécu sous son règne, ou essai sur les progrès des arts et de l'esprit humain, sous le règne de Louis XV.* 2 vols. [Paul-Philippe Gudin de la Brenellerie.] Deux Ponts, 1776. At least 1 other edition by 1777.

    A. STN

Major Dealers: Manoury, Caen 25 (1). }   25 (1)

Total: 25 (1)

    D. Customs Confiscations: 1 instance: 1778.

48. **Aux sages cabalistes ou le Nekiridian.*
    C. Police Confiscations: 1 of 10 lists: Prot.

49. *Aventures (les) de la Madonna et de François d'Assise, recueillies de plusieurs ouvrages des docteurs romains, écrites d'un style récréatif, en même temps capable de faire sentir le ridicule du papisme sans aucune controverse, par M. Renoult.* Jean-Baptiste Renoult. Amsterdam, 1701. At least 3 other editions by 1750.
    A. STN
    >   *Major Dealers:* Mauvelain, Troyes 7 (2). }   7   (2)
    >   Total: 7   (2)

    Aventures monacales. See #471, *Nouvelles monacales, ou les aventures divertissantes de frère Maurice, publiées par le Sr. D***.*

50. *Avocat (l') national, ou lettre d'un patriote au sieur Bouquet, dans laquelle on défend la vérité, les lois et la patrie contre le système qu'il a publié dans un ouvrage intitulé "Lettres provinciales."* n.p., n.d.
    C. Police Confiscations: 1 of 10 lists: Prot.

51. **Bacha dans son serrail.*
    A. STN
    >   *Colporteurs:* "Troisième" 2 (1).   }   2   (1)
    >   Total: 2   (1)

52. *Balai (le), poème héroï-comique en XVIII chants.* [Henri-Joseph Du Laurens.] Constantinople, 1761. At least 4 other editions by 1775.
    A. STN
    >   *Major Dealers:* Pavie, La Rochelle 6 (1). ⎫
    >   *Paris:* Barré 3 (1).   ⎬   9   (2)
    >   *Minor Dealers:* Malassis, Nantes 6 (1). }   6   (1)
    >   Total: 15   (3)
    B. Catalogues: 2 of 6 lists: (Décombaz: "12°. Constantinople, 1772, 1 1. 5 s."; Bern: "par Voltaire, 2 1.").
    C. Police Confiscations: 6 of 10 lists: Stockdorf, Pilon, Prot, Desauges, Paris, Versailles.
    D. Customs Confiscations: 1 instance: 1771.

53. **Ballet (le) de la soeur Ursule.*
    C. Police Confiscations: 1 of 10 lists: Prot.

54. *Bannissement (le) des jésuites hors du royaume de France.* [J. Mettayer and L'Huillier.] Paris, 1515 (actual date unknown).
   A. STN

Major Dealers: Blouet, Rennes 2 (1). }	2	(1)
Total:	2	(1)

   Beau (le) de la galanterie. See #16, *Amour (l') décent et délicat. . .*

55. *Bélisaire.* Jean-François Marmontel. Paris, 1767. At least 30 other editions by 1787.
   A. STN

Major Dealers: Buchet, Nîmes 2 (1); Letourmy, Orléans 7 (2); Robert et Gauthier, Bourg-en-Bresse 2 (1); Rigaud, Pons, Montpellier 4 (1). *Paris:* Desauges 6 (1). *Colporteurs:* Planquais 4 (1).	25	(7)
Minor Dealers: Jarfaut, Melun 6 (1). }	6	(1)
Total:	31	(8)

   D. Customs Confiscations: 7 instances: 1771 (3), 1772, 1774, 1775 (2).

56. *Belle Allemande (la), ou les galanteries de Thérèse.* [Claude Villaret?, or Antoine Bret?] Amsterdam, 1745. At least 9 other editions by 1776.
   A. STN

Major Dealers: Blouet, Rennes 12 (1); Letourmy, Orléans 2 (1); Malherbe, Loudun 10 (1). *Lorraine:* Choppin, Bar-le-Duc 4 (1). *Paris:* Védrène 6 (1): Prévost 6 (1); Lequay Morin 12 (1); Barré 3 (1).	55	(8)
Minor Dealers: Sens, Toulouse 12 (1); Billault, Tours 13 (1); Boisserand, Roanne 12 (2): Caldesaigues, Marseille 4 (1).	41	(5)
Total:	96	(13)

   B. Catalogues: 1 of 6 lists: (Décombaz: "12°. 1774, 15 s.").
   C. Police Confiscations: 2 of 10 lists: Prot, Paris.

57. *Belle Wolfienne (la), avec deux lettres philosophiques, l'une sur l'immortalité de l'âme, et l'autre sur l'harmonie préétablie.* 6 vols.

[Jean-Henri-Samuel Formey and Chambrier?] The Hague, 1741–53. At least 1 other edition by 1752.
C. Police Confiscations: 1 of 10 lists: Prot.

58. *Bible (la) enfin expliquée par plusieurs aumôniers de S.M.L.R.D.P.* 2 vols. [François-Marie Arouet de Voltaire.] London, 1776. At least 4 other editions by 1777.
   A. STN
      Major Dealers: Malherbe, Loudun 6 (1); Manoury, Caen 37 (2).
      Colporteurs: Gilles 6 (1). } 49 (4)

      Minor Dealers: Billault, Tours 13 (1); Habert, Bar-sur-Aube 10 (1); Laisney, Beauvais 6 (1): Resplandy, Toulouse 13 (1). } 42 (4)

      Total: 91 (8)
   B. Catalogues: 1 of 6 lists: (Chappuis et Didier: "2 vol. gr. 8°. 1777, 2 1.").
   C. Police Confiscations: 1 of 10 lists: Moureau.
   D. Customs Confiscations: 1 instance: 1786.

59. *Bibliothèque philosophique du législateur, du politique, du jurisconsulte.* 10 vols. ed. by Jacques-Pierre Brissot de Warville. Berlin, 1782–85.
   A. STN
      Major Dealers: Bergeret, Bordeaux 36 (3); Charmet, Besançon 1 (1); Mossy, Marseille 1 (1). } 38 (5)

      Total: 38 (5)

60. *Bigarrures (les) d'un citoyen de Genève et ses conseils, dédiées aux américains.* 2 vols. Philadelphia, 1776.
   A. STN
      Major Dealers: Charmet, Besançon 6 (1); Letourmy, Orléans 8 (1); Malherbe, Loudun 14 (2): Robert et Gauthier, Bourg-en-Bresse 1 (1).
      Lorraine: Choppin, Bar-le-Duc 3 (3).
      Paris: Barré 3 (1); Lequay Morin 3 (1). } 38 (10)

      Minor Dealers: Bonnard, Auxerre 3 (1); Sens, Toulouse 4 (1). } 7 (2)

      Total: 45 (12)

61. *Bijou (le) de société, ou l'amusement des Grâces.* A Paphos, l'an des plaisirs (c. 1784, according to Gay). (Pia cites as a reordering of *Le Cabinet de Lampsaque* [1784].)
    C. Police Confiscations: 1 of 10 lists: Moureau.
    D. Customs Confiscations: 2 instances: 1776 (2).

62. *Bijoux (les) indiscrets.* 2 vols. [Denis Diderot.] Monomotapa, [1748]. At least 11 other editions by 1785.
    A. STN
       Major Dealers: Mauvelain, Troyes 1 (1);   }   3   (2)
           Pavie, La Rochelle 2 (1).

                  Total: 3   (2)
    B. Catalogues: 2 of 6 lists: (Décombaz: "8°. fig. Amsterdam, 1772, 3 1."; Bern: "avec figures, 6 1.").
    C. Police Confiscations: 3 of 10 lists: Stockdorf, Pilon, Jouy, et al.
    D. Customs Confiscations: 4 instances: 1771, 1774, 1779, 1786.

63. *Blondine (la) ou aventures nocturnes entre les hommes et les femmes.* Amsterdam, 1762.
    B. Catalogues: 1 of 6 lists: (Bern: "24 s.").

64. *Bonheur (le), poème, en six chants. Avec des fragments de quelques épîtres, ouvrages posthumes de M. Helvétius.* Claude-Adrien Helvétius. London, 1772. At least 2 other editions by 1779.
    A. STN
       Major Dealers: Buchet, Nîmes 2 (1); Letourmy, Orléans 18 (2); Malherbe, Loudun 6 (1).
       Lorraine: Bertrand, Thionville 2 (1); Chénoux, Lunéville 6 (1); Audéart, Lunéville 10 (2).   }   77   (11)
       Lyon: Cellier 2 (1).
       Colporteurs: Blaisot 6 (1); Gilles 25 (1).
       Minor Dealers: Lair, Blois 1 (1).   }   1   (1)

                  Total: 78   (12)
    B. Catalogues: 2 of 6 lists: (Nouffer: bound with *De l'Homme;* Bern: "4 1.").
    C. Police Confiscations: 2 of 10 lists: Prot, Paris.

   D. Customs Confiscations: 4 instances: 1775, 1776, 1778, 1779.

65. *Bonhomme (le) anglais.* [Charles Théveneau de Morande.] n.p., 1783.
   A. STN
      Major Dealers: Mauvelain, Troyes 12 (2). } 12 (2)

      Total: 12 (2)

66. *Bon-Sens (le), ou idées naturelles opposées aux idées surnaturelles.* [Paul-Henri-Dietrich Thiry, baron d'Holbach.] London, 1772. At least 10 other editions by 1788.
   A. STN
      Major Dealers: Blouet, Rennes 50 (1); Charmet, Besançon 12 (1); Letourmy, Orléans 8 (1); Malherbe, Loudun 21 (2); Robert et Gauthier, Bourg-en-Bresse 12 (1).
      Lorraine: Audéart, Lunéville 10 (2); Matthieu, Nancy 4 (1).
      Paris: Desauges 25 (1).
      Colporteurs: Gilles 52 (1). } 194 (11)

      Minor Dealers: Chevrier, Poitiers 6 (1); Habert, Bar-sur-Aube 10 (1); Malassis, Nantes 9 (2); Petit, Reims 1 (1). } 26 (5)

      Total: 220 (16)
   B. Catalogues: 2 of 6 lists: (Décombaz: "8°. Londres, 1773, 2 l. 5 s."; Bern: "5 l.").
   C. Police Confiscations: 3 of 10 lists: Stockdorf, Prot, Paris.
   D. Customs Confiscations: 3 instances: 1776, 1781, 1784.

67. *Brunus redivivus, ou traité des erreurs populaires, ouvrage critique, historique, et philosophique imité de Pomponace.* n.p., n.d. (Also reprinted in *Pièces philosophiques.*)
   A. STN
      Major Dealers: Charmet, Besançon 6 (1). } 6 (1)
      Minor Dealers: Malassis, Nantes 1 (1). } 1 (1)
      Total: 7 (2)
   C. Police Confiscations: 2 of 10 lists: Stockdorf, Manoury.

68. *Bureau (le) d'esprit, comédie en cinq actes et en prose.* [James Rutledge.] Liège, 1776. At least 1 other edition by 1777.
    C. Police Confiscations: 1 of 10 lists: Desauges.

69. *Cabinet (le) d'amour et de Vénus.* 2 vols. Cologne, n.d. (An anthology containing *L'Ecole des filles* and *La Putain errante,* according to Pia.)
    A. STN
    Major Dealers: Pavie, La Rochelle 8 (2). }   8   (2)
                                       Total: 8   (2)
    C. Police Confiscations: 1 of 10 lists: Paris.
    D. Customs Confiscations: 1 instance: 1781.

70. *Cabinet (le) de Lampsaque, ou choix d'épigrammes érotiques des plus célèbres poètes français.* 2 vols. Paphos, 1784.
    A. STN
    Major Dealers: Mauvelain, Troyes 1 (1). }   1   (1)
                                        Total: 1   (1)

71. *Cacomonade (la), histoire politique et morale, traduite de l'allemand du docteur Pangloss, par le docteur lui-même, depuis son retour de Constantinople.* [Simon-Nicolas-Henri Linguet.] Cologne, 1756 (actually 1766, according to Martin-Mylne-Frautschi). At least 2 other editions by 1767.
    A. STN
    Colporteurs: Planquais 6 (1).   }   6   (1)
                                        Total: 6   (1)

72. *Café (le) politique d'Amsterdam, ou entretiens familiers d'un français, d'un anglais, d'un hollandais et d'un cosmopolite, sur divers intérêts économiques et politiques de France, de l'Espagne et de l'Angleterre, par Charles-Elie, Denis Roonptsij.* 2 vols. [pseud. of Roch-Antoine de Pellissery.] Amsterdam, 1776. At least 1 other edition by 1778.
    A. STN
    Major Dealers: Charmet, Besançon
       6 (1).   }   12   (2)
    Lorraine: Choppin, Bar-le-Duc 6 (1).
                                        Total: 12   (2)
    D. Customs Confiscations: 1 instance: 1778.

73. *Café (le) politique de Londres, ou Pasquin dans la loge des anti-gallicans à Londres.* 2 vols. [Jacques-Pierre Brissot de Warville] n.p., 1780.

28

A. STN
  Major Dealers: Charmet, Besançon
  6 (1).

$$\left.\right\}\quad 6\ \ (1)$$

Total: 6 (1)

74. *Campagne de Messieurs les maréchaux de Broglie et de Belle-Isle, en Bohème et en Bavière. L'an M.DCC.XLI–M.DCC.XLIII.* Vols. 9–16 of *Recueil des campagnes de divers maréchaux de France, publié par Du Moulin.* [ed. by Pierre-François Du Moulin.] Amsterdam, 1760–73.
  C. Police Confiscations: 2 of 10 lists: Pilon, Prot.

75. *Campagne de Monsieur le maréchal de Coigny en Allemagne l'an M.DCC.XLIV. contenant les lettres de ce maréchal et celles de plusieurs officiers généraux au roi, à M. le comte d'Argenson.* 5 vols. [ed. by Pierre-François Du Moulin.] Amsterdam, 1761–72. (Also as Vols. 19–26 of *Recueil des campagnes de divers maréchaux de France, publié par Du Moulin.* [ed. by Pierre-François Du Moulin.] Amsterdam, 1760–73.)
  C. Police Confiscations: 1 of 10 lists: Prot.

76. *Campagne de Monsieur le maréchal de Maillebois en Westphalie. L'an M.DCC.XLI & II.* Vol. 8 of *Recueil des campagnes de divers maréchaux de France, publié par Du Moulin.* [ed. by Pierre-François Du Moulin.] Amsterdam, 1760–73.
  C. Police Confiscations: 1 of 10 lists: Pilon.

  Campagnes (les) de l'abbé T***. See #350, *Lauriers (les) ecclésiastiques . . .*

77. *Canapé (le), couleur de feu, par M. de D***.* [Louis-Charles Fougeret de Monbron?] The Hague, n.d. (1714). At least 9 other editions by 1775.
  C. Police Confiscations: 2 of 10 lists: Prot, Lyon.
  D. Customs Confiscations: 1 instance: 1771.

78. *Candide, ou l'optimisme. Traduit de l'allemand de M. le docteur Ralph.* [François-Marie Arouet de Voltaire.] n.p., 1759. At least 40 other editions by 1787.
  A. STN
    Major Dealers: Rigaud, Pons, Montpellier 4 (1).

$$\left.\right\}\quad 4\ \ (1)$$

Total: 4 (1)

  B. Catalogues: 1 of 6 lists: (Bern: "2 1.").

C. Police Confiscations: 1 of 10 lists: Stockdorf.

D. Customs Confiscations: 4 instances: 1772, 1774, 1778, 1779.

79. *Cataractes de l'imagination, déluge de la scribomanie, vomissement littéraire, hémorrhagie encyclopédique, monstre des monstres par Epiménide l'Inspiré.* 4 vols. [Jean-Marie Chassaignon.] Dans l'antre de Trophonius, 1779.
    A. STN

      Major Dealers: Mauvelain, Troyes 6 (1). }   6   (1)

                       Total: 6   (1)

80. *Catéchisme de l'honnête homme, ou dialogue entre un caloyer et un homme de bien. Traduit du grec vulgaire par D.J.J.R.C.D.C.D.G.* [François-Marie Arouet de Voltaire.] n.p., 1758 (actually 1763, according to Cioranescu and Bengesco). At least 2 other editions by 1764.
    A. STN

      Major Dealers: Blouet, Rennes 11 (1);
          Malherbe, Loudun 26 (1). }   37   (2)

                      Total: 37   (2)

    B. Catalogues: 1 of 6 lists: (Cailler).
    C. Police Confiscations: 2 of 10 lists: Pilon, Paris.

81. *Catéchisme du citoyen, ou éléments du droit public français.* [Joseph Saige.] En France, 1785. At least 2 other editions by 1788.[2]
    A. STN

      Major Dealers: Buchet, Nîmes 13 (1);
          Pavie, La Rochelle 48 (2). }   61   (3)

                      Total: 61   (3)

82. *Catéchumène (le), traduit du chinois.* [Charles Borde.] Amsterdam, 1768. At least 4 other editions by 1769; also as *Le Voyageur catéchumène* and *L'Américain sensé par hasard en Europe, et fait chrétien par complaisance.*
    A. STN

      Major Dealers: Buchet, Nîmes 12 (1);
          Mauvelain, Troyes 7 (2).

continued

---

[2] Pavie (La Rochelle) orders the edition of 1775 on April 1, 1776. No available bibliographic sources cite an edition before 1785.

Lorraine: Sandré, Lunéville 6 (1); Augé, Lunéville 10 (1); Audéart, Lunéville 42 (5); Bergue, Thionville 6 (1). *Colporteurs:* Blaisot 6 (1); "Troisième" 6 (1). }   95   (13)

                           Total: 95   (13)

    B. Catalogues: 2 of 6 lists: (Grasset, "8°. 6 s"; Bern: "3 1.").
    C. Police Confiscations: 2 of 10 lists: Stockdorf, Pilon.

83. **Catecumeni (I) Lettera ad un Teologo, colla sua Risposta.*
    B. Catalogues: 1 of 6 lists: (Nouffer: "8°. Philadelphia, 1777").

84. **Catholicon (le) ou dictionnaire universelle des sciences.* 6 vols.
    C. Police Confiscations: 1 of 10 lists: Paris. (Possibly the same work as *Catholicon ou dictionnaire universelle de la langue française.*)
    D. Customs Confiscations: 1 instance: 1781.

85. *Cent Nouvelles Nouvelles (les).* [Antoine de La Sale?] Paris, 1486. At least 3 18th-century editions by 1736.
    A. STN

Major Dealers: Buchet, Nîmes 26 (1); Robert et Gauthier, Bourg-en-Bresse 4 (1). }   30   (2)

Minor Dealers: Caldesaigues, Marseille 6 (1). }   6   (1)

                           Total: 36   (3)

86. *Chandelle (la) d'Arras, poème héroï-comique en XVIII chants.* [Henri-Joseph Du Laurens.] Bern, 1765. At least 2 other editions by 1775; also as *Etrennes aux gens d'église ou la Chandelle . . .*
    A. STN

Major Dealers: Charmet, Besançon 12 (2); Letourmy, Orléans 49 (3); Pavie, La Rochelle 8 (1); Robert et Gauthier, Bourg-en-Bresse 24 (2). *Paris:* Barré 6 (1); Prévost 3 (1). }   102   (10)

Minor Dealers: Malassis, Nantes 15 (1); Billault, Tours 1 (1).   16   (2)

                           Total: 118   (12)

B. Catalogues: 4 of 6 lists: (Décombaz: "12°. Londres, 1774, 1 1. 10 s."; Cailler; Chappuis et Didier: "8°. 12 s."; Bern: "5 1.").

C. Police Confiscations: 4 of 10 lists: Prot, Desauges, Paris, Versailles.

D. Customs Confiscations: 3 instances: 1778, 1779, 1781.

87. *Chansons des francs-maçons.* (Possibly *Chansons de la Très vénérable confrérie des maçons libres.* The Hague, 1735.)
D. Customs Confiscations: 1 instance: 1776.

88. *Chien (le) après les moines. Lu et approuvé par une bande de défroqués.* [Honoré-Gabriel Riqueti, comte de Mirabeau?, or Louis-Sébastien Mercier?, or Charles Théveneau de Morande?] Amsterdam, 1784.
A. STN

Major Dealers: Mauvelain, Troyes 12 (2).	12 (2)
Total:	12 (2)

89. *Choses (les) utiles et agréables.* 3 vols. [François-Marie Arouet de Voltaire.] Berlin, 1769. At least 1 other edition in 1769.
A. STN

Major Dealers: Bergeret, Bordeaux 12 (1); Blouet, Rennes 14 (3); Letourmy, Orléans 2 (1); Robert et Gauthier, Bourg-en-Bresse 2 (1). *Lorraine:* Bergue, Thionville 12 (1). *Paris:* Lequay Morin 2 (1); Prévost 2 (1). *Colporteurs:* Blaisot 6 (1); "Troisième" 6 (1).	58 (11)
Minor Dealers: Bonnard, Auxerre 3 (1); Sens, Toulouse 2 (1).	5 (2)
Total:	63 (13)

B. Catalogues: 2 of 6 lists: (Grasset; Bern: "figures, 6 1.").
C. Police Confiscations: 1 of 10 lists: Stockdorf.
D. Customs Confiscations: 1 instance: 1771.

90. *Chrétien (un) contre six juifs.* [François-Marie Arouet de Voltaire.] The Hague, 1777. At least 3 other editions by 1785; also as *Le Vieillard du mont Caucase.*

A. STN

> *Major Dealers:* Charmet, Besançon 6
> (1); Letourmy, Orléans 6 (1); Rigaud,
> Pons, Montpellier 6 (1).
> *Paris:* Lequay Morin 125 (2); Barré
> 3 (1).

146 (6)

Total: 146 (6)

B. Catalogues: 2 of 6 lists: (Nouffer; Chappuis et Didier: "12°. portrait. 1777, 15 s.").

91. *Chrétiens anciens et modernes, ou abrégé des points les plus inté-ressants de l'histoire ecclésiastique.* [Benoît Sinsart, abbé de Münster] London, 1754.
    C. Police Confiscations: 1 of 10 lists: Prot.

92. *Christianisme (le) dévoilé, ou examen des principes et des effets de la religion chrétienne, par feu M. Boulanger.* [Paul-Henri-Dietrich Thiry, baron d'Holbach.] London, 1756. At least 11 other editions by 1777.
    A. STN

> *Major Dealers:* Bergeret, Bordeaux 16
> (2); Blouet, Rennes 40 (3); Buchet,
> Nîmes 26 (2); Charmet, Besançon 12
> (1); Letourmy, Orléans 10 (2); Mal-
> herbe, Loudun 52 (3); Mauvelain,
> Troyes 3 (3).
> *Lorraine:* Augé, Lunéville 4 (2); Gay,
> Lunéville 4 (1); Audéart, Lunéville 2
> (1); Matthieu, Nancy 1 (1).
> *Lyon:* Flandin 12 (1).
> *Paris:* Barré 7 (1); Védrène 6 (1).
> *Colporteurs:* Gilles 25 (1).

220 (25)

> *Minor Dealers:* Billault, Tours 13 (1);
> Chevrier, Poitiers 1 (1); Calde-
> saigues, Marseille 4 (1); Malassis,
> Nantes 3 (1); Sens, Toulouse 12 (1);
> Sombert, Châlons-sur-Marne 6 (1).

39 (6)

Total: 259 (31)

B. Catalogues: 3 of 6 lists: (Grasset; Décombaz: "12°. Lon-dres, 1774, 2 1. 5 s."; Bern: "6 1.").
C. Police Confiscations: 4 of 10 lists: Pilon, Prot, Desauges, Paris.

D. Customs Confiscations: 6 instances: 1771, 1772, 1778, 1779, 1786, n.d.

93. *Chronique (la) scandaleuse, ou mémoires pour servir à l'histoire des mœurs de la génération présente.* [Guillaume Imbert de Bourdeaux.] Paris, 1783. At least 4 other editions by 1788.
    A. STN

Major Dealers: Charmet, Besançon 13 (1); Mauvelain, Troyes 52 (5). *Lorraine:* Bonthoux, Nancy 6 (1).	71	(7)
Total:	71	(7)

D. Customs Confiscations: 1 instance: 1784.

94. *Ciel (le) ouvert à tous les hommes, ou traité théologique dans lequel, sans rien déranger des pratiques de la religion, on prouve solidement, par l'Ecriture-Sainte et la raison que tous les hommes seront sauvés.* [Pierre Cuppé.] n.p., 1768. At least 1 other edition by 1783.
    A. STN

Major Dealers: Mauvelain, Troyes 11 (4).	11	(4)
Total:	11	(4)

C. Police Confiscations: 1 of 10 lists: Pilon.

95. *Code de la nature, ou véritable esprit de ses lois, de tout temps négligé ou méconnu.* [Morelly.] Partout, chez le vrai sage, 1755. At least 2 other editions by 1760.
    B. Catalogues: 1 of 6 lists: (Décombaz: "12°. 1760, 1 1.").
    D. Customs Confiscations: 1 instance: 1774.

96. *Code (le) français, ou recueil de toutes les pièces intéressantes publiées en France, relativement aux troubles des parlements, avec des observations critiques et historiques, des pièces nouvelles et une table raisonnée.* 2 vols. [abbé Joseph-Honoré Rémy.] Brussels, 1771. Earlier version as *Recueil de toutes les pièces intéressantes . . .*
    A. STN

Major Dealers: Manoury, Caen 12 (1).	12	(1)
Total:	12	(1)

97. *Colimaçons (les) du Révérend Père L'Escarbotier, par la grâce de Dieu capucin indigne, prédicateur ordinaire et cuisinier du grand*

couvent de la ville de Clermont en Auvergne au Révérend Père Elie, carme chaussé, docteur en théologie. [François-Marie Arouet de Voltaire.] n.p., 1768.

A. STN

Major Dealers: Blouet, Rennes 6 (1);
Robert et Gauthier, Bourg-en-Bresse
4 (1).
Lorraine: Bergue, Thionville 6 (1).
Colporteurs: Blaisot 6 (1); Planquais 6
(1); "Troisième" 6 (1). } 34 (6)

Total: 34 (6)

B. Catalogues: 2 of 6 lists: (Grasset: "8°. 6 s."; Décombaz).
C. Police Confiscations: 2 of 10 lists: Stockdorf, Pilon.

98. *Collection complète de tous les ouvrages pour et contre M. Necker avec des notes critiques, politiques et secrètes, le tout par ordre chronologique.* 3 vols. Utrecht, 1782.

A. STN

Major Dealers: Charmet, Besançon 19
(2); Mauvelain, Troyes 10 (4);
Mossy, Marseille 4 (1).
Lorraine: Choppin, Bar-le-Duc 2 (2).
Paris: Prévost 2 (1). } 37 (10)

Minor Dealers: Petit, Reims 19 (2); Waroquier, Soissons 3 (2). } 22 (4)

Total: 59 (14)

D. Customs Confiscations: 2 instances: 1782 (2).

99. *Collection d'anciens évangiles, ou monuments du premier siècle du christianisme, extraits de Fabricius, Grabius et autres savants, par l'abbé B***.* [François-Marie Arouet de Voltaire.] London, 1769.

A. STN

Major Dealers: Blouet, Rennes 2 (1). } 2 (1)
Total: 2 (1)

B. Catalogues: 1 of 6 lists: (Bern: "6 l.").
C. Police Confiscations. 3 of 10 lists: Stockdorf, Pilon, Prot.
D. Customs Confiscations: 1 instance: 1786.

100. **Collection des pièces pour les mainmortables.*
B. Catalogues: 1 of 5 lists: (Grasset: "8°.").

35

Collection sur les miracles. See #589, *Questions sur les miracles à M. Claparède . . .*

101. *Colporteur (le), histoire morale et critique, par M. de Chevrier.* François-Antoine Chevrier. London, L'An de la vérité (c. 1761, according to Cioranescu). At least 5 other undated editions.
    A. STN

    Colporteurs: Planquais 3 (1).   }   3 (1)

                                            Total: 3 (1)
    C. Police Confiscations: 2 of 10 lists: Manoury, Jouy, et al.
    D. Customs Confiscations: 5 instances: 1771 (2), 1772, 1775, 1779.

102. *Commentaire historique sur les œuvres de l'auteur de la Henriade, etc., avec les pièces originales et les preuves.* [François-Marie Arouet de Voltaire.] Basel, 1776. At least 3 other editions by 1777.
    A. STN

Major Dealers: Bergeret, Bordeaux 2 (1); Buchet, Nîmes 26 (1); Malherbe, Loudun 4 (1); Mossy, Marseille 6 (1); Rigaud, Pons, Montpellier 9 (2). *Lorraine:* Choppin, Bar-le-Duc 3 (2); Gerlache, Metz 2 (2); Bernard, Lunéville 1 (1); L'Entretien, Lunéville 5 (2). *Paris:* Barré 3 (1); Cugnet 2 (2); Prévost 4 (1).	67	(17)
Minor Dealers: Cazin, Reims 25 (1); Sens, Toulouse 33 (3); Laisney, Beauvais 6 (1); Jarfaut, Melun 4 (1); Billault, Tours 13 (1); Caldesaigues, Marseille 12 (1).	93	(8)
Total:	160	(25)

103. *Commentaire sur le livre des Délits et des peines, par un avocat de province.* [François-Marie Arouet de Voltaire.] n.p., 1766. At least 1 other edition in 1767.
    A. STN

Major Dealers: Blouet, Rennes 2 (1).
Lorraine: Audéart, Lunéville 2 (1).

⎫
⎬
⎭

4 (2)

Total: 4 (2)

B. Catalogues: 2 of 6 lists: (Grasset: "8°. 12 s."; Décombaz).

C. Police Confiscations: 1 of 10 lists: Pilon.

D. Customs Confiscations: 1 instance: 1776.

104. *Commentaire sur l'Esprit des lois de Montesquieu, par M. de Voltaire.* François-Marie Arouet de Voltaire. n.p., 1778 (actually 1777?, according to Bengesco).

B. Catalogues: 1 of 6 lists: (Nouffer: "suivi du Prix de la justice & de l'Humanité. 8°. 2 part. Portrait. sous Presse." Bengesco suggests 1777 as the first edition that appeared with *Prix de la justice et de l'humanité par l'auteur de l'Henriade.*)

C. Police Confiscations: 1 of 10 lists: Desauges.

105. *Commentaires sur les lois anglaises par M. de Blackstone traduits par D. G***.* 6 vols. William Blackstone. (trans. by Auguste-Pierre Damiens de Gomicourt from Blackstone's *Commentaries on the Laws of England.*) Brussels, 1774–76.

D. Customs Confiscations: 5 instances: 1774 (4), 1776.

106. *Compère (le) Mathieu, ou les bigarrures de l'esprit humain.* 3 vols. [Henri-Joseph Du Laurens.] London, 1766. At least 15 other editions by 1788.

A. STN

Major Dealers: Charmet, Besançon 6 (1); Malherbe, Loudun 65 (5); Rigaud, Pons, Montpellier 4 (1); Robert et Gauthier, Bourg-en-Bresse 6 (1).
Lorraine: Choppin, Bar-le-Duc 4 (2).
Lyon: Baritel 6 (1).
Colporteurs: Gilles 51 (2).

⎫
⎬
⎭

142 (13)

Minor Dealers: Habert, Bar-sur-Aube 4 (1); Jarfaut, Melun 8 (2).

⎫
⎬
⎭

12 (3)

Total: 154 (16)

B. Catalogues: 3 of 6 lists: (Grasset; Décombaz: "8°. 3 vol. Londres, 1732, 6 l."; Bern: "15 l.").

C. Police Confiscations: 6 of 10 lists: Stockdorf, Pilon, Manoury, Prot, Desauges, Versailles.

D. Customs Confiscations: 8 instances: 1771 (2), 1772, 1774, 1775, 1778, 1779 (2).

107. *Concubitus sine Lucina, ou le plaisir sans peine. Réponse à la lettre intitulée "Lucina sine concubita." Traduit de l'anglais.* [Richard Roe.] (trans. by Anne-Gabriel Meusnier de Querlon?, or de Combes?) London, 1750. At least 3 other editions by 1786.

A. STN

Major Dealers: Charmet, Besançon 25 (1); Letourmy, Orléans 6 (1); Malherbe, Loudun 18 (2). *Lorraine:* L'Entretien, Lunéville 6 (1). *Paris:* Lequay Morin 2 (1).	57	(6)
Minor Dealers: Caldesaigues, Marseille 5 (1).	5	(1)
Total:	62	(7)

108. **Confession d'une jeune fille. Estampes.*
D. Customs Confiscations: 1 instance: 1771.

109. **Confessions d'une religieuse. Estampes.*
D. Customs Confiscations: 1 instance: 1771.

110. *Confessions (les) de J.-J. Rousseau.* Part 1. 2 vols. Jean-Jacques Rousseau. Geneva, 1782. At least 2 other editions of Part 1 in 1782.

A. STN

Major Dealers: Charmet, Besançon 54 (2); Mauvelain, Troyes 10 (4); Manoury, Caen 50 (1). *Lorraine:* Choppin, Bar-le-Duc 4 (1); Bertrand, Thionville 12 (1). *Paris:* Prévost 2 (1).	132	(10)
Total:	132	(10)

C. Customs Confiscations: 2 instances: 1782, 1785.

111. *Confessions (les) d'un fat par le chevalier de la B***.* 2 vols. [Jean-François de Bastide.] Paris, 1749. At least 1 other edition by 1750.

B. Catalogues: 1 of 6 lists: (Décombaz: "12°. Francfort, 1750. 1 l. 10 s.").

112. *Confidence philosophique.* [Jacques Vernes.] Geneva and London, 1771. At least 4 other editions by 1788.
    A. STN
       Major Dealers: Blouet, Rennes 6 (1); Mossy, Marseille 25 (1).
       Lorraine: Chénoux, Lunéville 10 (2); Matthieu, Nancy 4 (1).
       Lyon: Barret 6 (1).
       51 (6)
       Total: 51 (6)
    B. Catalogues: 1 of 6 lists: (Bern: "5 1.").
    C. Police Confiscations: 2 of 10 lists: Stockdorf, Pilon.

113. *Congrès (le) politique, ou entretiens libres des puissances de l'Europe sur le bal général prochain.* London, 1772.
    B. Catalogues: 1 of 6 lists: (Bern: "fig.").
    C. Police Confiscations: 1 of 10 lists: Stockdorf.

114. *Constitution de l'Angleterre comparée avec la forme républicaine et les monarchies de l'Europe.* [Jean-Louis de Lolme.] Amsterdam, 1771.
    A. STN
       Major Dealers: Blouet, Rennes 6 (1); Charmet, Besançon 2 (1).
       8 (2)
       Total: 8 (2)
    B. Catalogues: 1 of 6 lists: (Décombaz: "8°. Amsterdam, 1771, 3 1.").
    C. Police Confiscations: 1 of 10 lists: Prot.
    D. Customs Confiscations: 2 instances: 1773, 1785.

115. *Constitution (la) de l'hôtel du Roule, avec les cent une propositions de la très célèbre madame Pâris.* A Condom, l'an des c . . . , 10007 (c. 1755, according to Gay).
    B. Catalogues: 1 of 6 lists: (Décombaz: "avec la fameuse Messaline, 8°. 1770. 1 1. 10 s." Page 106 begins *La Fameuse Messaline, tragédie en un acte, par Pyron, dit Prepucius,* according to Gay.).

116. *Consultation sur la validité des mariages des protestants de*

France. [Jean-Etienne-Marie Portalis with André Pazery.] The Hague and Paris, 1771.

D. Customs Confiscations: 1 instance: 1771.

117. *Contagion (la) sacrée, ou histoire naturelle de la superstition. Ouvrage traduit de l'anglais.* 2 vols. [trans. by Paul-Henri-Dietrich Thiry, baron d'Holbach] (trans. from *A Natural History of Superstition* [1709], by John Trenchard and Thomas Gordon [according to Barbier] or Toland [according to Vercruysse].) London, 1768. At least 2 other editions by 1775.

A. STN

> *Major Dealers:* Bergeret, Bordeaux 6 (1); Blouet, Rennes 16 (2); Letourmy, Orléans 12 (2); Malherbe, Loudun 51 (2); Mauvelain, Troyes 2 (2); Pavie, La Rochelle 4 (1).
> *Lyon:* Flandin 12 (1).
> *Paris:* Barré 2 (1); Prévost 3 (1).

108 (13)

> *Minor Dealers:* Caldesaigues, Marseille 3 (1); Sens, Toulouse 6 (1); Billault, Tours 13 (1); Chevrier, Poitiers 1 (1).

23 (4)

Total: 131 (17)

B. Catalogues: 2 of 6 lists: (Décombaz; Bern: "9 1.").

C. Police Confiscations: 2 of 10 lists: Stockdorf, Desauges.

118. *Contes de Boccace.* (trans. from *Il Decamerone* [1354] by Giovanni Boccaccio.)

The first French translation by Antoine-Jean Le Maçon appeared in 1545. The work appeared in the 18th century as: *Le Décaméron,* trans. by Le Maçon (1702 and 3 later editions by 1777); *Contes et nouvelles de Boccace* (1732 and 2 later editions by 1744); and *Contes de J. Boccace,* trans. by Antoine Sabatier de Castres (1770 and 1 later edition in 1783).

A. STN

> *Major Dealers:* Charmet, Besançon 49 (3): Malherbe, Loudun 12 (1); Manoury, Caen 24 (2); Mauvelain, Troyes 2 (2).

continued

40

Lorraine: Gerlache, Metz 2 (1).	91	(10)
Lyon: Cellier 2 (1).		
Minor Dealers: Cazin, Reims 12 (1); Jarfaut, Melun 12 (2)	24	(3)
Total:	115	(13)

D. Customs Confiscations: 1 instance: 1782.

119. *Contes et nouvelles de la reine de Navarre.* Marguerite d'Angoulême, reine de Navarre, called Marguerite de Navarre. n.p., 1559. At least 14 editions in the 18th century; also as *Heptaméron, Heptaméron français,* and *Nouvelles de Marguerite de Navarre.*

A. STN

Major Dealers: Malherbe, Loudun 1 (1); Mauvelain, Troyes 1 (1); Robert et Gauthier, Bourg-en-Bresse 2 (1).	4	(3)
Minor Dealers: Jarfaut, Melun 12 (2)	12	(2)
Total:	16	(5)

120. *Contes et nouvelles en vers de M. de la Fontaine.* Jean de la Fontaine. Gay lists many editions beginning in 1665 and continuing through the 18th century; title varies.

A. STN

Major Dealers: Charmet, Besançon 6 (1); Manoury, Caen 12 (1); Mossy, Marseille 6 (1); Robert et Gauthier, Bourg-en-Bresse 2 (1).		
Lorraine: Choppin, Bar-le-Duc 1 (1); Bertrand, Thionville 15 (4); Bergue, Thionville 6 (1); Gay, Lunéville 4 (1); Audéart, Lunéville 15 (2); Matthieu, Nancy 1 (1).	74	(16)
Lyon: Cellier 2 (1).		
Colporteurs: Planquais 4 (1).		
Minor Dealers: Malassis, Nantes 6 (1); Cazin, Reims 1 (1); Sombert, Châlons-sur-Marne 8 (2); Jarfaut, Melun 10 (2); Boisserand, Roanne 4 (1).	29	(7)
Total:	103	(23)

B. Catalogues: 1 of 6 lists: (Décombaz: "12°. 2 vol. Londres,

1775, 2 1." and "les mêmes avec figures, 12°. 3 vol. Amsterdam, 1772. reliés en veau. 8 1.").

C. Police Confiscations: 2 of 10 lists: Jouy, et al., Prot.

D. Customs Confiscations: 5 instances: 1771 (3), 1772, 1779.

Contes et poésies de Grécourt. See #490, *Œuvres.* Grécourt.

121. *Contes théologiques, suivis des litanies des catholiques du XVIII siècle et de poésies érotico-philosophiques, ou recueil presque édifiant.* [Pub. by François-René-Joseph de Pommereul.] n.p., 1783. At least 1 other edition by 1784.

A. STN

Major Dealers: Mauvelain, Troyes 6 (1) }   6 (1)

Total: 6 (1)

122. *Contes très mogols, enrichis de notes, avis, avertissements curieux et instructifs, à l'usage des deux sexes, pour servir de suite ou de commencement à l'histoire des empereurs mogols, par un vieillard quelquefois jeune.* [Benoît-Joseph Marsollier des Vivetières?, or Simon-Pierre Mérard de Saint-Just?] Geneva, 1770.

A. STN

Lorraine: Bergue, Thionville 6 (1).
Colporteurs: Blaisot 6 (1); Planquais 1 (1). }   13 (3)

Total: 13 (3)

123. *Contrat conjugal, ou lois du mariage, de la répudiation et du divorce, avec une dissertation sur l'origine et le droit des dispenses par Le Scène des Maisons.* Jacques Le Scène-Desmaisons. n.p., 1781. At least 2 other editions by 1784.

C. Police Confiscations: 1 of 10 lists: Versailles.

124. *Contrat (du) social, ou principes du droit politique.* Jean-Jacques Rousseau. Amsterdam, 1762. At least 13 other editions by 1789.

A. STN

Colporteurs: Planquais 4 (1). }   4 (1)

Total: 4 (1)

D. Customs Confiscations: 3 instances: 1771, 1774, 1779.

125. *Conversation du roi de Prusse dans une course faite en 1779 pour visiter un district de ses états.* Frederick II. n.p., 1784.

D. Customs Confiscations: 1 instance: 1786.

126. **Conversations familières de M. le chancelier avec le Sr. le Brun.*
     C. Police Confiscations: 2 of 10 lists: Stockdorf, Pilon.

     Correspondance de madame Gourdan avec un recueil de chansons à l'usage des soupers chez madame Gourdan. See #563, *Portefeuille (le) de madame Gourdan . . .*

127. *Correspondance de M. le marquis de Montalembert, étant employé par le roi de France à l'armée suédoise, avec M. le marquis d'Havrincourt, M. le maréchal de Richelieu, les ministres du roi à Versailles, pour servir à l'histoire de la dernière guerre.* 3 vols. Marquis Marc-René de Montalembert. London, 1777.
     A. STN

     Major Dealers: Buchet, Nîmes 18 (2); Charmet, Besançon 6 (1); Robert et Gauthier, Bourg-en-Bresse 2 (1); Rigaud, Pons, Montpellier 12 (3). 〕 39 (8)
     Paris: Barrois 1 (1)
     Minor Dealers: Caldesaigues, Marseille 12 (2). 〕 12 (2)

     Total: 51 (10)

     D. Customs Confiscations: 3 instances: 1777, 1779, 1781.

128. *Correspondance politique, civile et littéraire pour servir à l'histoire du XVIII siècle.* 3 vols. Berlin, 1783.
     A. STN

     Major Dealers: Mauvelain, Troyes 12 (2). 〕 12 (2)

     Total: 12 (2)

129. *Correspondance secrète et familière de M. de Maupeou avec M. de Sor***, conseiller du nouveau parlement.* 3 vols. [Mathieu-François Pidansat de Mairobert, or possibly by Jacques-Mathieu Augeard.] n.p., 1771. At least 2 other editions by 1773; also as *Maupeouana, ou correspondance . . .*
     A. STN

     Major Dealers: Letourmy, Orléans 12 (1); Malherbe, Loudun 8 (2); Mauvelain, Troyes 1 (1); Rigaud, Pons, Montpellier 100 (1).
     Lorraine: Chénoux, Lunéville 12 (1);

continued

Bertrand, Thionville 12 (1); Bon-
thoux, Nancy 2 (1).   184   (10)
Colporteurs: Gilles 37 (2)
Minor Dealers: Malassis, Nantes 3 (1);
Jarfaut, Melun 2 (1).   5   (2)

Total: 189   (12)

   C. Police Confiscations: 4 of 10 lists: Stockdorf, Pilon, Moureau, Desauges.

   D. Customs Confiscations: 2 instances: 1772, 1777.

130. *Correspondance secrète, politique et littéraire, ou mémoires pour servir à l'histoire des cours, des sociétés et de la littérature en France, depuis la mort de Louis XV.* 18 vols. [Guillaume Imbert de Bourdeaux, Louis-François Métra, and others.] London, 1787–90.
   A. STN
      Major Dealers: Charmet, Besançon 1 (1)   1 (1)

                                Total: 1 (1)

131. *Cosmopolite (le), ou le citoyen du monde par M. Monbron.* [Louis-Charles Fougeret de Monbron.] n.p., 1750. At least 2 other editions by 1762.
   C. Police Confiscations: 1 of 10 lists: Paris.

132. *Cousin (le) de Mahomet, et la folie salutaire, histoire plus que galante.* 2 vols. [Nicolas Fromaget.] Leyden, 1742. At least 11 other editions by 1786.
   A. STN
      Major Dealers: Charmet, Besançon 12
      (1).
      Colporteurs: Blaisot 6 (1); Planquais 4   22   (3)
      (1).

                                Total: 22   (3)

   B. Catalogues: 1 of 6 lists: (Décombaz: "12°. 2 vol. fig. 1770, 2 1. 5s.").

   D. Customs Confiscations: 3 instances: 1771, 1773, 1774.

133. *Cri (le) du sang innocent.* [François-Marie Arouet de Voltaire.] n.p., 1775.
   B. Catalogues: 1 of 6 lists: (Cailler).

134. *Critique du siècle, ou lettres sur divers sujets par l'auteur des Lettres juives.* 2 vols. [Jean-Baptiste de Boyer, marquis d'Argens.] The Hague, 1755.

A. STN
   Lorraine: Augé, Lunéville 2 (1)   }   2 (1)
                                       Total: 2 (1)

135. *Cruauté (de la) religieuse.* [trans. by Paul-Henri-Dietrich Thiry, baron d'Holbach.] (B.M. Catalogue states, "purported to be translated from an English original.") London, 1769. At least 1 other edition by 1775.
   A. STN
      Major Dealers: Blouet, Rennes 6 (1);
        Letourmy, Orléans 16 (3); Malherbe,
        Loudun 50 (1); Mauvelain, Troyes 7
        (2); Pavie, La Rochelle 4 (1).   }   98 (12)
      Lyon: Flandin 4 (1); Jacquenod 3 (1).
      Paris: Barré 6 (1); Prévost 2 (1).
      Minor Dealers: Chevrier, Poitiers 1 (1);
        Sens, Toulouse 12 (1); Billault,   }   26   (3)
        Tours 13 (1).
                                Total: 124 (15)
   B. Catalogues: 2 of 6 lists: (Décombaz: "12°. 1775, 1 1." and "8°. 1.1."; Bern: "4 1.").
   C. Police Confiscations: 3 of 10 lists: Pilon, Prot, Desauges.

Cul d'Iris. See #298, *Histoire d'Iris.*

136. *Culte (du) des dieux fétiches, ou parallèle de l'ancienne religion d'Egypte avec la religion actuelle de Nigritie.* [Charles de Brosses.] n.p., 1760.
   B. Catalogues: 1 of 6 lists: (Bern: "4 1.").
   C. Police Confiscations: 1 of 10 lists: Stockdorf.

137. *David, ou l'histoire de l'homme selon le cœur de Dieu. Ouvrage traduit de l'anglais.* [trans. by Paul-Henri-Dietrich Thiry, baron d'Holbach.] (trans. from *The History of the Man after God's own Heart* [1756] by Peter Annet?) London, 1768. At least 1 other edition by 1778.
   A. STN
      Major Dealers: Malherbe, Loudun 1 (1). }   1 (1)
      Minor Dealers: Malassis, Nantes 2 (1);
        Chevrier, Poitiers 1 (1).   }   3 (2)
                                Total: 4   (3)
   B. Catalogues: 3 of 6 lists: (Décombaz: "8°. Londres, 1768,

45

3 1."; Chappuis et Didier: "suivi de *Saül,* tragédie, par M. de Voltaire. gr. 12°. 1778, 8 s."; Bern: "3 1.").

C. Police Confiscations: 4 of 10 lists: Stockdorf, Pilon, Prot, Desauges.

138. *Déclaration de M. de Voltaire sur le procès entre M. le comte de Morangiès et les Verron. Réponse à l'écrit d'un avocat intitulé "Preuves démonstratives en fait de justice."* [François-Marie Arouet de Voltaire.] Lausanne, 1773.
   B. Catalogues: 1 of 6 lists: Grasset: "8°. 4 s.").

139. *Défense de Louis XIV.* [François-Marie Arouet de Voltaire.] n.p., n.d. (1769, according to Cioranescu and Bengesco). At least 1 other edition by 1770.
   A. STN
   Major Dealers: Blouet, Rennes 1 (1).   }   <u>1</u>   <u>(1)</u>
                                        Total: 1   (1)
   B. Catalogues: 2 of 6 lists: (Grasset: "8°. 4 s."; Bern).

140. *Défense (la) de mon oncle contre ses infâmes persécuteurs. Par A . . . . T de V***.* [François-Marie Arouet de Voltaire?] Geneva, 1767. At least 4 other editions by 1773.
   B. Catalogues: 1 of 6 lists: (Bern: "3 1.").
   C. Police Confiscations: 2 of 10 lists: Stockdorf, Pilon.
   D. Customs Confiscations: 2 instances: 1774, 1779.

141. *Défense des livres de l'Ancien Testament contre l'écrit intitulé: "La Philosophie de l'histoire."* [Joseph-Guillaume Clémence.] Amsterdam, 1767. At least 1 other edition by 1768.
   B. Catalogues: 1 of 6 lists: (Bern: "6 1.").

142. *Défense du paganisme, par l'empereur Julien, en grec et en fran-çais, avec des dissertations et des notes pour servir d'éclaircissement au text et pour en réfuter les erreurs, par M. le marquis d'Argens.* Jean-Baptiste de Boyer, marquis d'Argens. Berlin, 1764.
   B. Catalogues: 1 of 6 lists: (Bern: "5 1.").
   C. Police Confiscations: 2 of 10 lists: Stockdorf, Prot.

143. *Dégoûts (les) du plaisir, frivolité.* Lampsaque, 1752.
   B. Catalogues: 1 of 6 lists: (Bern: "1 1. 10 s.").

144. *Déisme (le) réfuté par lui-même, ou examen des principes d'incrédulité répandus dans les divers ouvrages de M. Rousseau, en forme de lettres, par M. Bergier.* 2 vols. Nicolas-Sylvestre

Bergier. Paris, 1765. At least 1 other edition by 1771.
B. Catalogues: 1 of 6 lists: (Bern: "5 1.").

Délices (les) du cloître. See #697, *Vénus dans le cloître.*

145. *Désoeuvré (le), ou l'espion du boulevard du Temple.* [François-Marie Mayeur de Saint-Paul.] London, 1781. At least 5 other editions by 1783; also as *Le Chroniqueur désoeuvré, ou . . .*
A. STN

Major Dealers: Mauvelain, Troyes 8 (2) }	8	(2)
Total:	8	(2)

C. Police Confiscations: 1 of 10 lists: Versailles.
D. Customs Confiscations: 3 instances: 1784 (2), 1785.

146. *Dévirgineurs (les) et Combabus, contes en vers, précédés par des réflexions sur le conte, et suivis de Floricourt, histoire française.* [Claude-Joseph Dorat.] Amsterdam, 1765. At least 1 other edition in 1765; originally published as *Floricourt, histoire française* (1762).
B. Catalogues: 1 of 6 lists: (Bern: "30 s.").

147. *Devoirs (les), statuts ou règlements généraux des F∴ M∴ mis dans un nouvel ordre et approuvés par la grande loge des Sept Provinces Unies des Pays-Bas. (Dédié à la loge de l'union à Francfort.)* Amsterdam, 1761. At least 4 other editions by 1775.[†]
A. STN

Major Dealers: Bergeret, Bordeaux 11 (2); Charmet, Besançon 6 (1); Letourmy, Orléans 3 (1); Malherbe, Loudun 6 (1); Mossy, Marseille 13 (1); Pavie, La Rochelle 12 (1). *Lorraine:* Choppin, Bar-le-Duc 4 (1); Matthieu, Nancy 2 (1). *Lyon:* Cellier 6 (1). *Paris:* Prévost 6 (1); Barré 12 (1).	81	(12)
Minor Dealers: Cazin, Reims 6 (1); Petit, Reims 2 (1); Sens, Toulouse 6 (1); Sombert, Châlons-sur-Marne 6 (1); Billault, Tours 2 (1); Caldesaigues, Marseille 3 (1).	25	(6)
Total:	106	(18)

[†] The typographical sign ∴ was commonly used to indicate Freemasonry.

47

148. *Diable (le) dans un bénitier, et la métamorphose du Gazetier cuirassé en mouche, ou tentative du sieur Receveur, inspecteur de la police de Paris, chevalier de St. Louis, pour établir à Londres une police à l'instar de celle de Paris. Revu, corrigé, et augmenté par M. l'abbé Aubert, censeur-royal.* Pierre Le Roux. [pseud. of Anne-Gédéon La Fitte de Pellepore?] Paris, n.d. (c. 1784, according to Cioranescu).
    A. STN
    Major Dealers: Mauvelain, Troyes 6 (1). }   6   (1)
                                                       Total: 6   (1)

149. *Dialogue de Pégase et du vieillard.* [François-Marie Arouet de Voltaire.] n.p., n.d. (1774, according to Cioranescu).
    A. STN
    Lorraine: Choppin, Bar-le-Duc 6 (1); Bertrand, Thionville 4 (1); Audéart, Lunéville 6 (1). }   16   (3)
    Minor Dealers: Jarfaut, Melun 2 (1); Billault, Tours 2 (1). }   4   (2)
                                                       Total: 20   (5)
    D. Customs Confiscations: 1 instance: 1776.

Dialogue entre un caloyer et un honnête homme. See #80, *Catéchisme de l'honnête homme.*

150. *Dialogue entre un évêque et un curé sur les mariages des protestants.* [Louis Guidi.] n.p., 1775.
    A. STN
    Major Dealers: Blouet, Rennes 6 (1); Letourmy, Orléans 3 (1); Malherbe, Loudun 76 (2). }   85   (4)
    Minor Dealers: Fontaine, Colmar 2 (1); Billault, Tours 13 (1). }   15   (2)
                                                       Total: 100   (6)
    D. Customs Confiscations: 1 instance: 1778.

151. *Dialogues sur l'âme par les interlocuteurs en ce temps-là.* n.p., 1771. (NUC cites this title as appearing with d'Holbach's *Lettres philosophiques* [1768].)
    C. Police Confiscations: 1 of 10 lists: Stockdorf.

152. *Diatribe à l'auteur des Ephémérides.* [François-Marie Arouet de Voltaire.] Geneva and Paris, 1775.

A. STN
> *Major Dealers:* Manoury, Caen 25 (1). }   25   (1)
> Total: 25   (1)

153. *Dictionnaire philosophique portatif.* [François-Marie Arouet de Voltaire.] London 1764. At least 10 other editions by 1789; also as *La Raison par alphabet.*
   A. STN
   > *Major Dealers:* Blouet, Rennes 22 (4); Buchet, Nîmes 52 (2); Charmet, Besançon 6 (1); Letourmy, Orléans 12 (1); Malherbe, Loudun 16 (2); Manoury, Caen 50 (2); Rigaud, Pons, Montpellier 12 (4).
   > *Lorraine:* Bertrand, Thionville 8 (2); Audéart, Lunéville 2 (1); Matthieu, Nancy 2 (1).
   > *Colporteurs:* Planquais 3 (1).   185   (21)
   >
   > *Minor Dealers:* Chevrier, Poitiers 1 (1); Sens, Toulouse 6 (1); Bonnard, Auxerre 5 (2); Waroquier, Soissons 1 (1); Billault, Tours 2 (1); Caldesaigues, Marseille 4 (1).   19   (7)
   >
   > Total: 204   (28)

   B. Catalogues: 3 of 6 lists: (Grasset; Décombaz: "augmenté d'un supplément par l'auteur, 12°. 2 vol. *Berlin,* 1765, 4 1. 10 s." and as *"Raison par alphabet, par Mr. de Voltaire, 7me édition, corrigée & augmentée par l'auteur, 8°. 2 vol. 1763. 6 1.";* Bern: "12 1.", "6 1." and as *Raison par alphabet* "8 1.").
   C. Police Confiscations: 3 of 10 lists: Stockdorf, Prot, Paris.
   D. Customs Confiscations: 5 instances: 1772 (2), 1773, 1777, 1779.

154. *Dieu et les hommes. Œuvre théologique, mais raisonnable, par le Dr Obern. Traduit par Jacques Aimon.* [François-Marie Arouet de Voltaire.] Berlin, 1769.
   A. STN
   > *Major Dealers:* Mauvelain, Troyes 6 (1).
   > *Colporteurs:* Gilles 6 (1).   12   (2)

Minor Dealers: Malassis, Nantes 2 (1). }   2   (1)

Total: 14   (3)

B. Catalogues: 2 of 6 lists: (Grasset: Bern: "5 1.").
C. Police Confiscations: 2 of 10 lists: Pilon, Prot.
D. Customs Confiscations: 1 instance: 1771.

155. *Dieu. Réponse au Système de la nature.* [François-Marie Arouet de Voltaire.] n.p., n.d. (c. 1770, according to Bengesco).
  A. STN

Major Dealers: Rigaud, Pons, Montpel- } 50 (1)
  lier 50 (1)

Total: 50   (1)

C. Police Confiscations: 1 of 10 lists: Pilon.

156. *Dîner (le) du comte de Boulainvilliers, par M. St.-Hyacinthe.* [François-Marie Arouet de Voltaire.] n.p., 1728 (actually 1767, according to Bengesco and Cioranescu). At least 3 other editions by 1769.
  A. STN

Major Dealers: Blouet, Rennes 8 (2);
  Charmet, Besançon 6 (1); Letourmy,
  Orléans 24 (3); Robert et Gauthier,
  Bourg-en-Bresse 6 (1).
  Lorraine: Sandré, Lunéville 8 (1); Audé-
  art, Lunéville 6 (1). } 58 (9)

Minor Dealers: Malassis, Nantes 4 (1);
  Bonnard, Auxerre 3 (1); Billault,
  Tours 13 (1). } 20 (3)

Total: 78   (12)

B. Catalogues: 2 of 6 lists: (Grasset: "8°., 8 s."; Bern: "30 s.").
C. Police Confiscations: 1 of 10 lists: Pilon.
D. Customs Confiscations: 3 instances: 1778, 1779 (2).

157. *Discours aux confédérés catholiques de Kaminiek en Pologne par le major Kaiserling, au service du roi de Prusse.* Amsterdam, 1768.
  B. Catalogues: 1 of 6 lists: (Grasset).

158. **Discours céleste, traduit de l'italien en gaulois et de ce dernier en français.*
  A. STN

Major Dealers: Pavie, La Rochelle 12 (1). } 12 (1)

Total: 12 (1)

159. **Discours chrétien, le Christ est-il divisé?*
C. Police Confiscations: 1 of 10 lists: Prot.

160. *Discours de l'empereur Julien contre les chrétiens, traduit par M. le marquis d'Argens. Avec de nouvelles notes de divers auteurs.* [ed. by François-Marie Arouet de Voltaire.] Berlin, 1708 (actually 1769, according to Cioranescu).
A. STN

Major Dealers: Malherbe, Loudun 1 (1); Robert et Gauthier, Bourg-en-Bresse 10 (2). } 11 (3)

Minor Dealers: Chevrier, Poitiers 1 (1). } 1 (1)

Total: 12 (4)

B. Catalogues: 2 of 6 lists: (Grasset: "8°, 1 1. 10 s." Décombaz: "8°. Berlin, 1768, 1 1. 10 s.").
D. Customs Confiscations: 1 instance: 1771.

161. *Discours du roi de Suède sur la liberté de la presse, avec l'épître de M. de Voltaire au roi de Danemark, sur le même sujet.* n.p., 1775. (*Epître au roi de Danemark* by François-Marie Arouet de Voltaire appeared in 1770, according to Bengesco.)
A. STN

Major Dealers: Manoury, Caen 12 (1); Mossy, Marseille 4 (1); Rigaud, Pons, Montpellier 10 (2). } 26 (4)

Minor Dealers: Cazin, Reims 6 (1); Billault, Tours 2 (1). } 8 (2)

Total: 34 (6)

162. *Discours historique sur l'Apocalypse, par feu M. Abauzit.* Firmin Abauzit. London, 1770.
A. STN

Minor Dealers: Chevrier, Poitiers 1 (1). } 1 (1)

Total: 1 (1)

B. Catalogues: 1 of 6 lists: (Bern: "3 1.").
C. Police Confiscations: 3 of 10 lists: Stockdorf, Pilon, Prot.
D. Customs Confiscations: 1 instance: 1778.

51

163. *Discours sur la liberté de penser, écrit à l'occasion d'une nouvelle secte d'esprits forts. Traduit de l'anglais et augmenté d'une lettre d'un médecin arabe.* [trans. by Henri Scheurléer and pub. by Jean Rousset de Missy.] London, 1714. (trans. from *Discours of Free-Thinking* [1713] by Anthony Collins.) At least 3 other editions by 1774.

A. STN

Major Dealers: Blouet, Rennes 4 (1); Mauvelain, Troyes 7 (2). } 11 (3)

Minor Dealers: Chevrier, Poitiers 1 (1). } 1 (1)

Total: 12 (4)

B. Catalogues: 1 of 6 lists: (Bern: "2 vol., 5 l.").

C. Police Confiscations: 2 of 10 lists: Pilon, Prot.

164. *Discours sur l'économie politique par Jean-Jacques Rousseau, citoyen de Genève.* Jean-Jacques Rousseau. Geneva, 1758. At least 6 other editions by 1764. (Originally in *Encyclopédie,* Vol. V, pp. 337–49, 1755.)

A. STN

Major Dealers: Charmet, Besançon 6 (1).

Colporteurs: Planquais 4 (1). } 10 (2)

Total: 10 (2)

165. *Discours sur les miracles de Jésus-Christ. Traduit de l'anglais de Thomas Woolston.* [trans. by Paul-Henri-Dietrich Thiry, baron d'Holbach.] (trans. from *Six Discourses on the Miracles of Our Saviour* [1727–29] by Thomas Woolston.) Amsterdam, 1769.

A. STN

Major Dealers: Blouet, Rennes 4 (1); Manoury, Caen 25 (1).

Colporteurs: Gilles 12 (1). } 41 (3)

Minor Dealers: Chevrier, Poitiers 1 (1). } 1 (1)

Total: 42 (4)

B. Catalogues: 1 of 6 lists: (Bern: "6 l.").

C. Police Confiscations: 3 of 10 lists: Stockdorf, Pilon, Prot.

166. *Discours sur l'état actuel de la politique et de la science militaire en Europe avec le plan d'un ouvrage intitulé "La France politique*

et militaire." [Jacques-Antoine, Hippolyte de Guibert.] Geneva, 1773.

D. Customs Confiscations: 2 instances: 1773, 1776.

167. *Discussion si la polygamie est contre la loi naturelle ou divine, tant de l'Ancien que du Nouveau Testament, de ce qui a donné lieu de l'interdire aux chrétiens; si les souverains chrétiens sont autorisés de la réintroduire dans leurs états, et de quelle manière ils pourront s'y prendre sans occasionner des désordres dans les ménages, par Louis, comte de Rantzow.* St. Petersburg, 1774.

C. Police Confiscations: 1 of 10 lists: Prot.

168. *Dissertation sur Elie et Enoch par l'auteur des Recherches sur l'origine du despotisme oriental et servant de suite à cet ouvrage.* [Nicholas-Antoine Boulanger, ed. by Paul-Henri-Dietrich Thiry, baron d'Holbach.] n.p., "dix-huitième siècle" (1764, according to Vercruysse). At least 2 other editions in 1764.

A. STN

Major Dealers: Bergeret, Bordeaux 12 (1); Blouet, Rennes 2 (1); Malherbe, Loudun 1 (1).	15	(3)
Minor Dealers: Chevrier, Poitiers 1 (1).	1	(1)
Total:	16	(4)

C. Police Confiscations: 2 of 10 lists: Pilon, Prot.

169. *Dissertation sur Jeanne d'Arc, vulgairement nommée la Pucelle d'Orléans.* [Jean-Pierre-Louis de La Roche du Main, marquis de Luchet?] n.p., 1766.

A. STN

Major Dealers: Bergeret, Bordeaux 6 (1); Blouet, Rennes 2 (1); Letourmy, Orléans 3 (1); Pavie, La Rochelle 2 (1).	13	(4)
Minor Dealers: Jarfaut, Melun 4 (1); Billault, Tours 2 (1).	6	(2)
Total:	19	(6)

170. *Dissertation sur l'établissement de l'abbaye de St. Claude, ses chroniques, ses légendes, ses chartes, ses usurpations, et sur les droits des habitants de cette terre.* [Charles-Gabriel-Frédéric Christin.] Neuchâtel, 1772.

A. STN
Major Dealers: Charmet, Besançon 50
(1); Letourmy, Orléans 2 (1); Rigaud,
Pons, Montpellier 12 (1); Robert et
Gauthier, Bourg-en-Bresse 100 (1).   172   (6)
Lorraine: Chénoux, Lunéville 6 (1);
Augé, Lunéville 2 (1).

Minor Dealers: Chevrier, Poitiers 18
(2).   18   (2)
                                   Total: 190   (8)

171. *Dissertation sur l'honoraire des messes, où l'on traite de son ori-
gine, des illusions et autres abus qui s'en sont suivis.* [Dom
Antoine Guiard.] n.p., 1748. At least 1 other edition by
1757.
A. STN
Major Dealers: Mauvelain, Troyes 1 (1).   1   (1)
                                   Total: 1   (1)

172. *Dissertations mêlées sur divers sujets importants et curieux.* 2
vols. [Jean-Frédéric Bernard.] Amsterdam, 1740.
C. Police Confiscations: 1 of 10 lists: Prot.

173. **Dom Alphonse l'impuissant. Tragédie.*
A. STN
Major Dealers: Robert et Gauthier,
Bourg-en-Bresse 4 (1).   4   (1)
                                   Total: 4   (1)

Dom B, portier des Chartreux. See #287, *Histoire de dom B . . .*

174. *Doutes sur la liberté de l'Escaut, réclamée par l'empereur, sur les
causes et sur les conséquences probables de cette réclamation, par le
comte de Mirabeau.* [Honoré-Gabriel Riqueti, comte de Mirabeau.] London, 1784. At least 1 other edition by 1785.
D. Customs Confiscations: 1 instance: 1786.

175. *Doutes sur la religion, suivis de l'Analyse du traité théologi-poli-
tique de Spinosa.* [*Doutes* by Henri, comte de Boulainvilliers?;
Analyse by Gayot de Pitaval.] London, 1767.
A. STN
Major Dealers: Blouet, Rennes 4 (1).   4   (1)
Minor Dealers: Chevrier, Poitiers 1 (1).   1   (1)
                                   Total: 5   (2)

B. Catalogues: 1 of 6 lists: (Bern: "4 1.").
C. Police Confiscations: 1 of 10 lists: Stockdorf.

176. *Droits (les) de la couronne de Hongrie.* 2 vols.
D. Customs Confiscations: 2 instances: 1776 (2).

177. *Droits (les) des colonies britanniques.*
A. STN
Major Dealers: Mossy, Marseille 6 (1). } 6 (1)
Total: 6 (1)

178. *Droits (les) des hommes et les usurpations des autres. Traduit de l'italien.* [François-Marie Arouet de Voltaire.] Amsterdam, 1768. At least 1 other edition in 1768.
A. STN
Major Dealers: Blouet, Rennes 6 (1);
    Robert et Gauthier, Bourg-en-Bresse
    4 (1).   15 (4)
Paris: Prévost 4 (1).
Colporteurs: "Troisième" 1 (1).
Total: 15 (4)
B. Catalogues: 3 of 6 lists: (Grasset: "8°, 8 s."; Décombaz; Bern: "50 s.").
C. Police Confiscations: 1 of 10 lists: Paris.
D. Customs Confiscations: 1 instance: 1781.

179. *Druides (les), tragédie représentée pour la première fois sur le Théâtre-Français, le 7 mars 1772.* [Antoine Blanc, dit le Blanc de Guillet.] St. Petersburg, 1783. At least 1 other edition by 1784.
A. STN
Major Dealers: Chevrier, Poitiers 4 (1). } 4 (1)
Total: 4 (1)

180. *Ebauche de la religion naturelle, par Mr. Wollaston, traduite de l'anglais avec un supplément et autres additions considérables.* 3 vols. [trans. by Garrigue?] (trans. from *The Religion of Nature Delineated* [1772] by Thomas Wollaston.) The Hague, 1726.
A. STN
Minor Dealers: Blouet, Rennes 2 (1);
    Pavie, La Rochelle 10 (2).   12 (3)
Total: 12 (3)

181. *Eclaircissements sur les Mœurs par l'auteur des Mœurs.* [François-Vincent Toussaint.] Amsterdam, 1762.
    D. Customs Confiscations: 1 instance: 1771.

182. *Ecole (l') de l'homme, ou parallèle des portraits du siècle et des tableaux de l'Ecriture Sainte, ouvrage moral, critique et anecdotique.* 3 vols. [François Genard? or Dupuis?] London, 1752. At least 3 other editions by 1762.
    C. Police Confiscations: 1 of 10 lists: Jouy, et al.

183. *Ecole (l') des filles, ou la philosophie des dames, leur indiquant le secret pour se faire aimer des hommes quand même elles ne serait pas belles, et le plus sûr moyen d'avoir du plaisir tout le temps de leur vie, divisée en deux dialogues par A.D.P.* [Michel Milot, also spelled as Mililot or Hélot.] Paris, 1655. At least 2 other editions by 1772; also in *Le Cabinet d'amour et Vénus.*
    A. STN

Major Dealers: Charmet, Besançon 25 (1); Letourmy, Orléans 68 (4); Malherbe, Loudun 50 (1).		
Lorraine: Choppin, Bar-le-Duc 2 (1); L'Entretien, Lunéville 4 (1); Audéart, Lunéville 4 (1).	185	(13)
Lyon: Cellier 2 (1).		
Paris: Barré 6 (1); Lequay Morin 12 (1); Védrène 12 (1).		
Minor Dealers: Sens, Toulouse 12 (1); Resplandy, Toulouse 13 (1); Billault, Tours 13 (1).	38	(3)
Total:	223	(16)

    B. Catalogues: 2 of 6 lists: (Cailler; Bern: "belles figures, 18 l.").
    C. Police Confiscations: 1 of 10 lists: Prot.
    D. Customs Confiscations: 1 instance: 1778 (as *La Philosophie des dames*).

    Ecumoire (l'). See #668, *Tanzaï et Néadarné.*

184. **Efforts du despotisme.* (Probably *Efforts (les) de la liberté et du patriotisme contre le despotisme du Sr Maupeou, chancelier de France, ou recueil des écrits patriotiques publiés pour maintenir l'ancien gouvernement français.* 6 vols. London, 1775.)
    C. Police Confiscations: 1 of 10 lists: Prot.

185. *Egarements (les) de Julie.* [Jacques-Antoine-René Perrin?, or Claude-Joseph Dorat?] Paris, 1755. At least 13 other editions by 1788.
    A. STN

Major Dealers: Charmet, Besançon 6 (1).	}	6 (1)
Minor Dealers: Malassis, Nantes 6 (1).	}	6 (1)
	Total:	12 (2)

186. *Eglise (de l') du pape, de quelques points de controverse et moyens de réunion de toutes les églises chrétiennes.* [Louis Dutens.] Geneva, 1781.
    A. STN

Major Dealers: Manoury, Caen 12 (1).	}	12 (1)
	Total:	12 (1)

187. *Eléments de la politique ou recherches des vrais principes de l'économie sociale.* 6 vols. [Louis-Gabriel Dubuat Nançay.] London, 1773.
    C. Police Confiscations: 1 of 10 lists: Prot.

188. *Elève (l') de la nature. Par J.-J. R.* 2 vols. [Gaspard Guillard de Beaurieu.] The Hague and Paris, 1763. At least 14 other editions by 1783.
    D. Customs Confiscations: 2 instances: 1778, 1779.

189. *Eloge de Louis XV, prononcé dans une académie, le 25 mai 1774.* [François-Marie Arouet de Voltaire.] Ferney and Geneva, 1774.
    A. STN

Major Dealers: Blouet, Rennes 6 (1). *Colporteurs:* Blaisot 6 (1); Planquais 6 (1); "Troisième" 2 (1).	}	20 (4)
	Total:	20 (4)

190. *Eloge de M. de Voltaire par M.P.* Charles Palissot de Montenoy. London, 1778. At least 1 other edition by 1779.
    A. STN

Lorraine: Bertrand, Thionville 8 (1); L'Entretien, Lunéville 12 (1).	}	20 (2)
	Total:	20 (2)

    D. Customs Confiscations: 1 instance: 1783.

191. *Eloge de M. Helvétius.* [François-Jean, marquis de Chastellux.] n.p., 1774.

A. STN
   Colporteurs: Planquais 6 (1).   }   6   (1)
                                  Total: 6   (1)

Eloge (l') des tétons. See #719, *Yeux (les), le nez et les tétons.*

192. *Eloge historique de la raison, prononcé dans une académie de province, par M. de Chambon.* [François-Marie Arouet de Voltaire.] n.p., 1775.
   A. STN
      Major Dealers: Buchet, Nîmes 13 (1); Charmet, Besançon 44 (3); Letourmy, Orléans 12 (1); Manoury, Caen 24 (1); Rigaud, Pons, Montpellier 2 (1).   }   95   (7)
      Minor Dealers: Malassis, Nantes 3 (1); Laisney, Beauvais 2 (1); Boisserand, Roanne 6 (1).   }   11   (3)
                          Total: 106   (10)

193. *Emile ou de l'éducation.* 4 vols. Jean-Jacques Rousseau. The Hague, 1762. At least 28 other editions by 1788.
   A. STN
      Major Dealers: Charmet, Besançon 4 (2).   }   6   (3)
      Colporteurs: Planquais 2 (1).
                          Total: 6   (3)
   B. Catalogues: 1 of 6 lists: (Décombaz: "12°. 4 vol. fig. Amsterd. 1765, 7 1. 10 s.").
   C. Police Confiscations: 2 of 10 lists: Pilon, Jouy, et al.
   D. Customs Confiscations: 12 instances: 1771 (7), 1772, 1773, 1775, 1778 (2).

194. *Enchiridion Leonis papae.* n.p., 1623. At least 5 other editions by 1777. French edition: *Manuel ou enchiridion de prières contenant les sept psaumes et diverses oraisons mystérieuses de Léon Pape, contre les périls du monde et pour acquérir divers secrets merveilleux.* Lyon, 1784.
   D. Customs Confiscations: 1 instance: 1777.

195. *Enfantement (l') de Jupiter ou la fille sans mère.* [François-Charles Huerne de La Mothe.] Amsterdam, 1762. At least 3

other editions by 1776; also as *Histoire nouvelle de Margot des pelotons, ou la galanterie naturelle.*

A. STN

Major Dealers: Malherbe, Loudun 33
  (2); Pavie, La Rochelle 12 (1). } 51 (4)
Lorraine: L'Entretien, Lunéville 6 (1).

Minor Dealers: Resplandy, Toulouse 13
  (1); Jarfaut, Melun 4 (1). } 17 (2)

Total: 68 (6)

C. Police Confiscations: 1 of 10 lists: Lyon.

196. *Enfer (l') détruit ou examen raisonné du dogme de l'éternité des peines, ouvrage traduit de l'anglais.* [trans. by Paul-Henri-Dietrich Thiry, baron d'Holbach.] (no available sources list the original title). London, 1769.

A. STN

Major Dealers: Blouet, Rennes 6 (1);
  Malherbe, Loudun 1 (1). } 11 (3)
Colporteurs: Gilles 4 (1).

Minor Dealers: Chevrier, Poitiers 1 (1). } 1 (1)

Total: 12 (4)

B. Catalogues: 1 of 6 lists: (Bern: "4 1.").

C. Police Confiscations: 1 of 10 lists: Prot.

197. *Entretiens (les) de l'autre monde sur ce qui se passe dans celui-ci, ou dialogues grotesques et pittoresques entre feu Louis XV, feu le prince de Conti, feu M. Turgot, Saint-Germain et autres personnages.* 2 vols. London, 1784.

A. STN

Major Dealers: Mauvelain, Troyes 50
  (6). } 50 (6)

Total: 50 (6)

198. **Entretiens de Louis XV avec le prince de Conti aux Champs-Elysées.* (Probably a version of the preceding work.)

A. STN

Minor Dealers: Laisney, Beauvais 25 (1).} 25 (1)

Total: 25 (1)

199. *Epître à Horace.* [François-Marie Arouet de Voltaire.] n.p., n.d. (1772, according to Bengesco).

B. Catalogues: 1 of 6 lists: (Grasset).

200. *Epître à Ninon de l'Enclos, et réponse à M. de V., publié par M. Asinoff, ancien pasteur d'Oldenbourg.* [*Epître* by Count Andrei Petrovich Schuvalov?, and *Réponse* by Jean-François La Harpe? or Etienne Marchand?, according to Cioranescu.] Geneva, 1774.
   A. STN
       Major Dealers: Manoury, Caen 12 (1). }   12 (1)
                                    Total: 12 (1)

201. *Epître (l') aux Romains, par le comte Passeran. Traduit de l'italien.* [François-Marie Arouet de Voltaire.] n.p., n.d. (1768, according to Cioranescu and Bengesco).
   A. STN
       Major Dealers: Blouet, Rennes 4 (1). }   4 (1)
                                    Total: 4 (1)
   B. Catalogues: 2 of 6 lists: (Grasset: "7° [sic]. 8 s."; Bern: "30 s.").
   D. Customs Confiscations: 1 instance: 1776.

202. *Epîtres, satires, contes, odes et pièces fugitives du poète philosophe, dont plusieurs n'ont point encore paru. Enrichis de notes curieuses et intéressantes.* [François-Marie Arouet de Voltaire.] London, 1771.
   A. STN
       Major Dealers: Blouet, Rennes 1 (1); Malherbe, Loudun 6 (1); Manoury, Caen 12 (1); Rigaud, Pons, Montpellier 6 (1); Robert et Gauthier, Bourg-en-Bresse 18 (2).
       Lorraine: Bertrand, Thionville 2 (1); Gay, Lunéville 12 (1); Audéart, Lunéville 12 (3); Matthieu, Nancy 4 (1); Bonthoux, Nancy 6 (1).
       Lyon: Barret 50 (2).
       Colporteurs: Blaisot 4 (1). }   133 (16)

       Minor Dealers: Malassis, Nantes 3 (1); Chevrier, Poitiers 15 (2); Fontaine, Colmar 2 (1); Boisserand, Roanne 7 (2). }   27 (6)
                                    Total: 160 (22)

B. Catalogues: 1 of 6 lists: (Bern: "5 1.").
C. Police Confiscations: 1 of 10 lists: Pilon.
D. Customs Confiscations: 1 instance: 1771.

203. *Erreurs (des) et de la verité, ou les hommes rappelés au principe universel de la science, par un Ph*** Inc . . .* [Louis-Claude, marquis de Saint-Martin.] Edinburgh, 1775. At least 2 other editions by 1784.
D. Customs Confiscations: 2 instances: 1781, 1784.

204. *Errotika Biblion.* [Honoré-Gabriel Riqueti, comte de Mirabeau.] n.p., 1783. At least 1 other edition by 1785.
A. STN

Major Dealers: Mauvelain, Troyes 24 (4)	}	24	(4)
Minor Dealers: Petit, Reims 2 (1).	}	2	(1)
	Total:	26	(5)

Espion (l') anglais. See #474, *Observateur (l') anglais . . .*

205. *Espion (l') chinois, ou l'envoyé secret de la cour de Pékin pour examiner l'état présent de l'Europe, traduit du chinois.* 6 vols. [Ange Goudar.] Cologne, 1764. At least 8 other editions by 1783.
A. STN

Major Dealers: Blouet, Rennes 4 (1); Charmet, Besançon 6 (1); Mauvelain, Troyes 3 (2); Pavie, La Rochelle 2 (1). *Colporteurs:* Gilles 6 (1); Planquais 1 (1).	}	22	(7)
Minor Dealers: Malassis, Nantes 2 (1); Chevrier, Poitiers 2 (1).	}	4	(2)
	Total:	26	(9)

B. Catalogues: 3 of 6 lists: (Grasset; Décombaz: "12°. 9 vol. 1773, 10 1."; Bern: "en feuille, 18 1., et relié, 24 1.").
C. Police Confiscations: 5 of 10 lists: Pilon, Moureau, Prot, Desauges, Paris.
D. Customs Confiscations: 2 instances: 1778, 1779.

Espion (l') des boulevards. See #145, *Désœuvré (le), ou l'espion du boulevard du Temple.*

206. *Espion (l') dévalisé.* [Baudouin de Guémadeuc.] London, 1782. At least 2 other editions by 1784.
  A. STN
      Major Dealers: Charmet, Besançon 60 (2); Mauvelain, Troyes 31 (9); Robert et Gauthier, Bourg-en-Bresse 6 (1). } 110 (13)
      Lorraine: Henry, Nancy 13 (1).

      Total: 110 (13)
  C. Police Confiscations: 2 of 10 lists: Lyon, Versailles.

207. *Espion (l') français à Londres, ou observations critiques sur l'Angleterre et sur les anglais, par M. le chevalier Goudard.* 2 vols. Ange Goudar. London, 1779. At least 1 other edition by 1780.
  A. STN
      Major Dealers: Charmet, Besançon 2 (1); Mauvelain, Troyes 4 (2).
      Lorraine: Choppin, Bar-le-Duc 2 (1). } 9 (5)
      Paris: Prévost 1 (1).
      Minor Dealers: Waroquier, Soissons 4 (3) } 4 (3)

      Total: 13 (8)

208. *Espion (l') turc dans les cours des princes chrétiens.* 6 vols. n.p., 1742. (partially trans. by Isidore-François Pidou de Saint-Olon? from *L'Esploratore turco* [1684] by Giovanni-Paolo Marana.) At least 12 other editions by 1756. (Some editions omit *"turc"* from the title.)
  A. STN
      Colporteurs: Planquais 1 (1). } 1 (1)
      Total: 1 (1)
  B. Catalogues: 1 of 6 lists: (Bern: "avec figures 24 1. relié").
  C. Police Confiscations: 1 of 10 lists: Stockdorf.
  D. Customs Confiscations: 1 instance: 1774.

209. *Esprit (de l').* [Claude-Adrien Helvétius.] Paris, 1758. At least 2 other editions in 1758.
  A. STN
      Major Dealers: Charmet, Besançon 12 (1); Malherbe, Loudun 2 (1).

continued

Lorraine: Chénoux, Lunéville 6 (1);
   Audéart, Lunéville 4 (1).   51 (6)

Lyon: Baritel 24 (1).

Paris: Barré 3 (1).

Minor Dealers: Malassis, Nantes 3 (1);
   Lair, Blois 1 (1).   4 (2)

                          Total: 55 (8)

B. Catalogues: 2 of 6 lists: (Décombaz: "8°. 3 vol. Francfort, 1768, 4 1. 10 s."; Bern: "7 1. 10 s. relié").

C. Police Confiscations: 2 of 10 lists: Stockdorf, Prot.

D. Customs Confiscations: 4 instances: 1774, 1775 (2), 1779.

210. *Esprit (l') de l'Encyclopédie, ou choix des articles les plus curieux, les plus agréables, les plus piquants, et les plus philosophiques de ce grand dictionnaire.* 5 vols. [Joseph de La Porte.] Geneva, 1768. At least 1 other edition by 1769.

A. STN

Major Dealers: Malherbe, Loudun 2 (1).

Paris: Lequay Morin 6 (1).

Colporteurs: Gilles 12 (1); Planquais 2   22 (4)
   (1).

                          Total: 22 (4)

D. Customs Confiscations: 1 instance: 1779.

211. *Esprit de l'histoire générale de l'Europe, depuis l'an 476 jusqu'à la paix de Westphalie.* [Simon-Nicolas-Henri Linguet.] London, 1783.

D. Customs Confiscations: 1 instance: 1786.

212. **Esprit (de l') de parti, dialogue du poète et de son ami.*
  B. Catalogues: 1 of 6 lists: (Décombaz: "8°. 1774, 3 s.").

213. *Esprit (l') du clergé ou le christianisme primitif vengé des entreprises et des excès de nos prêtres modernes. Traduit de l'anglais.* 2 vols. [trans. by Paul-Henri-Dietrich Thiry, baron d'Holbach, with notes by Jacques-André Naigeon.] London, 1767. (trans. from *The Independent Whig* by John Trenchard and Thomas Gordon.) At least 1 other edition by 1768 as *Les Prêtres démasqués ou des iniquités du clergé chrétien.*

A. STN

Major Dealers: Blouet, Rennes 16 (1);
Malherbe, Loudun 4 (1); Mauvelain,   27   (4)
Troyes 7 (2).

Minor Dealers: Chevrier, Poitiers 1 (1). }   1   (1)

Total: 28   (5)

    B. Catalogues: 1 of 6 lists: (Bern: "6 1." and as "Les Prêtres démasqués, 4 1.").
    C. Police Confiscations: 3 of 10 lists: Stockdorf, Pilon, Prot.

214. *Esprit (l') du judaïsme, ou examen raisonné de la loi de Moïse et de son influence sur la religion chrétienne.* [trans. by Paul-Henri-Dietrich Thiry, baron d'Holbach.] London, 1770. (trans. from *A Discourse of the Grounds and Reasons of the Christian Religion* [1724] by Anthony Collins.)
    A. STN

Major Dealers: Malherbe, Loudun 1 (1). }   1   (1)

Minor Dealers: Chevrier, Poitiers 1 (1);
Malassis, Nantes 2 (1).   3   (2)

Total: 4   (3)

    B. Catalogues: 1 of 6 lists: (Bern: "3 1.").
    C. Police Confiscations: 3 of 10 lists: Stockdorf, Pilon, Prot.

215. *Esprit et génie de l'abbé Raynal, tiré de ses ouvrages.* [Jean-Baptiste-Antoine Hédouin.] Montargis, 1777. At least 1 other edition by 1782.
    C. Police Confiscations: 1 of 10 lists: Versailles.

216. *Essai contre l'abus du pouvoir des souverains, et juste idée du gouvernement d'un bon prince. Suivi du Tocsin contre le despotisme du souverain. Par M.**, avocat.* London, 1776.
    C. Police Confiscations: 1 of 10 lists: Prot.

217. *Essai général de tactique précédé d'un discours sur l'état actuel de la politique et la science militaire en Europe.* 2 vols. [Jacques-Antoine-Hippolyte de Guibert.] London, 1772.
    B. Catalogues: 1 of 6 lists: (Bern: "Avec le plan d'un ouvrage intitulé: la France politique & militaire, 22 1.").
    D. Customs Confiscations: 1 instance: 1774.

218. *Essai historique sur la vie de Marie Antoinette d'Autriche, reine de France, pour servir à l'histoire de cette princesse.* [Pierre-Etienne-Auguste Goupil?] London, 1789.

A. STN
   Major Dealers: Mauvelain, Troyes 6 (1). }   6   (1)
                   Total: 6   (1)

219. *Essai philosophique sur l'âme des bêtes où l'on traite de son existence et de sa nature et où l'on mêle par occasion diverses réflexions
   sur la nature de la liberté, sur celle de nos sensations, sur l'union
   de l'âme et du corps, sur l'immortalité de l'âme, et où l'on réfute
   diverses objections de M. Bayle.* [David-Renaud Boullier.]
   Amsterdam, 1728. At least 1 other edition by 1737.
   D. Customs Confiscations: 1 instance: 1779.

220. *Essai philosophique sur le monachisme, par M.L.* [Simon-Nico-
   las-Henri Linguet.] Paris, 1775. At least 1 other edition by
   1777.
   A. STN
   Major Dealers: Bergeret, Bordeaux 6 ⎤
       (1); Charmet, Besançon 93 (5); Le- ⎟
       tourmy, Orléans 4 (1); Malherbe, ⎟
       Loudun 75 (2); Mossy, Marseille 26 ⎬   208   (12)
       (1). ⎟
   Lorraine: d'Alancourt, Nancy 2 (1). ⎟
   Paris: Cugnet 2 (1). ⎦
   Minor Dealers: Sens, Toulouse 61 (3); ⎤
       Resplandy, Toulouse 26 (1); Som- ⎟
       bert, Châlons-sur-Marne 6 (1); Lais- ⎬   108   (7)
       ney, Beauvais 13 (1); Billault, Tours ⎟
       2 (1). ⎦
                      Total: 316   (19)

221. *Essai politique sur la véritable liberté civile, discours adressé au
   peuple d'Angleterre.* London, 1771.
   C. Police Confiscations: 1 of 10 lists: Prot.

222. *Essai sur la liberté de produire ses sentiments.* [Elie Luzac.] Au
   pays libres, 1749.
   C. Police Confiscations: 1 of 10 lists: Paris.

223. *Essai sur la nature et la destination de l'âme.* [trans. by Paul-
   Henri-Dietrich Thiry, baron d'Holbach?] (trans. from pam-
   phlets by Anthony Collins, including *Letter to Dodwell*
   [1707].) London, 1769.

A. STN

    Major Dealers: Blouet, Rennes 6 (1).   }   6 (1)

    Minor Dealers: Chevrier, Poitiers 1 (1). }   <u>1 (1)</u>

                                Total: 7 (2)

B. Catalogues: 1 of 6 lists: (Bern: "4 1.").

C. Police Confiscations: 3 of 10 lists: Stockdorf, Pilon, Prot.

224. *Essai sur la providence et sur la possibilité physique de la resurrection. Traduit de l'anglais du Dr. B***.* [Jean Bion and Prosper Marchand.] The Hague, 1719. (Not a translation, according to Barbier.) At least 1 other edition by 1731.

A. STN

    Major Dealers: Letourmy, Orléans 4 (1);

    Malherbe, Loudun 12 (1); Manoury,   28   (3)

    Caen 12 (1).

                           Total: <u>28   (3)</u>

225. *Essai sur le despotisme.* [Honoré-Gabriel Riqueti, comte de Mirabeau.] London, 1775. At least 2 other editions by 1786.

A. STN

    Major Dealers: Blouet, Rennes 4 (1);

    Letourmy, Orléans 8 (2); Pavie, La

    Rochelle 32 (2).

    Lorraine: Bertrand, Thionville 3 (1).   112   (11)

    Lyon: Flandin 30 (1); Jacquenod 1 (1).

    Paris: Barré 3 (1); Prévost 6 (1).

    Colporteurs: Gilles 25 (1).

    Minor Dealers: Sens, Toulouse 6 (1);

    Bonnard, Auxerre 3 (1); Fontaine,   15   (5)

    Colmar 2 (1); Jarfaut, Melun 2 (1);

    Billault, Tours 2 (1).

                           Total: <u>127   (16)</u>

C. Police Confiscations: 1 of 10 lists: Prot.

226. *Essai sur les préjugés, ou de l'influence des opinions sur les mœurs et sur le bonheur des hommes. Ouvrage contenant l'apologie de la philosophie, par Mr. D.M.* [Paul-Henri-Dietrich Thiry, baron d'Holbach, or César-Chesneau Du Marsais?, with notes by Jacques-André Naigeon.] London, 1770. At least 2 other editions by 1777.

A. STN

Major Dealers: Blouet, Rennes 4 (1);
   Malherbe, Loudun 1 (1); Mauvelain,   11 (3)
   Troyes 6 (1).

Minor Dealers: Malassis, Nantes 1 (1);
   Chevrier, Poitiers 1 (1).   2 (2)

                                  Total: 13 (5)

C. Police Confiscations: 2 of 10 lists: Stockdorf, Pilon.

D. Customs Confiscations: 1 instance: 1779.

227. *Essai sur les probabilités en fait de justice.* [François-Marie Arouet de Voltaire.] n.p., n.d. (1772, according to Bengesco). At least 2 other undated editions.

C. Customs Confiscations: 1 instance: 1772.

228. *Essai sur l'histoire générale et sur les mœurs et l'esprit des nations, depuis Charlemagne jusqu'à nos jours.* 7 vols. [François-Marie Arouet de Voltaire.] n.p., 1756. At least 6 other editions by 1775; 1775 as *Essai sur les mœurs et l'esprit.*

C. Police Confiscations: 1 of 10 lists: Prot.

229. *Essais historiques, critiques, littéraires et philosophiques, par M. Ma . . .* [Louis-Pierre Manuel.] Geneva, 1783.

A. STN

Major Dealers: Mauvelain, Troyes 16
   (4).   16 (4)

                                    Total: 16 (4)

230. *Essais politiques sur l'état actuel de quelques puissances, par M.R.C.B.* [James Rutledge.] London, 1777.

D. Customs Confiscations: 1 instance: 1781.

Essais sur le bal général prochain des puissances européens. See #113, *Congrès (le) politique . . .*

231. *Essais sur les mystères et le véritable objet de la confrérie des Francs-Maçons.* [Karl-Friedrich Koeppen.] The Hague, 1771. At least 1 other edition by 1776.

A. STN

Lorraine: Choppin, Bar-le-Duc 1 (1)
Paris: Prévost 6 (1).   7 (2)

                                  Total: 7 (2)

232. *Essais sur Paris.* (Possibly *Essais historiques sur Paris de M. de Saint-Foix.* 2 vols. Germain-François Poullain de Saint-Foix. London, 1754–55. At least 7 other editions by 1776.)
    D. Customs Confiscations: 3 instances: 1774, 1775 (2).

233. *Etat (de l') de l'Eglise, et de la puissance légitime du pontife romain.* 2 vols. [abridged and trans. by Remacle Lissoir.] Wurtzburg, 1766. (trans. from *Justini Febronii . . . de statu ecclesiae et legitima potestate romani pontificus* [1763] by Johann Nicolas Von Hontheim.) At least 1 other edition by 1786.
    B. Catalogues: 1 of 6 lists: (Bern: "6.1.").
    C. Police Confiscations: 3 of 10 lists: Stockdorf, Pilon, Prot.

234. *Etat de l'homme dans le péché originel où l'on fait voir quelle est la source et quelles sont les causes et les suites de ce péché dans le monde.* [trans. by Jean-Frédéric Bernard.] Imprimé dans le monde, 1714. (trans. from *Peccatum originale . . .* [1678] by Adriaan Beverland.) At least 5 other editions by 1774.
    C. Police Confiscations: 1 of 10 lists: Prot.

235. *Etat présent de la Pennsylvanie où l'on trouve le détail de ce qui s'y est passé depuis la defaite du général Braddock jusqu'à la prise d'Oswego, avec une carte particulière de cette colonie.* [trans. by Jean-Ignace de la Ville.] n.p., n.d. (trans. from *A Brief View of the Conduct of Pennsylvania for the Year 1755* by H. W. Smith.)
    D. Customs Confiscations: 1 instance: 1779.

236. *Etrennes aux désœuvrés ou lettre d'un Quaker à ses frères et à un grand docteur.* Lewis Penn. London, 1767.
    A. STN
       Major Dealers: Blouet, Rennes 6 (1).   }   6 (1)
       Minor Dealers: Chevrier, Poitiers 1 (1). }   1 (1)
                                         Total: 7 (2)
    B. Catalogues: 1 of 6 lists: (Bern: "30 s.").
    C. Police Confiscations: 1 of 10 lists: Prot.

237. *Etrennes voluptueuses dédiées aux Grâces, par Mme L.M.D.P., contenant la jouissance des cinq sens et plusieurs autres pièces.* [François-Antoine Chevrier?] London, n.d. (c. 1760, according to Gay).
    D. Customs Confiscations: 1 instance: 1771.

238. *Evangile (l') de la raison. Ouvrage posthume de M.D.M. . . . Y.*

[ed. by François-Marie Arouet de Voltaire.] n.p., n.d. (1764, according to Cioranescu and Bengesco). At least 6 other editions by 1768.

A. STN

> *Major Dealers:* Charmet, Besançon 6 (1).   6 (1)
>
> *Minor Dealers:* Malassis, Nantes 3 (1); Chevrier, Poitiers 3 (1).   6 (2)
>
> Total: 12 (3)

B. Catalogues: 2 of 6 lists: (Grasset; Bern: "12 1.").
C. Police Confiscations: 1 of 10 lists: Stockdorf.
D. Customs Confiscations: 1 instance: 1779.

239. *Evangile (l') du jour.* 16 vols. [François-Marie Arouet de Voltaire.] London, 1769–80.

A. STN

> *Major Dealers:* Blouet, Rennes 6 (1); Malherbe, Loudun 20 (1); Mauvelain, Troyes 7 (2).
> *Colporteurs:* Gilles 39 (3).   72 (7)
>
> *Minor Dealers:* Malassis, Nantes 3 (1); Chevrier, Poitiers 1 (1).   4 (2)
>
> Total: 76 (9)

B. Catalogues: 1 of 6 lists: (Bern: "18 1.").
C. Police Confiscations: 1 of 10 lists: Prot.
D. Customs Confiscations: 1 instance: 1772.

240. *Examen critique de la vie et des ouvrages de Saint Paul. Avec un dissertation sur Saint Pierre, par feu M. Boulanger.* [trans. by Paul-Henri-Dietrich Thiry, baron d'Holbach.] (trans. from *The History and Character of St. Paul Examined* [1742?] by Peter Annet.) London, 1770.

A. STN

> *Major Dealers:* Blouet, Rennes 4 (1); Robert et Gauthier, Bourg-en-Bresse 7 (2).   11 (3)
>
> *Minor Dealers:* Malassis, Nantes 3 (1); Chevrier, Poitiers 1 (1).   4 (2)
>
> Total: 15 (5)

B. Catalogues: 1 of 6 lists: (Bern: "4 1.").
C. Police Confiscations: 2 of 10 lists: Stockdorf, Prot.

241. *Examen critique des apologistes de la religion chrétienne, par M. Fréret.* [Jean Lévesque de Burigny?] n.p., 1766.
   A. STN

Major Dealers: Bergeret, Bordeaux 12 (2); Blouet, Rennes 10 (2); Le-tourmy, Orléans 12 (2); Manoury, Caen 25 (1).		
Lorraine: Audéart, Lunéville 2 (1); Augé, Lunéville 4 (2); Sandré, Lunéville 3 (1).	86	(15)
Paris: Barré 3 (1); Prévost 9 (2); Védrène 6 (1).		
Minor Dealers: Chevrier, Poitiers 1 (1); Cazin, Reims 25 (1); Billault, Tours 3 (1); Caldesaigues, Marseille 8 (1).	37	(4)
Total:	123	(19)

   B. Catalogues: 3 of 6 lists: (Grasset; Décombaz: "8°. 1767, "1 1. 10 s"; Bern: "4 1.").
   C. Police Confiscations: 4 of 10 lists: Stockdorf, Pilon, Prot, Desauges.
   D. Customs Confiscations: 2 instances: 1771, 1772.

242. *Examen critique du militaire français, suivi des principes qui doivent déterminer sa constitution, sa discipline et son instruction, par M. le M.B.D.B.* 3 vols. [Baron François-Philippe Loubat de Bohan.] Geneva, 1781.
   A. STN

Major Dealers: Charmet, Besançon 8 (2).	8	(2)
Total:	8	(2)

   Examen critique du Nouveau Testament. See #612, *Réflexions impartiales sur l'Evangile par feu M. de Mirabaud.*

243. *Examen de la doctrine touchant le salut des païens, ou nouvelle apologie pour Socrate, par Mr Jean Auguste Eberhard, traduit de l'allemand.* [trans. by Charles-Guillaume-Frédéric Dumas.] Amsterdam, 1773. (trans. from *Neue Apologie des Sokrates oder Untersuchung der Lehre von der Seligkeit der Heiden* [1772–78] by Johann August Eberhard.)
   C. Police Confiscations: 1 of 10 lists: Prot.

244. *Examen de la religion dont on cherche l'éclaircissement de bonne foi, ouvrage attribué à Mr. de Saint-Evremond, traduit de l'anglais de Gilbert Burnet.* [Charles de Marguetel de Saint-Denis, seigneur de Saint-Evremond.] London, 1745. (Attribution to St.-Evremond is apocryphal; the author is De La Serre, according to the B.N. catalogue, which also lists *La Vraie Religion démontrée par l'Ecriture Sainte, traduite de l'anglais par Gilbert Burnet* as a 1767 edition of the above.)
   B. Catalogues: 1 of 6 lists: (Bern: "4 1." and as "La Vraie religion, 4 1.").

245. *Examen de l'Essai sur les préjugés.* [Frederick II.] London, 1770.
   A. STN

Minor Dealers: Chevrier, Poitiers 1 (1). }	1	(1)
Total:	1	(1)

   B. Catalogues: 1 of 6 lists: (Bern: "4 1.").
   C. Police Confiscations: 2 of 10 lists: Stockdorf, Pilon.

246. **Examen de l'évidence du Christianisme.*
   C. Police Confiscations: 1 of 10 lists: Desauges.

247. *Examen des prophéties qui servent de fondement à la religion chrétienne. Avec un essai de critique sur les prophètes et les prophéties en général. Ouvrages traduits de l'anglais.* [trans. by Paul-Henri-Dietrich Thiry, baron d'Holbach.] (Freely translated and summarized from *A Discourse on the Grounds and Reasons of the Christian Religion* [1724] and *The Scheme of Literal Prophecy Considered* [1726], both by Anthony Collins.) London, 1768.
   A. STN

Major Dealers: Blouet, Rennes 2 (1). }	2	(1)
Minor Dealers: Chevrier, Poitiers 1 (1). }	1	(1)
Total:	3	(2)

   B. Catalogues: 1 of 6 lists: (Bern: "4 1.").
   C. Police Confiscations: 2 of 10 lists: Stockdorf, Pilon.

248. *Examen impartial des principales religions du monde.* Paris, n.d. (Condemned by the Parlement of Paris in 1770, according to Peignot.)
   A. STN

Major Dealers: Blouet, Rennes 6 (1);
    Mauvelain, Troyes 6 (1).   }   12   (2)

Minor Dealers: Malassis, Nantes 2 (1). }   2   (1)

                          Total: 14   (3)

B. Catalogues: 1 of 6 lists: (Bern: "4 1.").

C. Police Confiscations: 3 of 10 lists: Stockdorf, Pilon, Prot.

249. *Examen important de Milord Bolingbroke, écrit sur la fin de 1736.* [François-Marie-Arouet de Voltaire.] n.p., 1767 (first appeared in *Recueil nécessaire* [1765], according to Cioranescu and Bengesco). At least 4 other editions by 1776.

A. STN

Major Dealers: Bergeret, Bordeaux 6
(1); Blouet, Rennes 4 (1); Buchet,
Nîmes 13 (1); Malherbe, Loudun 1
(1); Letourmy, Orléans 6 (1); Pavie,
La Rochelle 6 (1).

Lorraine: Bonthoux, Nancy 2 (1); Ché-
noux, Lunéville 18 (2); Gerlache,
Metz 42 (4); Gay, Lunéville 16 (2).   }   128   (18)

Lyon: Barret 6 (1).

Paris: Lequay Morin 2 (1); Prévost 6
(1).

Minor Dealers: Chevrier, Poitiers 1 (1);
Sens, Toulouse 4 (1); Resplandy,   }   18   (3)
Toulouse 13 (1).

                          Total: 146   (21)

B. Catalogues: 5 of 6 lists: (Grasset: "8°, 1 1. 10 s."; Décom-
baz: "8°. 1767, 2 1."; Cailler; Chappuis et Didier: "8°. 15
s."; Bern).

C. Police Confiscations: 1 of 10 lists: Stockdorf.

D. Customs Confiscations: 1 instance: 1772.

250. *Exposé des motifs qui ont engagé Sa Majesté le roi de Prusse à s'opposer au démembrement de la Bavière.* [Ewald Friedrich, Graf von Hertzberg.] n.p., 1778.

A. STN

Major Dealers: Manoury, Caen 12 (1). }   12   (1)

                          Total: 12   (1)

251. *Extrait des assertions dangereuses et pernicieuses en tout genre,*

que les soi-disant jésuites ont soutenues, enseignées et publiées dans leurs livres. 3 vols. Amsterdam, 1763.
  B. Catalogues: 1 of 6 lists: (Bern).

252. *Extrait du Dictionnaire historique et critique de Bayle, divisé en deux volumes, avec une préface.* 2 vols. [Frederick II and Jean-Baptiste de Boyer, marquis d'Argens?] Berlin, 1765. At least 2 other editions by 1780.
  C. Police Confiscations: 1 of 10 lists: Prot.

253. *Extrait du droit public de la France, par Louis Brancas, comte de Lauraguais.* [Louis-Léon-Félicité de Brancas, comte de Lauraguais.] En France, 1771.
  C. Police Confiscations: 1 of 10 lists: Pilon.

254. *Fanatisme (le) des philosophes.* [Simon-Nicolas-Henri Linguet.] London, 1764.
  B. Catalogues: 1 of 6 lists: (Bern: "30 s.").

255. *Fastes (les) de Louis XV, de ses ministres, maîtresses, généraux et autres notables personnages de son règne.* 2 vols. [Bouffonidor, i.e., Ange Goudar.] Villefranche, 1782.
  A. STN
    Major Dealers: Manoury, Caen 25 (1); Mauvelain, Troyes 97 (2); Robert et Gauthier, Bourg-en-Bresse 39 (1). *Lorraine:* Carez, Toul 6 (1); Bonthoux, Nancy 4 (1); Henri, Nancy 4 (1).   175 (7)

                         Total: 175 (7)
  D. Customs Confiscations: 3 instances: 1783, 1784, 1787.

256. *Fausseté (la) des miracles des deux testaments, prouvée par le parallèle avec de semblables prodiges opérés dans diverses sectes, ouvrage traduit du manuscrit latin intitulé "Theophrastus redivivus."* London, 1775.
  A. STN
    Major Dealers: Blouet, Rennes 6 (1); Letourmy, Orléans 6 (1); Malherbe, Loudun 6 (1); Mauvelain, Troyes 7 (2); Pavie, La Rochelle 4 (1). *Lorraine:* Audéart, Lunéville 6 (1). *Lyon:* Flandin 6 (1). *Paris:* Barré 6 (1).   47 (9)

Minor Dealers: Malassis, Nantes 3 (1);
   Chevrier, Poitiers 3 (2); Sens, Tou-
   louse 4 (1); Billault, Tours 13 (1);   31   (6)
   Caldesaigues, Marseille 8 (1).

                         Total: 78 (15)

  B. Catalogues: 2 of 6 lists: (Décombaz: "8°. Lond. 1774, 1
     1. 10 s."; Bern: "3 1.").
  C. Police Confiscations: 3 of 10 lists: Stockdorf, Pilon,
    Desauges.
  D. Customs Confiscations: 1 instance: 1778.

257. *Félicia ou mes fredaines.* [André-Robert Andréa de Nerciat.]
    London, 1775. At least 13 other editions by 1786.
    A. STN

      Major Dealers: Manoury, Caen 25 (1). }   25 (1)
                        Total: 25 (1)

258. *Félicité (de la) publique, ou considérations sur le sort des hommes
    dans les différentes époques de l'histoire.* 2 vols. [François-Jean,
    marquis de Chastellux.] Amsterdam, 1772. At least 1 other
    edition by 1776.
    A. STN

      Major Dealers: Blouet, Rennes 12 (1);
        Malherbe, Loudun 26 (1); Mossy,
        Marseille 10 (2).   61   (6)
      Lorraine: Chénoux, Lunéville 12 (1);
        Bertrand, Thionville 1 (1).
      Minor Dealers: Chevrier, Poitiers 2 (1). }   2   (1)
                        Total: 63 (7)

  B. Catalogues: 1 of 6 lists: (Bern: "9 1.").
  C. Police Confiscations: 3 of 10 lists: Stockdorf, Pilon, Prot.

259. *Fille (la) de joie, ouvrage quintessencié de l'anglais.* Lampsaque,
    1751. [trans. by Lambert? or Charles-Louis Fougeret de
    Monbron?] (trans. from *Memoirs of a Woman of Pleasure*
    [1748–49] by John Cleland.) At least 15 other editions by
    1788.
    A. STN

      Major Dealers: Charmet, Besançon 12
        (1); Letourmy, Orléans 61 (4); Mal-
        herbe, Loudun 65 (2); Pavie, La
        Rochelle 20 (2).

continued

Lorraine: Choppin, Bar-le-Duc 4 (1); Bertrand, Thionville 4 (1); Bergue, Thionville 25 (1); Matthieu, Nancy 2 (1); Babin, Nancy 1 (1).   306 (24)

Lyon: Baritel 6 (1); Cellier 2 (1).

Paris: Barré 6 (1); Lequay Morin 12 (1); Prévost 4 (1).

Colporteurs: Blaisot 12 (1); Planquais 6 (1); "Troisième" 19 (1); Gilles 54 (2).

Minor Dealers: Malassis, Nantes 15 (1); Sens, Toulouse 12 (1); Resplandy, Toulouse 13 (1); Bonnard, Auxerre 3 (1); Billault, Tours 13 (1); Caldesaigues, Marseille 19 (1).   66 (6)

Total: 372 (30)

B. Catalogues: 4 of 6 lists: (Grasset; Décombaz: "8°. fig. Lampsaque, 1770, 2 1. 5 s." and "8°. 2 part. fig. Londres, 1774, 12 1."; Cailler; Bern: "avec figures 18 1.").

C. Police Confiscations: 4 of 10 lists: Moureau, Prot, Lyon, Paris.

D. Customs Confiscations: 5 instances: 1774, 1777, 1778, 1781, 1786.

260. *Fille (la) naturelle.* [Nicolas-Edmé Restif de la Bretonne.] The Hague and Paris, 1769. At least 7 other editions by 1776.

A. STN

Major Dealers: Bergeret, Bordeaux 4 (1); Charmet, Besançon 25 (1); Letourmy, Orléans 31 (2); Mossy, Marseille 25 (2); Robert et Gauthier, Bourg-en-Bresse 18 (2).   112 (11)

Lorraine: Choppin, Bar-le-Duc 4 (1); Bernard, Lunéville 1 (1); L'Entretien, Lunéville 4 (1).

Minor Dealers: Chevrier, Poitiers 3 (1); Petit, Reims 5 (2); Jarfaut, Melun 10 (1); Billault, Tours 2 (1).   20 (5)

Total: 132 (16)

D. Customs Confiscations: 1 instance: 1777.

261. *Folies philosophiques par un homme retiré du monde.* 2 vols. [Jean-Pierre-Louis de la Roche du Maine, marquis de Luchet.] n.p., 1784. At least 1 other edition in 1784.
   D. Customs Confiscations: 1 instance: 1786.

262. *Fond (le) du sac ou restant des babioles de M. X***, membre éveillé de l'Académie des dormants.* 2 vols. [François-Félix Nogaret.] Venice, 1780.
   D. Customs Confiscations: 1 instance: 1783.

263. *Foutro-manie (la), poème lubrique en six chants.* [Gabriel Sénac de Meilhan?, or Claude-François-Xavier Mercier de Compiègne?] Sardanapolis, 1780. (Weller suggests that the first edition was 1775; Gay suggests c. 1778.)
   A. STN
   Major Dealers: Manoury, Caen 100 (1). }   100   (1)
                                     Total: 100   (1)
   C. Police Confiscations: 1 of 10 lists: Prot.
   D. Customs Confiscations: 1 instance: 1784.

264. *Fragment des instructions pour le prince royal de* *** [François-Marie Arouet de Voltaire.] Berlin, 1766. At least 4 other editions by 1768.
   B. Catalogues: 2 of 6 lists: (Grasset: "8°. 12 s."; Décombaz).
   C. Police Confiscations: 1 of 10 lists: Pilon.

265. *Fragments sur l'Inde et sur le général Lalli.* [François-Marie Arouet de Voltaire.] n.p., 1773. At least 5 other editions by 1779; also as *Fragments sur quelques révolutions de l'Inde et sur la mort du comte de Lally.*
   A. STN
   Major Dealers: Charmet, Besançon 20 (1); Mossy, Marseille 20 (1); Rigaud, Pons, Montpellier 6 (1); Robert et Gauthier, Bourg-en-Bresse 4 (1).   64   (8)
   Lorraine: Bertrand, Thionville 4 (1); Bernard, Lunéville 1 (1); Audéart, Lunéville 9 (2).
   Minor Dealers: Chevrier, Poitiers 3 (1); Jarfaut, Melun 2 (1).   5   (2)
                                     Total: 69   (10)

266. *Galanteries des rois de France, depuis le commencement de la monarchie jusqu'à présent.* [Claude Vanel.] Brussels, 1694. At least 9 other editions by 1753; 1740 as *Intrigues galantes de la cour de France;* 1753 as *Galanteries de la cour de France.*
   A. STN

   Major Dealers: Mauvelain, Troyes 1 (1) }   1   (1)
                                       Total: 1   (1)

267. *Gazetier (le) cuirassé, ou anecdotes scandaleuses de la cour de France.* [Charles Théveneau de Morande.] A cent lieues de la Bastille, 1771. At least 2 other editions by 1777; also as *Mélanges confus sur les matières fort claires . . .*
   A. STN

   Major Dealers: Blouet, Rennes 18 (3);   ⎫
       Charmet, Besançon 12 (1); Robert et   ⎪
       Gauthier, Bourg-en-Bresse 6 (1).   ⎪
   Lorraine: Chénoux, Lunéville 24 (2);   ⎪
       Augé, Lunéville 2 (1); Gerlache,   ⎬   124   (5)
       Metz 6 (1); Orbelin, Thionville 1 (1);   ⎪
       Matthieu, Nancy 6 (1).   ⎪
   Lyon: Barret 6 (1).   ⎪
   Paris: Desauges 25 (1).   ⎪
   Colporteurs: Gilles 18 (2).   ⎭
   Minor Dealers: Petit, Reims 1 (1); Calde-⎫
       saigues, Marseille 10 (1).   ⎬   11   (2)
                                    Total: 135   (7)
   B. Catalogues: 1 of 6 lists: (Décombaz: "8°. 1771, 3 l.").
   C. Police Confiscations: 4 of 10 lists: Stockdorf, Pilon, Prot, Versailles.
   D. Customs Confiscations: 4 instances: 1775, 1778, 1781, 1784.

268. **Gazetier (le) monastique.* 2 vols.
   A. STN

   Major Dealers: Mauvelian, Troyes 12 }   12   (2)
       (2).
                                      Total: 12   (2)

269. *Gazette (la) de Cythère, ou aventures galantes et récentes arrivées dans les principales villes de l'Europe, traduite de l'anglais, à la fin de laquelle on a joint le Précis historique de la vie de Mad. la*

comtesse du Barry. [François Bernard.] London, 1774. At least 2 other editions by 1776.

A. STN

    Major Dealers: Manoury, Caen 100 (1)   }   100 (1)

                              Total: 100 (1)

C. Police Confiscations: 3 of 10 lists: Manoury, Prot, Versailles.

D. Customs Confiscations: 2 instances: 1775 (2).

270. *Gazette (la) noire, par un homme qui n'est pas blanc, ou œuvres posthumes du Gazetier cuirassé.* [Charles Théveneau de Morande.] A cent lieues de la Bastille, 1784.

A. STN

    Major Dealers: Mauvelain, Troyes 12   }   12 (2)

      (2).

                            Total: 12 (2)

271. *Génération (la) de l'homme, ou le tableau de l'amour conjugal considéré dans l'état de mariage.* [Nicolas Venette.] Amsterdam, 1687.

D. Customs Confiscations: 1 instance: 1779.

Grand Albert (le). See #7, *Admirables Secrets (les) d'Albert le Grand . . .*

272. *Grand Grimoire (le), avec la clavicule de Salomon, et la magie noire, ou les forces infernales du grand Agrippa, pour découvrir tous les trésors cachés, et se faire obéir de tous les esprits: suivis de tous les arts magiques.* n.p., 1202 [sic].

B. Catalogues: 2 of 6 lists: (Décombaz: "12°. fig. 1702. 1 1. 15 s."; Cailler: "12°. fig. 1702.").

273. *Grand-Œuvre (le) dévoilé en faveur des personnes qui ont grand besoin d'argent. Par celui qui l'a fait.* Paris, 1779.

B. Catalogues: 1 of 6 lists: (Chappuis et Didier: "8°. 1780, 5 s.").

C. Police Confiscations: 1 of 10 lists: Desauges.

274. *Grélot (le) ou les etc., etc., etc., ouvrage dédié à moi.* [Paul Baret.] Ici, à présent (1754, according to Martin-Mylne-Frautschi). At least 5 other editions by 1782.

C. Police Confiscations: 1 of 10 lists: Paris.

275. *Grigri, histoire véritable traduite du japonais en portugais par Didaque Hadeczuca, compagnon d'un missionnaire à Yendo, et du portugais en français par l'abbé de ***, aumônier d'un vaisseau hollandais, Dernière édition.* 2 vols. [ed. by Louis de Cahusac.] Nagazaki, l'an du monde 59749 (1739, according to Martin-Mylne-Frautschi). At least 6 other editions by 1782.
   C. Police Confiscations: 2 of 10 lists: Manoury, Prot.

276. *Grimoire, ou la magie naturelle.* The Hague, n.d.
   B. Catalogues: 1 of 6 lists: (Décombaz: "12°. La Haye, 1770. 2 1. 10 s.").

277. *Guèbres (les), ou la tolérance, tragédie par M. D*** M***.* [François-Marie Arouet de Voltaire.] n.p., 1769. At least 5 other editions by 1777.
   A. STN

Colporteurs: Blaisot 1 (1); "Troisième" 2 (1).	3	(2)
Minor Dealers: Blouet, Rennes 2 (1); Robert et Gauthier, Bourg-en-Bresse 1 (1).	3	(2)
Total:	6	(4)

278. *Guerre (la) civile de Genève, ou les amours de Robert Covelle. Poème héroïque avec des notes instructives.* [François-Marie Arouet de Voltaire.] Besançon, 1768. At least 4 other editions by 1775.
   A. STN

Lorraine: Audéart, Lunéville 8 (2).	8	(2)
Total:	8	(2)

   B. Catalogues: 2 of 6 lists: (Grasset: "8°. 12 s."; Bern: "30 s.").

279. *Guzmanade (la), ou l'établissement de l'Inquisition, poème en XII chants.* [Honoré-Gabriel Riqueti, comte de Mirabeau?] Amsterdam, 1778.
   A. STN

Major Dealers: Mauvelain, Troyes 7 (1).	7	(1)
Total:	7	(1)

280. **Haquenettes ou étrennes au seigneur de Maupeou.*
   C. Police Confiscations: 2 of 10 lists: Pilon, Manoury.

281. *Haute messe célébrée par l'abbé Perchel, conseiller-clerc du ci-devant soi-disant conseil supérieur de Rouen.* [Anne-Louis-François Percel?] Aux dépens du Conseil Supérieur, 1774. At least 1 other edition by 1777.
    C. Police Confiscations: 1 of 10 lists: Manoury.

282. *Hazard (le) du coin du feu, dialogue moral.* Claude-Prosper Jolyot de Crébillon, fils. The Hague, 1763. At least 2 other editions by 1764.
    B. Catalogues: 1 of 6 lists: (Décombaz: "12°. la Haye, 1763. 1 1. 5 s.").

    Heptaméron. See #119, *Contes et nouvelles de la reine de Navarre.*

283. *Heureux Jour (l'), épitre à mon ami.* Paris, 1768.
    C. Police Confiscations: 1 of 10 lists: Pilon.

284. *Histoire abrégée des religions du monde, ou l'analyse de l'Encyclo-pédie de Voltaire.* Geneva, 1770.
    D. Customs Confiscations: 1 instance: 1771.

285. **Histoire abrégée du sacerdoce ancien et moderne.*
    A. STN
        Lorraine: Chénoux, Lunéville 3 (1). }   3   (1)
        Minor Dealers: Chevrier, Poitiers 2 (1). }   2   (1)
                                            Total: 5   (2)

286. *Histoire critique de Jésus-Christ, ou, analyse raisonnée des Evangiles.* [Paul-Henri-Dietrich Thiry, baron d'Holbach.] n.p., n.d. (1770, according to Vercruysse.) At least 2 other editions by 1778.
    A. STN
        Major Dealers: Blouet, Rennes 190 (5); Malherbe, Loudun 28 (3); Mauvelain, Troyes 22 (7); Pavie, La Rochelle 12 (1); Robert et Gauthier, Bourg-en-Bresse 4 (1).
        Lorraine: Chénoux, Lunéville 6 (1); Augé, Lunéville 2 (1); Bertrand, Thionville 2 (1); Bergue, Thionville 6 (1); Orbelin, Thionville 6 (1); Gay, Lunéville 4 (1); Audéart, Lunéville 22 (7).

continued

Lyon: Barret 6 (1).

Colporteurs: Blaisot 6 (1); Planquais 6
(1); "Troisième" 2 (1).

324 (34)

Minor Dealers: Malassis, Nantes 2 (1);
Chevrier, Poitiers 1 (1).

3 (2)

Total: 327 (36)

B. Catalogues: 4 of 6 lists: (Grasset: "8°., 2 1."; Décombaz:
"8°., 1774, 2 1. 10 s."; Chappuis et Didier: "gr. 8°. 1778,
1 1. 10 s."; Bern: "6 1.").

C. Police Confiscations: 2 of 10 lists: Stockdorf, Pilon.

D. Customs Confiscations: 2 instances: 1775, 1776.

287. *Histoire de dom B . . . , portier des Chartreux, écrite par lui-même.* [Jean-Charles Gervaise de Latouche?, or Charles Nourry?] Rome, n.d., (c. 1745, according to Martin-Mylne-Frautschi). At least 19 other editions by 1788; also as *Le Portier des Chartreux, Histoire de Gouberdom,* and *Mémoires de Saturnin.*

A. STN

Major Dealers: Blouet, Rennes 8 (2);
Malherbe, Loudun 52 (1); Pavie, La
Rochelle 1 (1); Robert et Gauthier,
Bourg-en-Bresse 36 (3).

Lorraine: Sandré, Lunéville 2 (1); Bertrand, Thionville 6 (1); Orbelin, Thionville 6 (1); Gay, Lunéville 4 (1);
Audéart, Lunéville 2 (1).

Lyon: Baritel 6 (1).

Colporteurs: Gilles 29 (2).

152 (15)

Minor Dealers: Malassis, Nantes 6 (1);
Petit, Reims 2 (1); Habert, Bar-sur-
Aube 4 (1); Lair, Blois 1 (1); Calde-
saigues, Marseille 25 (1).

38 (5)

Total: 190 (20)

B. Catalogues: 5 of 6 lists: (Grasset; Décombaz: "8°. 2 vol. fig. 1774, 12 1." and "8°. 2 vol. fig. Hollande, 1772, 16 1.": Nouffer: "nouv. édit. très-bien exécutée sur papier superfin, avec 21 fig. très-bien gravées, 8°. 2 vol. Londres, 1777."; Chappuis et Didier: "2 vol. 8°. 1777, 3 1. 5 s."; Bern: "Belles estampes, 36 1.").

81

C. Police Confiscations: 5 of 10 lists: Stockdorf, Pilon, Manoury, Prot, Paris.

D. Customs Confiscations: 2 instances: 1772, 1786.

288. *Histoire de Jenni, ou le sage et l'athée, par M. Sherloc. Traduit par M. de La Caille.* [François-Marie Arouet de Voltaire.] London, 1775. At least 2 other editions by 1776.
A. STN

Major Dealers: Buchet, Nîmes 26 (1); Charmet, Besançon 25 (1); Letourmy, Orléans 12 (1); Malherbe, Loudun 25 (2); Manoury, Caen 12 (1).		
Lorraine: Choppin, Bar-le-Duc 1 (1); Bertrand, Thionville 4 (1); Bernard, Lunéville 1 (1); L'Entretien, Lunéville 6 (1).	114	(11)
Paris: Prévost 2 (1).		
Minor Dealers: Cazin, Reims 6 (1); Bonnard, Auxerre 3 (1); Fontaine, Colmar 2 (1); Billault, Tours 4 (1).	15	(4)
Total:	129	(15)

B. Catalogues: 1 of 6 lists: (Décombaz: "8°. Londres, 1775, 15 s.").

D. Customs Confiscations: 2 instances: 1776, 1778.

Histoire de la coureuse. See #584, *Putain (la) errante.*

289. *Histoire de la pairie de France et du parlement de Paris, où l'on traite aussi des électeurs de l'empire, et du cardinalat, par Monsieur D.B. On y a joint des traités touchant les pairies d'Angleterre et l'origine des grands d'Espagne, par monsieur de G***.* [Jean Le Laboureur?, or Henri de Boulainvillier?] London, 1740. At least 3 other editions by 1753.
C. Police Confiscations: 1 of 10 lists: Prot.

290. *Histoire de la tourière des Carmélites. Ouvrage fait pour servir de pendant au Portier des Chartreux.* [Anne-Gabriel Meusnier de Querlon.] Paris, 1770 (actually 1745, according to Martin-Mylne-Frautschi). At least 11 other editions by 1784; "17000" as *La Tourière des Carmélites.*

A. STN

Major Dealers: Blouet, Rennes 2 (1);
 Pavie, La Rochelle 50 (1); Robert et   } 58 (3)
 Gauthier, Bourg-en-Bresse 6 (1).

Minor Dealers: Malassis, Nantes 6 (1). }   6 (1)
         Total: 64 (4)

B. Catalogues: 1 of 6 lists: (Bern: "fig. 40 s.").
C. Police Confiscations: 2 of 10 lists: Stockdorf, Paris.
D. Customs Confiscations: 4 instances: 1774, 1778, 1781, 1786.

291. *Histoire de la vie et mœurs de Mademoiselle Cronel, dite Frétillon, écrite par elle-même, actrice de la comédie de Rouen.* [Pierre-Alexandre Gaillard, dit de la Bataille?, or Anne-Claude-Philippe de Tubières de Grimoard de Pestels de Lévy, comte de Caylus?] The Hague, 1739. At least 15 other editions by 1782.

A. STN

Major Dealers: Charmet, Besançon 6 (2).   } 13 (4)
Colporteurs: Planquais 6 (1); "Troisième" 1 (1).

         Total: 13 (4)

D. Customs Confiscations: 2 instances: 1771, 1775.

292. *Histoire de l'établissement du christianisme.* [Pub. by François-Marie Arouet de Voltaire.] n.p., n.d. (c. 1776, according to Bengesco).

A. STN

Major Dealers: Malherbe, Loudun 12 (1).   } 12 (1)

Minor Dealers: Cazin, Reims 25 (1). } 25 (1)
        Total: 37 (2)

293. **Histoire de Louis XI.* (Possibly *Histoire de Louis XI.* 4 vols. [Charles Pinot Duclos.] Paris, 1745–46.)
B. Catalogues: 1 of 6 lists: (Cailler: "12°. 2 vol. 1777").

294. *Histoire de Mademoiselle Brion, dite comtesse de Launay.* n.p., 1754. At least 4 other editions by 1783; 1774 as *La Nouvelle Académie des dames ou histoire de Mlle B*** D.C.D.L.;* 1783 as *Histoire de Mademoiselle Brion, honnête putain.*

A. STN

Major Dealers: Mauvelain, Troyes 7 (2):
Pavie, La Rochelle 30 (3).   43 (6)
Lorraine: Orbelin, Thionville 6 (1).

Minor Dealers: Caldesaigues, Marseille
6 (1).   6 (1)

Total: 49 (7)

B. Catalogues: 2 of 6 lists: (Chappuis et Didier: "12° fig. 15 s."; Bern: "3 1.").
C. Police Confiscations: 5 of 10 lists: Stockdorf, Manoury, Prot, Lyon, Paris.
D. Customs Confiscations: 1 instance: 1781.

Histoire de Mlle Frétillon. See #291, *Histoire de la vie et mœurs de Mademoiselle Cronel* . . .

295. *Histoire de MM Paris, ouvrage dans lequel on montre comment un royaume peut passer dans l'espace de cinq années de l'état le plus déplorable à l'état le plus florissant par M. de L***.* [Jean-Pierre-Louis de la Roche du Maine, marquis de Luchet.] n.p., 1776.

A. STN

Major Dealers: Bergeret, Bordeaux 12
(1); Blouet, Rennes 1 (1); Buchet,
Nîmes 6 (1); Charmet, Besançon 12
(1); Letourmy, Orléans 1 (1);
Manoury, Caen 12 (1); Mossy, Mar-   54 (10)
seille 2 (1); Pavie, La Rochelle 2 (1);
Rigaud, Pons, Montpellier 4 (1).
Lorraine: Bernard, Lunéville 2 (1).

Total: 54 (10)

D. Customs Confiscations: 1 instance: 1777.

296. *Histoire des diables modernes, par M. A***.* London, 1763. At least 2 other editions by 1771 as . . . *par le feu Mr. Adolphus. Juif anglais, docteur en médecine, troisième édition.*

A. STN

Major Dealers: Bergeret, Bordeaux 4
(1); Buchet, Nîmes 26 (1); Charmet,
Besançon 10 (1); Mauvelain, Troyes   53 (5)
1 (1).
Lyon: Baritel 12 (1).

Minor Dealers: Malassis, Nantes, 3 (1); Fontaine, Colmar 2 (1). }   5 (2)

Total: 58 (7)

297. *Histoire des religieux de la Compagnie de Jésus, contenant ce qui s'est passé dans cet ordre depuis son établissement jusqu'à présent. Pour servir de supplément à l'histoire ecclésiastique des XVI, XVII, XVIIIe siècles.* 4 vols. [Pierre Quesnel.] Soleure, 1740. At least 2 other editions by 1751.

A. STN

Lorraine: Bernard, Lunéville 1 (1). }   1 (1)

Minor Dealers: Billault, Tours 1 (1). }   1 (1)

Total: 2 (2)

298. *Histoire d'Iris, par M.C.* [M.-C. Poisson.] The Hague, 1746.

A. STN

Major Dealers: Buchet, Nîmes 2 (1); Charmet, Besançon 6 (1); Malherbe, Loudun 12 (1); Rigaud, Pons, Montpellier 12 (1). }   32 (4)

Total: 32 (4)

299. *Histoire du Calvinisme et celle du papisme mises en parallèle ou apologie pour les réformateurs, pour la réformation et pour les réformes, divisée en quatre parties; contre un libelle intitulé "l'Histoire du Calvinisme par Mr. Maimbourg."* 4 vols. [Pierre Jurieu.] Rotterdam, 1683.

A. STN

Major Dealers: Buchet, Nîmes 6 (1); Letourmy, Orléans 1 (1). }   7 (2)

300. *Histoire d'une détention de trente-neuf ans, dans les prisons d'état, écrite par le prisonnier lui-même.* [Jean-Yrieix de Beaupoil, marquis de Saint-Aulaire.] Amsterdam, 1787. At least 3 other editions in 1787; also as *Le Donjon de Vincennes, la Bastille et Bicêtre, ou mémoires de M. Masers de Latude.*

A. STN

Major Dealers: Charmet, Besançon 2 (1). }   2 (1)

Total: 2 (1)

301. *Histoire du Paraguay sous les jésuites et de la royauté qu'ils y ont exercée pendant un siècle et demi.* 3 vols. [Bernardo Ibañez de

Echavarri.] Amsterdam and Leipzig, 1780. At least 1 other edition by 1782.

A. STN

    Major Dealers: Manoury, Caen 12 (1). }   12   (1)

                                  Total: 12   (1)

302. *Histoire du parlement de Paris, par Mr. l'abbé Big . . .* 2 vols. [François-Marie Arouet de Voltaire.] Amsterdam, 1769. At least 8 other editions by 1773.

A. STN

    Major Dealers: Blouet, Rennes 4 (1);
        Letourmy, Orléans 2 (1); Malherbe,
        Loudun 18 (2); Mossy, Marseille 6
        (1); Rigaud, Pons, Montpellier 4 (2).
    Lorraine: Audéart, Lunéville 3 (1).   }   46   (11)
    Paris: Prévost 2 (1).
    Colporteurs: Planquais 6 (1); "Troi-
        sième" 1 (1).

    Minor Dealers: Chevrier, Poitiers 6 (1). }   6   (1)

                                    Total: 52   (12)

B. Catalogues: 1 of 6 lists: (Bern: "6 1.").

C. Police Confiscations: 5 of 10 lists: Stockdorf, Moureau, Prot, Desauges, Paris.

D. Customs Confiscations: 3 instances: 1774 (2), 1775.

303. *Histoire du prince Apprius. Extraite des fastes du monde depuis sa création, manuscrit persan trouvé dans la bibliothèque de Schah-Hussein, roi de Perse, détrôné par Mamouth en 1722. Traduction française par Messire Esprit, gentilhomme provençal servant dans les troupes de la Perse.* [Pierre-François Godart de Beauchamps.] Constantinople, 1728. At least 6 other editions by 1764.

B. Catalogues: 1 of 6 lists: (Décombaz: "8°. la Haye, 1748, 1 l. 5 s.").

304. *Histoire du siège de Cythère.* Lampsaque, 1748.

A. STN

    Major Dealers: Robert et Gauthier,
        Bourg-en-Bresse 4 (1).   }   4   (1)

                             Total: 4   (1)

305. *Histoire ecclésiastique, ancienne et moderne, depuis la naissance*

de Jésus-Christ jusqu'au XVIIIe siècle. Traduit en français sur la version anglaise du latin de feu M. le baron de Mosheim, par le Dr. Archibald Maclaine. 6 vols. [trans. by Marc-Antoine Eidous.] (trans. from Maclaine's 1764 translation of *Institutionum historiae ecclesiasticae* [1726] by Johann Lorenz Mosheim.) Yverdon, 1776.

> *Major Dealers:* Blouet, Rennes 1 (1); Malherbe, Loudun 1 (1); Manoury, Caen 3 (1); Rigaud, Pons, Montpellier 1 (1). } 6 (4)

Total: 6 (4)

C. Police Confiscations: 1 of 10 lists: Desauges.
D. Customs Confiscations: 6 instances: 1777 (2), 1779, 1780 (2), 1781.

Histoire et vie d'Arétin. See #584, *Putain (la) errante.*

306. *Histoire (l') générale de l'état présent de l'Europe, traduite de l'anglais.* 2 vols. [trans. by Marc-Antoine-Eidous.] London, 1774.
C. Police Confiscations: 1 of 10 lists: Pilon.
D. Customs Confiscations: 1 instance: 1773.

307. *Histoire générale des dogmes et opinions philosophiques, depuis les plus anciens temps jusqu'à nos jours, tirée du Dictionnaire encyclopédique.* 3 vols. [Denis Diderot.] London, 1769.
A. STN

> *Lorraine:* Gay, Lunéville 2 (1); Audéart, Lunéville 2 (1). } 4 (2)
> *Minor Dealers:* Laisney, Beauvais 12 (1). } 12 (1)

Total: 16 (3)

D. Customs Confiscations: 3 instances: 1771 (2), 1775.

308. *Histoire naturelle de la religion, traduite de l'anglais de M. Hume.* [trans. by Jean-Baptiste de Mérian.] Amsterdam, 1759. (trans. from *The Natural History of Religion* [1757] by David Hume).
A. STN

> *Major Dealers:* Mauvelain, Troyes 1 (1); Robert et Gauthier, Bourg-en-Bresse 6 (1). } 7 (2)

Total: 7 (2)

309. *Histoire naturelle de la religion universelle, ou la fille de la nature.* (Possibly another version of *Imirce, ou la fille de la nature.*)
     A. STN
     Major Dealers: Pavie, La Rochelle 8 (1). }   8 (1)
                                    Total: 8 (1)

Histoire nouvelle de Margot des pelotons, ou la galanterie naturelle. See #195, *Enfantement (l') de Jupiter ou la fille sans mère.*

Histoire philosophique de la papauté. See #626, *Rendez à César . . .*

310. *Histoire philosophique de la religion.* 2 vols. [Claude Yvon.] Liège, 1779. At least 1 other edition by 1785.
     A. STN
     Lorraine: Gay, Lunéville 1 (1).

311. *Histoire philosophique et politique des établissements et du commerce des Européens dans les deux Indes.* 6 vols. [Guillaume-Thomas-François Raynal.] Amsterdam, 1770. Perhaps 50 other editions by 1789.
     A. STN
     Major Dealers: Bergeret, Bordeaux 42 (5); Blouet, Rennes 3 (2); Buchet, Nîmes 19 (2); Charmet, Besançon 59 (7); Letourmy, Orléans 7 (3); Malherbe, Loudun 55 (5); Manoury, Caen 70 (7); Mossy, Marseille 100 (3); Mauvelain, Troyes 17 (10); Rigaud, Pons, Montpellier 35 (4); Robert et Gauthier, Bourg-en-Bresse 14 (2).
     Lorraine: Carez, Toul 3 (1); Chénoux, Lunéville 18 (2); Choppin, Bar-le-Duc 6 (2); Bernard, Lunéville 20 (5); L'Entretien, Lunéville 4 (1); Gay, Lunéville 2 (1); Audéart, Lunéville 3 (2); d'Alancourt, Nancy 1 (1).

continued

Paris: Desauges 12 (1); Prévost 5 (2).   }   510   (70)
Colporteurs: Planquais 3 (1); Gilles 12 (1).

Minor Dealers: Malassis, Nantes 4 (1); Chevrier, Poitiers 16 (2); Petit, Reims 19 (3); Resplandy, Toulouse 6 (1); Sombert, Châlons-sur-Marne 2 (1); Bonnard, Auxerre 8 (2); Waroquier, Soissons 1 (1); Fontaine, Colmar 7 (2); Laisney, Beauvais 43 (3); Jarfaut, Melun 2 (1); Lair, Blois 2 (2).   }   110   (19)

Total: 620   (89)

B. Catalogues: 2 of 6 lists: (Décombaz: "12°. 7 vol. fig. la Haye, 1774, 10 1. 10 s." and "8°. 7 vol. fig. Hollande, 1775, 20 1."; Bern: "20 1.").

C. Police Confiscations: 4 of 10 lists: Stockdorf, Pilon, Jouy, et al., Prot.

D. Customs Confiscations: 45 instances: 1772 (2), 1773 (8), 1774 (7), 1775 (6), 1776 (2), 1778 (2), 1779 (5), 1781 (3), 1782 (4), 1783 (2), 1784 (2), 1785, 1786.

312. *Histoire secrète de Louis XIV.*
A. STN

Major Dealers: Blouet, Rennes 1 (1).   }   1   (1)

Total: 1   (1)

313. *Histoire secrète des femmes galantes de l'antiquité.* 3 vols. [François-Nicolas Dubois?, or Jacques Roergas de Serviez?] Paris, 1726–32. At least 1 other edition by 1745.
A. STN

Major Dealers: Mauvelain, Troyes 3 (3). }   3   (3)

Total: 3   (3)

314. *Histoire secrète des intrigues de la France en diverses cours de l'Europe.* [George Lockhard.] London, 1713.
A. STN

Major Dealers: Mauvelain, Troyes 3 (3).   }   3   (3)

Total: 3   (3)

315. *Histoire véritable de l'établissement du christianisme, par M. Mallé.*

B. Catalogues: 1 of 6 lists: (Décombaz: "8°. 1775, 3 1. 10 s.").

316. *Homélie du pasteur Bourn, prêchée à Londres le jour de la Pente-côte.* [François-Marie Arouet de Voltaire.] n.p., 1768.
B. Catalogues: 1 of 6 lists: (Grasset: "8°. 2 s.").

317. *Homme (l') aux quarante écus.* [François-Marie Arouet de Vol-taire.] n.p., 1768. At least 15 other editions in 1768.
A. STN

> *Major Dealers:* Bergeret, Bordeaux 12 (1); Malherbe, Loudun 12 (1).
> *Colporteurs:* Planquais 6 (1).

$\left.\right\}$ 30 (3)

Total: 30 (3)

B. Catalogues: 4 of 6 lists: (Grasset: "8°. 12 s."; Décombaz; Cailler; Bern: "30 s.").
C. Police Confiscations: 2 of 10 lists: Stockdorf, Pilon.
D. Customs Confiscations: 3 instances: 1774, 1778, 1779.

318. *Homme (de l'), de ses facultés intellectuelles et de son éducation. Ouvrage posthume de M. Helvétius.* 2 vols. [Claude-Adrien Helvétius.] London, 1773. At least 5 other editions by 1786.
A. STN

> *Major Dealers:* Letourmy, Orléans 7 (2); Malherbe, Loudun 55 (2); Robert et Gauthier, Bourg-en-Bresse 6 (1).
> *Lorraine:* Chénoux, Lunéville 18 (2); Bergue, Thionville 6 (1); Audéart, Lunéville 16 (3).
> *Lyon:* Cellier 4 (1).
> *Paris:* Barré 3 (1).
> *Colporteurs:* Planquais 6 (1); Gilles 25 (1).

$\left.\right\}$ 146 (15)

> *Minor Dealers:* Malassis, Nantes 8 (2); Chevrier, Poitiers 6 (1); Bonnard, Auxerre 3 (1); Laisney, Beauvais 52 (2).

$\left.\right\}$ 69 (6)

Total: 215 (21)

B. Catalogues: 2 of 6 lists: (Décombaz: "8°. 2 vol. Londres, 1772, 6 1."; Nouffer: bound with *Le Bonheur*).

    C. Police Confiscations: 4 of 10 lists: Pilon, Jouy, et al., Prot, Desauges.

    D. Customs Confiscations: 3 instances: 1774, 1779 (2).

319. *Homme (de l'); ou des principes et des lois de l'influence de l'âme sur le corps et du corps sur l'âme par J. P. Marat.* 3 vols. [Jean-Paul Marat.] Amsterdam, 1775–76.

    D. Customs Confiscations: 1 instance: 1775.

320. *Homme (l') dieu, ou l'univers seule famille. Poëme épique.* [Genu Soalhat, chevalier de Mainvilliers.] London, 1754.

    A. STN

Major Dealers: Pavie, La Rochelle 12 (1).	12	(1)
Total:	12	(1)

321. *Homme (l') plante.* [Julien Offray de La Mettrie.] Potsdam, n.d. (c. 1748, according to Barbier).

    D. Customs Confiscations: 1 instance: 1776.

322. *Homme (l') sauvage, histoire traduite de . . . par M. Mercier.* trans. by Louis-Sébastien Mercier. (trans. from *Der Wilde* [1757] by Johann Gottlob Benjamin Pfeil.) Paris, 1767. At least 10 other editions by 1785.

    A. STN

Major Dealers: Charmet, Besançon 3 (1); Rigaud, Pons, Montpellier 26 (1); Robert et Gauthier, Bourg-en-Bresse 12 (1).	41	(3)
Total:	41	(3)

    D. Customs Confiscations: 1 instance: 1775.

323. *Honny soit qui mal y pense, ou histoire des filles célèbres du XVIIIe siècle.* 2 vols. [Jean-Auguste Jullien, dit Desboulmiers.] London, 1761. At least 11 other editions by 1786.

    C. Police Confiscations: 2 of 10 lists: Pilon, Paris.

324. *Horoscope (l') politique de la Pologne, de la Prusse, de l'Angleterre, où se trouve le portrait caractéristique du prince héréditaire de Prusse.* [Stephano Zannowich.] Porto-Vecchio, 1779.

    A. STN

Major Dealers: Mauvelain, Troyes 8 (2).	8	(2)
Total:	8	(2)

325. *Humanité (l'), poème en six chants.* [B. Voiron.] n.p., n.d.
 A. STN
   Major Dealers: Charmet, Besançon 25 (1); Letourmy, Orléans 6 (1). } 31 (2)
   Total: 31 (2)

Huron (le) ou l'Ingénu. See #333, *Ingénu (l')* . . .

326. *Idées républicaines, par un membre d'un corps.* [François-Marie Arouet de Voltaire.] n.p., n.d. (c. 1762, according to Bengesco).
 A. STN
   Major Dealers: Blouet, Rennes 2 (1). } 2 (1)
   Total: 2 (1)

327. **Idées sur l'administration des villes municipales.*
 B. Catalogues: 1 of 6 lists: (Grasset: "8°. 6 s.").

328. **Il était seul. Pourquoi le choisir?*
 A. STN
   Minor Dealers: Chevrier, Poitiers 3 (1). } 3 (1)
   Total: 3 (1)

329. *Imirce, ou la fille de la nature.* [Henri-Joseph Du Laurens.] Berlin, 1765. At least 8 other editions by 1782.
 A. STN
   Major Dealers: Blouet, Rennes 4 (1); Mauvelain, Troyes 2 (1); Pavie, La Rochelle 2 (1); Robert et Gauthier, Bourg-en-Bresse 12 (1).
   Lorraine: Audéart, Lunéville 2 (1); d'Alancourt, Nancy 2 (1). } 24 (6)
   Total: 24 (6)
 B. Catalogues: 1 of 6 lists: (Bern: "4 1.").
 C. Police Confiscations: 4 of 10 lists: Stockdorf, Pilon, Prot, Paris.

330. *Imposture (de l') sacerdotale ou recueil de pièces sur le clergé. Traduites de l'anglais.* [trans. by Paul-Henri-Dietrich Thiry, baron d'Holbach.] [trans. from *A True Picture of Popery* by Davisson? and works of Bourn de Birmingham? and Thomas Gordon?] London, 1767. At least 1 other edition by 1772 as

De la Monstruosité pontificale ou tableau fidèle des papes (part 1 only).

A. STN

> *Major Dealers:* Blouet, Rennes 16 (2). }   16   (2)
> *Minor Dealers:* Malassis, Nantes 1 (1). }   1   (1)
>
> Total: 17   (3)

B. Catalogues: 1 of 6 lists: (Bern: "3 1.").

331. *Inconvénients (les) du célibat des prêtres, prouvés par des recherches historiques.* [Jacques-Maurice Gaudin.] Geneva, 1781. At least 1 other edition by 1783 as *Recherches philosophiques et historiques sur le célibat des prêtres.*

A. STN

> *Major Dealers:* Mauvelain, Troyes 12 (2)   }   12   (2)
>
> Total: 12   (2)

332. *Indépendant (un) à l'ordre des avocats, sur la décadence du barreau en France.* [Jacques-Pierre Brissot de Warville.] Berlin, 1781.

A. STN

> *Major Dealers:* Charmet, Besançon 18 (2); Robert et Gauthier, Bourg-en-Bresse 3 (1).   }   21   (3)
>
> Total: 21   (3)

333. *Ingénu (l'), histoire véritable tirée des manuscrits du Père Quesnel.* [François-Marie Arouet de Voltaire.] Utrecht, 1767. At least 18 other editions by 1768; also as *Le Huron ou l'Ingénu.*

A. STN

> *Major Dealers:* Blouet, Rennes 4 (1); Malherbe, Loudun 10 (1).
> *Colporteurs:* Planquais 6 (1).   }   20   (3)
>
> Total: 20   (3)

B. Catalogues: 3 of 6 lists: (Grasset: "8°. 15 s."; Cailler; Bern: "40 s." and as "Le Huron ou l'ingenu 40 s.").

D. Customs Confiscations: 2 instances: 1771, 1772.

334. *Inoculation du bons sens.* [Nicolas-Joseph Sélis.] London, 1761. At least 3 other editions by 1766.

D. Customs Confiscations: 1 instance: 1779.

335. *Instruction donnée par S. M. Catherine II à la commission chargée de dresser le projet d'un nouveau code des lois; traduit en français.* [Joseph-Antoine Félix de Balthasar?] Lausanne, 1769.
   A. STN
   Major Dealers: Blouet, Rennes 4 (1); Manoury, Caen 24 (2); Mossy, Marseille 6 (1); Robert et Gauthier, Bourg-en-Bresse 2 (1). } 36 (5)
   Total: 36 (5)

336. *Introduction à l'histoire de la guerre en Allemagne, en 1756, ou mémoires militaires et politiques, traduits de l'anglais et augmentés de notes et d'un précis sur la vie de Lloyd, par un officier français.* [de Romance, marquis de Mesmon?] London, 1784.
   D. Customs Confiscations: 1 instance: 1785.

337. *Israël vengé, ou Exposition naturelle des prophéties hébraïques que les chrétiens appliquent à Jésus, leur prétendu Messie. Par Isaac Orobio.* [trans. and ed. by Paul-Henri-Dietrich Thiry, baron d'Holbach, and Denis Diderot.] London, 1770.
   A. STN
   Major Dealers: Blouet, Rennes 4 (1). } 4 (1)
   Minor Dealers: Chevrier, Poitiers 2 (1). } 2 (1)
   Total: 6 (2)
   B. Catalogues: 1 of 6 lists: (Bern: "4 1.").
   C. Police Confiscations: 2 of 10 lists: Stockdorf, Prot.
   D. Customs Confiscations: 1 instance: 1778.

338. *Jean Hennuyer, évêque de Lisieux, drame en trois actes.* Louis-Sébastien Mercier. London, 1773. At least 1 other edition by 1775.
   A. STN
   Major Dealers: Malherbe, Loudun 1 (1). } 1 (1)
   Total: 1 (1)
   C. Police Confiscations: 2 of 10 lists: Manoury, Prot.
   D. Customs Confiscations: 1 instance: 1774.

339. **Jean-Jacques Rousseau, citoyen de Genève, à Christophe de Beaumont, archevêque de Paris, duc de S. Cloud, pair de France, commandeur de l'ordre du Saint-Esprit, proviseur de Sorbonne, etc.*

Avec sa lettre au conseil de Genève. Jean-Jacques Rousseau. Amsterdam, 1763. At least 11 other editions by 1766.
D. Customs Confiscations: 1 instance: 1771.

340. *Je suis pucelle, histoire véritable.* 2 vols. [Henri-Joseph Du Laurens?] The Hague, 1767.
    B. Catalogues: 1 of 6 lists: (Bern: "2 1. 10 s.").
    C. Police Confiscations: 1 of 10 lists: Stockdorf.

341. *Jésuites (les) de la maison professe de Paris en belle humeur et leurs intrigues galantes avec les dames de la cour.* 2 vols. Pampelune, 1696. At least 4 other editions by 1761; Vol. 2 sometimes entitled *Les Moines en belle humeur.*
    A. STN
      Major Dealers: Mauvelain, Troyes 7 (2);
        Pavie, La Rochelle 12 (1).
      Colporteurs: Planquais 2 (1); "Troi-
        sième" 2 (1).
      } 23 (5)

                                    Total: 23 (5)
    B. Catalogues: 3 of 6 lists: (Grasset: "12°. 1 1. 4 s."; Décombaz: "12°. fig. 1761, 1 1. 5 s."; Bern: "avec fig. 3 1.").
    C. Police Confiscations: 1 of 10 lists: Stockdorf.

342. *Jeune (le) philosophe, ou lettres amoureuses de Florival et de Sophie.* n.p., 1774.
    A. STN
      Major Dealers: Buchet, Nîmes 8 (2);
        Charmet, Besançon 12 (1); Pavie, La
        Rochelle 4 (1).
      Lyon: Cellier 4 (1).
      Paris: Prévost 2 (1).
      } 30 (6)

      Minor Dealers: Malassis, Nantes 1 (1);
        Jarfaut, Melun 4 (1); Billault, Tours
        2 (1).
      } 7 (3)

                                    Total: 37 (9)

343. *Jezennemours, roman-dramatique.* 2 vols. [Louis-Sébastien Mercier.] Neuchâtel, 1776. At least 8 other editions by 1786; 1785 as *Histoire d'une jeune luthérienne.*
    A. STN

95

Major Dealers: Charmet, Besançon 12
(1); Letourmy, Orléans 2 (1);
Manoury, Caen 25 (1); Mossy, Marseille 12 (1); Rigaud, Pons, Montpellier 6 (1); Robert et Gauthier,
Bourg-en-Bresse 3 (1).   60 (6)

Minor Dealers: Caldesaigues, Marseille
12 (1).   12 (1)

Total: 72 (7)

D. Customs Confiscations: 1 instance: 1778.

344. *Joujou (le) des demoiselles, nouveau choix de poésies luxurieuses.* 3
vols. [Joffreau de Lagerie?] Vitapolis, du boudoir de Conine,
1783 (first edition c. 1750, according to Pia and Weller).
   B. Catalogues: 1 of 6 lists: (Décombaz: "8 °. Londres, 1758,
   1 1.").
   D. Customs Confiscations: 1 instance (listed as *Joujou*):
   1786.

345. *Journal historique de la révolution opérée dans la constitution de
la monarchie française, par M. de Maupeou, chancelier de France.*
7 vols. [Mathieu-François Pidansat de Mairobert and Barthélemy-François-Joseph Moufle d'Angerville.] London,
1774–76. At least 2 other editions by 1776.
   A. STN
   Major Dealers: Bergeret, Bordeaux 30
   (1); Blouet, Rennes 66 (2); Buchet,
   Nîmes 54 (1); Charmet, Besançon 31
   (2); Letourmy, Orléans 75 (3); Mal-
   herbe, Loudun 76 (6); Mauvelain,
   Troyes 4 (3); Mossy, Marseille 30
   (6); Pavie, La Rochelle 31 (2);   515 (35)
   Rigaud, Pons, Montpellier 25 (1).
   Lorraine: Chénoux, Lunéville 12 (1);
   Bertrand, Thionville 7 (2); Audéart,
   Lunéville 20 (2).
   Paris: Prévost 4 (1).
   Colporteurs: Gilles 50 (2)
   Minor Dealers: Malassis, Nantes 6 (1);
   Sens, Toulouse 4 (1); Sombert, Châ-

continued

lons-sur-Marne 8 (2); Fontaine, Col-
mar 12 (2); Jarfaut, Melun 10 (3);
Billault, Tours 3 (1); Caldesaigues,
Marseille 3 (1). } 46 (11)

Total: 561 (46)

C. Police Confiscations: 2 of 10 lists: Pilon, Prot.

D. Customs Confiscations: 2 instances: 1777, 1778.

346. *Journal historique, ou fastes du règne de Louis XV surnommé le Bien-Aimé.* [Jean-Baptiste-Michel de Lévy.] n.p., 1757. At least 1 other edition by 1766.

A. STN

Major Dealers: Manoury, Caen 37 (2). } 37 (2)

Total: 37 (2)

347. *Journée de l'amour ou les heures de Cythère.* [Comtesse du Turpin de Crissé, Nicolas-François Guillard, Charles-Simon Favart, and Claude-Henri de Fusée de Voisenon.] Gnide, 1776.

D. Customs Confiscations: 1 instance: 1784.

348. *Jurisprudence (la) du grand-conseil examinée dans les maximes du royaume; ouvrage précieux contenant l'Histoire de l'Inquisition en France.* 2 vols. [Louis-Valentin de Goezmann.] Avignon, 1775.

C. Police Confiscations: 1 of 10 lists: Prot.

349. *Larmes (les) de Saint Ignace, ou dialogue entre S. Thomas et S. Ignace l'an de la destruction du colosse de Rhodes 9999, par un cousin du prophète Malagrida.* [Louis, duc d'Ayen, puis de Noailles.] n.p., n.d., (1762, according to Martin-Mylne-Frautschi).

B. Catalogues: 1 of 6 lists: (Bern: "30 s.").

350. *Lauriers (les) ecclésiastiques, ou campagnes de l'abbé de T***.* [Charles-Jacques-Louis-Auguste Rochette de La Morlière.] Luxuropolis, 1748. At least 12 other editions by 1788.

A. STN

Major Dealers: Letourmy, Orléans 18 (3); Malherbe, Loudun 50 (3); Pavie, La Rochelle 12 (1); Robert et Gauthier, Bourg-en-Bresse 22 (3).

continued

97

Lorraine: Bertrand, Thionville 4 (1);
Bergue, Thionville 12 (1); Audéart,
Lunéville 29 (3).
Lyon: Flandin 6 (1).
Colporteurs: Planquais 10 (2); "Troi-
sième" 4 (1).   167 (19)

Minor Dealers: Malassis, Nantes 3 (1);
Resplandy, Toulouse 13 (1); Caldesaigues, Marseille 8 (1).   24 (3)

Total: 191 (22)

B. Catalogues: 1 of 6 lists: (Bern: "3 1.").
C. Police Confiscations: 3 of 10 lists: Stockdorf, Pilon, Prot.

351. *Leçons (les) de la volupté ou la jeunesse du chevalier de Manon-
ville.* [Hubert d'Orléans.] Cythère, 1775. Original edition:
Confession générale du chevalier de Wilfort. Leipzig, 1755. At
least 7 other editions by 1787.
C. Police Confiscations: 1 of 10 lists: Paris.
D. Customs Confiscations: 1 instance: 1786.

352. *Législation (de la), ou principes des lois.* Gabriel Bonnot de
Mably. Amsterdam, 1776.
A. STN
Major Dealers: Buchet, Nîmes 39 (2);
Letourmy, Orléans 4 (1); Malherbe,
Loudun 16 (2); Mossy, Marseille 25
(2); Robert et Gauthier, Bourg-en-
Bresse 2 (1); Rigaud, Pons, Montpel-
lier 12 (1).
Lorraine: Bernard, Lunéville 4 (1).
Paris: Cugnet 2 (1).   104 (11)

Minor Dealers: Bonnard, Auxerre 3 (1);
Jarfaut, Melun 4 (1); Resplandy, Tou-
louse 13 (1); Laisney, Beauvais 6 (1);
Caldesaigues, Marseille 4 (1).   30 (5)

Total: 134 (16)

353. *Légitimité de l'usure légale, où l'on prouve son utilité.* [Joachim
Faiguet de Villeneuve.] Amsterdam, 1770.
A. STN
Major Dealers: Blouet, Rennes 6 (1). }   6 (1)

Total: 6 (1)

354. *Lettre au R. P. Berthier sur le matérialisme.* [Gabriel-François Coyer.] Geneva, 1759.
   A. STN
   > *Minor Dealers:* Chevrier, Poitiers 1 (1). }   1   (1)
   > Total: 1   (1)

   C. Police Confiscations: 2 of 10 lists: Pilon, Prot.

355. *Lettre de M. Linguet à M. le Comte de Vergennes, ministre des affaires étrangères en France.* Simon-Nicolas-Henri Linguet. London, 1777.
   A. STN
   > *Major Dealers:* Charmet, Besançon 6
   > (1); Malherbe, Loudun 10 (1); }   216   (4)
   > Rigaud, Pons, Montpellier 200 (2).
   > Total: 216   (4)

356. *Lettre de Monseigneur l'évêque d'A*** à M. de V***, avec les réponses du 11 avril 1768.* [François-Marie Arouet de Voltaire.] n.p., n.d. (1769, according to Bengesco). At least 2 other editions by 1772.
   A. STN
   > *Major Dealers:* Manoury, Caen 12 (1). }
   > *Lorraine:* Bertrand, Thionville 4 (1). }   16   (2)
   > *Minor Dealers:* Billault, Tours 6 (1). }   6   (1)
   > Total: 22   (3)

357. *Lettre de Thrasibule à Leucippe, ouvrage posthume de M. F . . .* [Nicolas Fréret?, or Paul-Henri-Dietrich Thiry, baron d'Holbach?, or Jacques-André Naigeon?] London, n.d. (c. 1766, according to Vercruysse).
   A. STN
   > *Major Dealers:* Bergeret, Bordeaux 12
   > (1); Blouet, Rennes 4 (1); Malherbe,
   > Loudun 1 (1); Manoury, Caen 75 (3);
   > Mauvelain, Troyes 1 (1). }   109   (10)
   > *Lorraine:* Chénoux, Lunéville 12 (1);
   > Augé, Lunéville 2 (1): Gay, Lunéville
   > 2 (1).
   > *Minor Dealers:* Chevrier, Poitiers 1 (1); }
   > Laisney, Beauvais 12 (1). }   13   (2)
   > Total: 122   (12)

B. Catalogues 1 of 6 lists: (Bern: "9 1.").
C. Police Confiscations: 1 of 10 lists: Pilon.

358. *Lettre d'un théologien à l'auteur du dictionnaire des Trois siècles littéraires.* [Jean-Antoine-Nicolas de Caritat, marquis de Condorcet.] Berlin, 1774.
A. STN

Major Dealers: Buchet, Nîmes 2 (1);
Rigaud, Pons, Montpellier 70 (3).   } 90 (6)
Lorraine: Audéart, Lunéville 18 (2).

Total: 90   (6)

359. *Lettre philosophique par M. de V*** avec plusieurs pièces galantes et nouvelles de différents auteurs.* The Hague, 1738. (This compilation of bawdy and irreligious essays, poems, and *pièces fugitives* should not be confused with Voltaire's *Lettres philosophiques* of 1734. According to Bengesco, Voltaire's *Lettres* went through a dozen editions but were not published as a separate work after 1739. The compilation first appeared in 1738 as *Lettres de M. de V*** avec plusieurs pièces de différents auteurs.* It was reprinted in 1739 and then reappeared, much expanded, throughout the second half of the century under the more common title given above. Pia lists 7 editions of the *Lettre philosophique:* one in 1756, one in 1760, two in 1774, two in 1775, and one in 1776. Their contents varied, but most began with a genuine excerpt from Voltaire's *Lettres philosophiques,* his audacious "Lettre sur l'âme," and then continued with unrelated works such as Prion's *Ode à Priape.*)
A. STN

Major Dealers: Bergeret, Bordeaux 18
(2); Blouet, Rennes 1 (1); Buchet,
Nîmes 12 (1); Charmet, Besançon
150 (3); Letourmy, Orléans 61 (5);
Malherbe, Loudun 3 (2): Pavie, La
Rochelle 16 (3); Rigaud, Pons, Mont-
pellier 20 (1); Robert et Gauthier,
Bourg-en-Bresse 6 (1).
Lorraine: Chénoux, Lunéville 12 (2);
Sandré, Lunéville 12 (1); Bertrand,
Thionville 4 (1); Bergue, Thionville

continued

100

6 (1); L'Entretien, Lunéville 6 (1):   432   (39)
Audéart, Lunéville 38 (7).
Paris: Barré 6 (1); Prévost 6 (1).
Colporteurs: Planquais 2 (1): "Troi-
sième" 4 (1); Gilles 54 (2).

Minor Dealers: Malassis, Nantes 25 (1);
Bonnard, Auxerre 3 (1); Laisney,   59   (4)
Beauvais 25 (1): Caldesaigues, Mar-
seille 6 (1).

Total: 491   (43)

B. Catalogues: 5 of 6 lists: (Grasset; Décombaz: "avec plusieurs pièces galantes & nouvelles, 12°. Londres, 1757,
1 1. 5 s."; Cailler; Nouffer: "dernière édit. encadrée 8°.
Londres 1777"; Chappuis et Didier: "avec plusieurs
pièces galantes de divers auteurs. 8°. bonne édition, 17
s.").

C. Police Confiscations: 4 of 10 lists: Stockdorf, Manoury,
Prot, Paris.

D. Customs Confiscations: 6 instances: 1771, 1773, 1777,
1779 (2), 1781.

360. *Lettre sur la prétendue comète.* [François-Marie Arouet de Voltaire.] Lausanne, 1773.
   B. Catalogues: 1 of 6 lists: (Grasset).

361. **Lettre sur le rappel des jésuites en France.*
   A. STN
      Major Dealers: Buchet, Nîmes 6 (1); Le-
         tourmy, Orléans 4 (1).
      Colporteurs: Blaisot 6 (1); Planquais 1   19   (5)
         (1); "Troisième" 2 (1).
      Minor Dealers: Sens, Toulouse 4 (1); Jar-   6   (2)
         faut, Melun 2 (1).

   Total: 25   (7)

362. *Lettre sur les aveugles à l'usage de ceux qui voient.* [Denis Diderot.] London, 1749. At least 1 other edition by 1772.
   A. STN
      Minor Dealers: Malassis, Nantes 2 (1);
         Chevrier, Poitiers 1 (1).   3   (2)

   Total: 3   (2)

   C. Police Confiscations: 1 of 10 lists: Prot.

363. *Lettre sur les panégyriques, par Irénée Aléthès, professeur en droit dans le canton suisse d'Uri.* [François-Marie Arouet de Voltaire.] n.p., n.d. (1767, according to Cioranescu and Bengesco). At least 2 other editions in 1767.
   A. STN
      Major Dealers: Blouet, Rennes 6 (1). ⎫
      Lorraine: Bergue, Thionville 6 (1). ⎬   12   (2)
                                      Total: 12   (2)
   B. Catalogues: 1 of 6 lists: (Grasset: "8°. 2 s.").

364. *Lettre sur les sourds et muets, à l'usage de ceux qui entendent et qui parlent, adressée à M***.* [Denis Diderot.] n.p., 1751. At least 1 other edition in 1751.
   B. Catalogues: 1 of 6 lists: (Bern: "4 l.").
   C. Police Confiscations: 1 of 10 lists: Prot.

365. *Lettre sur l'homme et ses rapports.* [François Hemsterhuys, fils.] Paris, 1772.
   B. Catalogues: 1 of 6 lists: (Bern: "4 l.").
   C. Police Confiscations: 1 of 10 lists: Stockdorf.
   D. Customs Confiscations: 1 instance: 1775.

366. **Lettres adressées à Jean-Jacques R.*
   D. Customs Confiscations: 1 instance: 1779.

367. *Lettres à Eugénie, ou préservatif contre les préjugés.* 2 vols. [Paul-Henri-Dietrich Thiry, baron d'Holbach.] London, 1768. At least 2 other editions by 1787.
   A. STN
      Major Dealers: Blouet, Rennes 12 (1); ⎫
      Letourmy, Orléans 4 (1); Malherbe, ⎪
      Loudun 7 (2); Manoury, Caen 25 (1); ⎬   60   (7)
      Mauvelain, Troyes 6 (1). ⎪
      Colporteurs: Gilles 6 (1). ⎭
      Minor Dealers: Malassis, Nantes 6 (1); ⎫
      Chevrier, Poitiers 1 (1); Laisney, ⎬   19   (3)
      Beauvais 12 (1). ⎭
                                        Total: 79   (10)
   B. Catalogues: 1 of 6 lists: (Bern: "9 l.").
   C. Police Confiscations: 3 of 10 lists: Stockdorf, Pilon, Prot.

368. *Lettres allemandes, traduites en français.* The Hague, n.d.
   D. Customs Confiscations: 1 instance: 1771.

369. *Lettres amoureuses d'Héloïse à Abaillard.* (Identification uncertain, possibly *Lettre d'Héloïse à Abailard, réponse d'Abailard à Héloïse.* [trans. by Nicolas Rémond des Cours.] Amsterdam, 1693; or *Les Véritables Lettres d'Abeilard et d'Héloïse, avec le latin à côté, traduites par l'auteur de leur vie.* 2 vols. [trans. by Gervaise.] Paris, 1723.)
    B. Catalogues: 1 of 6 lists: (Bern: "3 1.").

370. *Lettres à son Altesse Monseigneur le prince de *** sur Rabelais et sur d'autres auteurs accusés d'avoir mal parlé de la religion chrétienne.* [François-Marie Arouet de Voltaire.] Amsterdam, 1767. At least 1 other edition in 1767.
    B. Catalogues: 2 of 6 lists: (Grasset; Bern).

371. *Lettres à Sophie, contenant un examen des fondements de la religion chrétienne et diverses objections contre l'immortalité de l'âme.* 2 vols. [Nicolas Fréret?] London, n.d.
    A. STN

Major Dealers: Blouet, Rennes 12 (1); Manoury, Caen 25 (1).	37	(2)
Minor Dealers: Malassis, Nantes 6 (1): Chevrier, Poitiers 3 (2).	9	(3)
Total:	46	(5)

    B. Catalogues: 1 of 6 lists: (Bern: "5 1.").
    C. Police Confiscations: 3 of 10 lists: Stockdorf, Pilon, Prot.

372. *Lettres cabalistiques, ou correspondance philosophique, historique et critique, entre deux cabalistes, divers esprits élémentaires et le Seigneur Astaroth. Par l'auteur des Lettres juives.* 4 vols. [Jean-Baptiste de Boyer, marquis d'Argens.] The Hague, 1737–38. At least 7 other editions by 1769.
    A. STN

Lorraine: Bernard, Lunéville 3 (2); L'Entretien, Lunéville 7 (2); d'Alancourt, Nancy 2 (1). *Paris:* Prévost 4 (1).	16	(6)
Minor Dealers: Laisney, Beauvais 1 (1).	1	(1)
Total:	17	(7)

    D. Customs Confiscations: 3 instances: 1771 (2), 1773.

Lettres cherakéesiennes, mises en français, de la traduction italienne. Par J.-J. Rufus, sauvage européen. See #390, *Lettres iroquoises.* This collection contains 37 of the 43 "lettres."

103

373. *Lettres chinoises, indiennes et tartares, à M. Pauw, par un bénédictin. Avec plusieurs autres pièces intéressantes.* [François-Marie Arouet de Voltaire.] Paris, 1776. At least 1 other edition in 1776.

A. STN

Major Dealers: Bergeret, Bordeaux 25 (1); Blouet, Rennes 25 (1); Buchet, Nîmes 26 (1); Pavie, La Rochelle 2 (1).

Lorraine: Bernard, Lunéville 1 (1); L'Entretien, Lunéville 9 (2).

Paris: Cugnet 2 (2); Prévost 4 (1).

} 94 (10)

Minor Dealers: Sens, Toulouse 6 (1); Bonnard, Auxerre 3 (1); Billault, Tours 6 (1).

} 15 (3)

Total: 109 (13)

374. *Lettres chinoises, ou correspondance philosophique, historique et critique entre un chinois voyageur à Paris et ses correspondants à la Chine, en Moscovie, en Perse et au Japon, par l'auteur des Lettres juives et des Lettres cabalistiques.* 5 vols. [Jean-Baptiste de Boyer, marquis d'Argens.] The Hague, 1739. At least 5 other editions by 1779.

A. STN

Major Dealers: Malherbe, Loudun 54 (2).

Lorraine: Bernard, Lunéville 1 (1); L'Entretien, Lunéville 5 (2); d'Alancourt, Nancy 2 (1).

} 62 (6)

Minor Dealers: Cazin, Reims 1 (1); Bonnard, Auxerre 2 (1); Laisney, Beauvais 1 (1).

} 4 (3)

Total: 66 (9)

C. Police Confiscations: 1 of 10 lists: Prot.

D. Customs Confiscations: 5 instances: 1771, 1772, 1773 (2), 1776.

375. *Lettres (les) d'Amabed, traduites par l'abbé Tamponet.* [François-Marie Arouet de Voltaire.] Geneva, 1769. At least 4 other editions by 1772. (First appeared in *Les Choses utiles et agréables* [1769], according to Bengesco.)

B. Catalogues: 1 of 6 lists: (Bern: "24 s.").

376. *Lettres (des) de cachet et des prisons d'état. Ouvrage posthume, composé en 1778.* 2 vols. [Honoré-Gabriel Riqueti, comte de Mirabeau.] Hamburg, 1782.
    A. STN
      Major Dealers: Charmet, Besançon 44
        (3); Manoury, Caen 25 (1); } 96 (10)
        Mauvelain, Troyes 27 (6).
                                    Total: 96 (10)
    C. Police Confiscations: 2 of 10 lists: Lyon, Versailles.
    D. Customs Confiscations: 1 instance: 1783.

377. *Lettres de Julie à Eulalie ou tableau du libertinage de Paris.* London, 1784. (First appeared as *Ma Conversion, par M.D.R.C.D.M.F.,* in 1784. This title is not the same as *Ma Conversion* [1783] by Mirabeau, according to Martin-Mylne-Frautschi.) At least 1 other edition by 1785.
    A. STN
      Major Dealers: Mauvelain, Troyes 32 } 32 (3)
        (3).
                                    Total: 32 (3)

378. *Lettres de Mme la marquise de Pompadour depuis 1746 jusqu'en 1762 inclusivement.* 2 vols. [François, marquis de Barbé-Marbois?, or Claude-Prosper Jolyot de Crébillon, fils?] London, 1771. At least 4 other editions by 1776.
    A. STN
      Major Dealers: Charmet, Besançon 6
        (1); Letourmy, Orléans 3 (1); Robert
        et Gauthier, Bourg-en-Bresse 6 (1). } 30 (7)
      Paris: Prévost 6 (2); Lequay Morin 3
        (1); Védrène 6 (1).
      Minor Dealers: Bonnard, Auxerre 4 (1);
        Jarfaut, Melun 6 (1); Billault, Tours } 16 (4)
        2 (1); Caldesaigues, Marseille 4 (1).
                                    Total: 46 (11)
    B. Catalogues: 1 of 6 lists: (Bern: "6 1.").
    C. Police Confiscations: 2 of 10 lists: Stockdorf, Prot.
    D. Customs Confiscations: 5 instances: 1772, 1775, 1778 (2), 1786.

379. *Lettres de Memmius à Ciceron.* [François-Marie Arouet de Voltaire.] n.p., n.d. (Bengesco cites this title only as a compo-

nent of *Œuvres,* 1771, and *Questions sur l'Encyclopédie,* 1772.)
A. STN

Major Dealers: Charmet, Besançon 6 (1). } 6 (1)

Total: 6 (1)

380. *Lettres de M. de Voltaire à ses amis de Parnasse, avec des notes historiques et critiques.* [Jean-Baptiste-René Robinet.] Geneva, 1766.
D. Customs Confiscations: 1 instance: 1771.

381. *Lettres de Ninon de l'Enclos au marquis de Sévigné.* 2 vols. [Claude-Prosper Jolyot de Crébillon, fils.] Amsterdam, 1750. At least 25 other editions by 1787.
A. STN

Major Dealers: Manoury, Caen 12 (1). } 12 (1)

Total: 12 (1)

382. *Lettres d'un membre du Congrès américain à divers membres du parlement d'Angleterre.* [Vincent.] Philadelphia and Paris, 1779.
A. STN

Major Dealers: Mauvelain, Troyes 8 (2). } 8 (2)

Total: 8 (2)

383. *Lettres d'un Persan en Angleterre à son ami à Ispahan, ou nouvelles lettres persanes, où l'on trouve la continuation de l'histoire des Troglodites commencée par M. de Montesquieu, nouvelle traduction libre de l'anglais.* [trans. by Jean-François Peyron.] London and Paris, 1770. (trans. from *Letters from a Persian in England to His Friend in Ispahan* [1735] by George Lyttleton.) At least 1 other edition in 1770.
B. Catalogues: 1 of 6 lists: (Bern: "3 1.").

384. *Lettres d'un sauvage dépaysé, contenant une critique des mœurs du siècle et des réflexions sur des matières de religion et de politique.* [Jean-Baptiste de Boyer, marquis d'Argens?, or Jean Joubert de la Rue?] Amsterdam, 1738.
A. STN

Major Dealers: Malherbe, Loudun 1 (1). } 1 (1)

Total: 1 (1)

385. *Lettres écrites de la montagne par J.-J. Rousseau.* Jean-Jacques

Rousseau. Amsterdam, 1764. At least 10 other editions by 1767.

A. STN

    Colporteurs: Planquais 6 (1).   }   6 (1)

                                        Total: 6 (1)

B. Catalogues: 4 of 6 lists: (Grasset: "8°. 2 l."; Décombaz: "12°. 2 part. 1775, 2 l." and "8°. 2 vol. Amsterd. 1765, 3 l."; Cailler; Bern: "4 l.").

D. Customs Confiscations: 3 instances: 1771, 1774, 1775.

386. *Lettres galantes et philosophiques de deux nonnes, publiées par un apôtre du libertinage, avec des notes.* Au Paraclet, 1777.

    C. Police Confiscations: 2 of 10 lists: Moureau, Prot.

387. *Lettres historiques et dogmatiques sur les jubilés et les indulgences.* 3 vols. [Charles Chais.] The Hague, 1751.

A. STN

    Major Dealers: Malherbe, Loudun 15 (2).   }   15 (2)

    Minor Dealers: Chevrier, Poitiers 1 (1). }   1 (1)

                                          Total: 16 (3)

B. Catalogues: 1 of 6 lists: (Bern: "5 l.")

C. Police Confiscations: 2 of 10 lists: Stockdorf, Prot.

388. *Lettres historiques et galantes de Mme de C. . . .* 7 vols. [Anne-Marguerite Petit, dame du Noyer.] Cologne, 1704. At least 13 other editions by 1761.

A. STN

    Major Dealers: Manoury, Caen 3 (1); Mauvelain, Troyes 3 (3).   }   6 (4)

                                          Total: 6 (4)

D. Customs Confiscations: 1 instance (listed as *Lettres historiques et galantes*): 1779.

389. *Lettres hollandaises ou correspondance politique sur l'état présent de l'Europe, notamment de la république des sept Provinces-Unies.* [Auguste-Pierre Damiens de Gomicourt.] Amsterdam, 1779–81.

    C. Police Confiscations: 1 of 10 lists: Versailles.

390. *Lettres iroquoises.* 2 vols. [Jean-Henril Maubert de Gouvest.] Irocopolis, 1752. At least 3 other editions by 1769; also as

Lettres cherakéesiennes (contains 37 of the 43 original letters).
A. STN

Major Dealers: Blouet, Rennes 18 (1); Mauvelain, Troyes 12 (2).	30	(3)
Minor Dealers: Chevrier, Poitiers 3 (2).	3	(2)
Total:	33	(5)

391. *Lettres juives, ou correspondance philosophique, historique, et critique, entre un juif voyageur à Paris et ses correspondants en divers endroits.* 6 vols. [Jean-Baptiste de Boyer, marquis d'Argens.] The Hague, 1736. At least 12 other editions by 1777.
A. STN

Paris: Prévost 4 (1).	4	(1)
Total:	4	(1)

D. Customs Confiscations: 3 instances: 1771 (2); 1779.

392. *Lettres, mémoires et négociations particulières du chevalier d'Eon, ministre plénipotentiaire de France auprès du roi de la Grande Bretagne avec M.M. lec ducs de Praslin, de Nivernois, de Sainte-Foy et Régnier de Guerchy, ambassadeur extraordinaire, etc. etc. etc.* Charles-Geneviève-Louis-Auguste-André-Timothée d'Eon de Beaumont. London, 1764.
A. STN

Major Dealers: Manoury, Caen 12 (1).	12	(1)
Total:	12	(1)

393. *Lettres morales et critiques sur les différents états et les diverses occupations des hommes par M. le marquis d'Argens.* [Jean-Baptiste de Boyer, marquis d'Argens.] Amsterdam, 1748.
D. Customs Confiscations: 1 instance: 1779.

394. *Lettres originales de Madame la comtesse du Barry, avec celles des princes, seigneurs, ministres et autres qui lui ont écrit et qu'on a pu recueillir.* [Mathieu-François Pidansat de Mairobert?, or Charles Théveneau de Morande?] London, 1779.
A. STN

Major Dealers: Charmet, Besançon 12 (1).	12	(1)
Total:	12	(1)

B. Catalogues: 1 of 6 lists: (Chappuis et Didier: "8°. 1779, 15 s.").

Lettres philosophiques par M. de V***. See #359, *Lettre philosophique par M. de V****.

395. *Lettres philosophiques sur l'origine des préjugés, du dogme de l'immortalité de l'âme, de l'idolâtrie, et de la superstition; sur le système de Spinoza et sur l'origine du mouvement dans la matière. Traduites de l'anglais de J. Toland.*
A. STN
    Major Dealers: Blouet, Rennes 4 (1).   }   4   (1)
    Minor Dealers: Chevrier, Poitiers 1 (1). }   1   (1)
                              Total: 5   (2)
B. Catalogues: 1 of 6 lists: (Bern: "4 1.").
C. Police Confiscations: 2 of 10 lists: Stockdorf, Pilon.

396. *Lettres philosophiques sur Saint Paul, sur sa doctrine politique, morale et religieuse et sur plusieurs points de la religion chrétienne considérés politiquement. Traduit de l'anglais par le philosophe de Ferney et trouvés dans le portefeuille de M.V., son ancien secrétaire.* [Jacques-Pierre Brissot de Warville.] Neuchâtel, 1783.
A. STN
    Major Dealers: Mauvelain, Troyes 6 (1) }   6   (1)
                              Total: 6   (1)

397. *Lettres politiques sur l'état actuel de la France, écrites de la Hollande par M . . . à M . . . à Versailles à l'occasion du réquisitoire de M. Séguier, avocat du roi, demandant la suppression de deux brochures répandues depuis peu dans Paris.* The Hague, 1775.
C. Police Confiscations: 1 of 10 lists: Prot.

398. **Lettres profanes à l'abbé Baudeau.*
A. STN
    Major Dealers: Letourmy, Orléans 25 }   25   (1)
    (1).
                              Total: 25   (1)

399. *Lettres provinciales, ou examen impartial de l'origine, de la constitution et des révolutions de la monarchie française, par un avocat de province.* 2 vols. [Pierre Bouquet.] The Hague, 1772.
C. Police Confiscations: 2 of 10 lists: Pilon, Prot.

400. *Lettres secrètes de M. de Voltaire publiées par M.L.B.* [ed. by Jean-Baptiste-René Robinet.] Geneva, 1765. At least 1 other edition by 1785.

B. Catalogues: 1 of 6 lists: (Bern: "2 1.").
C. Police Confiscations: 1 of 10 lists: Stockdorf.

401. *Lettres secrètes, sur l'état actuel de la religion et du clergé de France, à M. le marquis de . . . . ancien mestre de camp de cavalerie, retiré dans ses terres.* [Nicolas Thyrel de Boismont?, or Cardinal Jean-Siffrein de Maury?, or abbé de Bourmont?] n.p., 1783.
A. STN

Major Dealers: Mauvelain, Troyes 12 (2).	12	(2)
Total:	12	(2)

402. *Lettres sur la législation, ou l'ordre légal dépravé, rétabli et perpétué. Par L.D.H.* 3 vols. [Victor Riqueti, marquis de Mirabeau.] Bern, 1775.
A. STN

Major Dealers: Letourmy, Orléans 6 (1).	6	(1)
Total:	6	(1)

403. **Lettres sur la philosophie nouvelle.*
A. STN

Major Dealers: Malherbe, Loudun 12 (1). *Paris:* Prévost 6 (1).	18	(2)
Minor Dealers: Billault, Tours 6 (1); Caldesaigues, Marseille 3 (1).	9	(2)
Total:	27	(4)

B. Catalogues: 1 of 6 lists: (Cailler: "8°. 1776").

404. *Lettres sur la religion essentielle à l'homme, distinguée de ce qui n'en est qu'accessoire.* [Marie Huber.] Amsterdam, 1738. At least 4 other editions by 1759.
A. STN

Minor Dealers: Chevrier, Poitiers 1 (1).	1	(1)
Total:	1	(1)

B. Catalogues: 1 of 6 lists: (Bern: "15 1.").
C. Police Confiscations: 2 of 10 lists: Stockdorf, Prot.
D. Customs Confiscations: 1 instance: 1775.

Lettres sur les jubilés et les indulgences. See #387, *Lettres historiques et dogmatiques sur les jubilés et les indulgences.*

405. *Liberté (la) de conscience resserrée dans ses bornes légitimes.* [Claude Yvon.] London, 1754–55.
    A. STN
       Minor Dealers: Chevrier, Poitiers 1 (1). }   1   (1)
                                                 Total: 1   (1)
    C. Police Confiscations: 2 of 10 lists: Stockdorf, Prot.

Libertin (le) de qualité ou confidences d'un prisonnier de Vincennes. See #412, *Ma Conversion* . . .

406. *Lindamine, ou l'optimisme des pays chauds.* [J. Baudouin.] London, 1778. (Martin-Mylne-Frautschi gives the original edition as *Lucrèce ou l'optimisme des Pays-Bas* [1745].)
    B. Catalogues: 2 of 6 lists: (Nouffer: ". . . suivi des Contes moraux, mis en vers libres par l'auteur de Lyndamine, pour servir de suite à l'Histoire de sa belle vie, enrichi de 23 planches, 12°. 2 vol. Londres 1778. Sous presse."; Chappuis et Didier: ". . . avec un recueil de contes libres. 2 vol. 12°. ornés de 22 figures. 1779, 3 1.")
    C. Police Confiscations: 1 of 10 lists: Paris.
    D. Customs Confiscations: 1 instance: 1781.

407. *Logique à mon usage, ouvrage traduit du chinois.* [Jakob Heinrich Meister.] Amsterdam, 1772.
    D. Customs Confiscations: 1 instance: 1773.

408. *Lois (les) de Minos, ou Astérie, tragédie en cinq actes par M. de Voltaire.* François-Marie Arouet de Voltaire. Geneva, 1773. At least 4 other editions in 1773.
    C. Police Confiscations: 1 of 10 lists: Pilon.

409. *Loisirs (les) du chevalier d'Eon de Beaumont, ancien ministre plénipotentiaire de France, sur divers sujets importants d'administration, etc. pendant son séjour en Angleterre.* 13 parts or vols. Charles-Geneviève-Louis-Auguste-André-Timothée d'Eon de Beaumont. Amsterdam, 1774.
    A. STN
       Major Dealers: Bergeret, Bordeaux 1 (1); Charmet, Besançon 4 (1); Malherbe, Loudun 6 (2); Manoury, Caen 12 (1).
       Lorraine: Bernard, Lunéville 3 (2);

continued

111

L'Entretien, Lunéville 1 (1); Mat-
thieu, Nancy 1 (1).   40   (10)
Colporteurs: Gilles 12 (1).
Minor Dealers: Sombert, Châlons-sur-
Marne 2 (2); Laisney, Beauvais 2 (1).   4   (3)
                                   Total: ‾44‾ ‾(13)‾
C. Police Confiscations: 1 of 10 lists: Prot.

Lucina sine concubitu. See #107, *Concubitus sine lucina . . .*

410. *Lucrèce. Traduction nouvelle avec des notes par M. L*G*.* 2 vols. [trans. by La Grange and revised by Jacques-André Naigeon?] Paris, 1768.
A. STN
    Minor Dealers: Chevrier, Poitiers 2 (1).   2   (1)
                                         Total: ‾2‾ ‾(1)‾

411. *Lyre (la) gaillarde, ou nouveau recueil d'amusements.* Aux Porcherons, 1776. At least 1 other edition by 1783.
A. STN
    Major Dealers: Charmet, Besançon 105
        (3); Letourmy, Orléans 12 (2); Pavie,
        La Rochelle 6 (1).
    Lorraine: Henry, Nancy 13 (1).   152   (10)
    Lyon: Cellier 2 (1).
    Paris: Barré 2 (1); Védrène 12 (1).
    Minor Dealers: Sens, Toulouse 6 (1);
        Resplandy, Toulouse 13 (1); Billault,
        Tours 13 (1); Caldesaigues, Marseille   45   (4)
        13 (1).
                                   Total: ‾197‾ ‾(14)‾
B. Catalogues: 1 of 6 lists: (Décombaz).
C. Police Confiscations: 1 of 10 lists: Paris.
D. Customs Confiscations: 1 instance: 1781.

412. *Ma Conversion, par M.D.R.C.D.M.F.* [Honoré-Gabriel Riqueti, comte de Mirabeau.] London, 1783. At least 1 other edition in 1784 as *Le Libertin de qualité, ou confidences d'un prisonnier de Vincennes.*
A. STN

112

Major Dealers: Charmet, Besançon 32 }
(2); Mauvelain, Troyes 12 (1).   44   (3)

Total: <u>44   (3)</u>

Mânes de Louis XV. See #47, *Aux Mânes de Louis XV* . . .

413. *Mannequins (les), conte ou histoire, comme l'on voudra.* [comte de Provence, later Louis XVIII?] n.p., n.d. (1777, according to Martin-Mylne-Frautschi.) At least 4 other undated editions.
  A. STN
    Major Dealers: Mossy, Marseille 6 (1). }   <u>6   (1)</u>
                                Total: 6   (1)
  B. Catalogues: 1 of 6 lists: (Chappuis et Didier: as ". . . satyre contre M. Turgot. 8°. 3 s").

414. *Manuel du philosophe ou dictionnaire des vertus ou des qualités intellectuelles de l'âme, dans lequel on en développe la connaissance, l'usage et l'alliance, etc.* Berlin, 1769.
  A. STN
    Major Dealers: Bergeret, Bordeaux 6
      (1); Buchet, Nîmes 2 (1).
    Lorraine: Chénoux, Lunéville 12 (1);   22   (4)
      Bernard, Lunéville 2 (1).

                                Total: <u>22   (4)</u>

415. *Manuel gaillard ou anecdotes voluptueuses recueillies par un bon vivant à l'usage de concitoyennes.* [comte d'Estaing?, according to Weller.] Glasgow, 1774.
  A. STN
    Minor Dealers: Malassis, Nantes 15 (1). }   <u>15   (1)</u>
                                Total: 15   (1)

Margot des pelotons. See #195, *Enfantement (l') de Jupiter* . . .

416. *Margot la ravaudeuse, par M. de M***.* [Charles-Louis Fougeret de Monbron.] Hamburg, 1750. (Cioranescu cites a suppressed 1748 edition.) At least 6 other editions by 1784.
  A. STN
    Major Dealers: Malherbe, Loudun 6 (1);
      Pavie, La Rochelle 12 (1).   22   (3)
    Colporteurs: Gilles 4 (1).

Minor Dealers: Chevrier, Poitiers 1 (1);
    Jarfaut, Melun 4 (1); Caldesaigues,   15 (3)
    Marseille 10 (1).

                                        Total: 37 (6)

B. Catalogues: 2 of 6 lists: (Décombaz: "8°. Hambourg, 1775, 1 1. 5 s."; Cailler).

C. Police Confiscations: 2 of 10 lists: Manoury, Prot.

D. Customs Confiscations: 3 instances: 1774, 1778, 1781.

417. *Marie-Thérèse à son fils.* (Probably *Marie-Thérèse d'Autriche, Impératrice apostolique à son fils, l'Empereur Joseph II.* n.p., 1782.)

D. Customs Confiscations: 1 instance: 1782.

418. *Matinées (les) du roi de. Prusse, écrites par lui-même.* [Baron Benoît Patono?, or comte de Schwerin?] Berlin, 1766. At least 2 other editions by 1788.

A. STN
    Major Dealers: Charmet, Besançon 6
        (1); Malherbe, Loudun 6 (1).
    Paris: Lequay Morin 1 (1); Prévost 6   19 (4)
        (1).
    Minor Dealers: Malassis, Nantes 3 (1).   3 (1)

                                          Total: 22 (5)

D. Customs Confiscations: 1 instance: 1786.

419. *Matinées (les) liégeoises ou l'art de prendre le thé en s'amusant.* Liège, 1778. *Soirées (les) liégeoises ou les délices du sentiment.* Liège, 1778. At least 1 other edition of *Les Soirées* in 1778. (*Les Soirées* is a sequel to *Les Matinées,* according to Martin-Mylne-Frautschi.)

C. Police Confiscations: 1 of 10 lists: Paris.

Maupeouana, ou correspondance secrète et familière du chancelier Maupeou avec son cœur Sorhouet, membre inamovible de la cour de pairs de France. See #129, *Correspondance secrète . . .*

420. *Maximes du droit public français tirées des capitulaires des ordonnances du royaume, et des autres monuments de l'histoire de France.* 2 vols. [Claude Mey.] En France, 1772. At least 1 other edition by 1775; second edition augmented by Gabriel-Nicolas Maultrot, G.-C. Aubry, and others.

A. STN

    Major Dealers: Blouet, Rennes 75 (2). } 75 (2)
                                Total: 75 (2)

C. Police Confiscations: 1 of 10 lists: Prot.

D. Customs Confiscations: 2 instances: 1775, 1785.

421. *Maximes (les) du gouvernement monarchique pour servir de suite aux Eléments de la politique par le même auteur.* 4 vols. [Louis-Gabriel Dubuat-Nançay.] London, 1778.

    A. STN

        Major Dealers: Charmet, Besançon 6 } 6 (1)
        (1).

                                  Total: 6 (1)

422. *Méditations philosophiques sur Dieu, le monde et l'homme.* [Thédore-Louis Lau.] Königsberg, 1770.

    A. STN

        Minor Dealers: Malassis, Nantes 2 (1). } 2 (1)
                                  Total: 2 (1)

    C. Police Confiscations: 1 of 10 lists: Stockdorf.

Mélanges confus sur des matières fort claires, par l'auteur du Gazetier cuirassé. See #267, *Gazetier (le) curaissé* . . .

Mélanges de Voltaire. See #468, *Nouveaux Mélanges philosophiques* . . .

423. **Mémoire à présenter au contrôleur général.*

    A. STN

        Major Dealers: Charmet, Besançon 20
        (1); Malherbe, Loudun 4 (1). } 30 (3)
        Paris: Prévost 6 (1).

                                  Total: 30 (3)

424. *Mémoire pour les souverains de la communion de Rome par M***, D***, C***. 1 juillet 1778. Traduit de l'italien.* n.p., 1779. (Trans. from *Pro Memoria per i sovrani della comunione di Roma de 1600, 1 iuglio, 1778.*)

    A. STN

        Major Dealers: Rigaud, Pons, Montpel-
        lier 2 (1). } 2 (1)

                                  Total: 2 (1)

425. *Mémoires authentiques de Mme la comtesse du Barry, par le chevalier Fr. N . . . London, 1772.*
    A. STN
        Major Dealers: Letourmy, Orléans 6 (1);
        Rigaud, Pons, Montpellier 2 (1).   58 (3)
        Paris: Védrène 50 (1).
        Minor Dealers: Malassis, Nantes 20 (1);
        Cazin, Reims 6 (1); Boisserand,   51 (3)
        Roanne 25 (1).

        Total: 109 (6)
    B. Catalogues: 2 of 6 lists: (Décombaz: "8°. Londres, 1775, 2 l. 5 s."; Bern: "4 l.").
    C. Police Confiscations: 2 of 10 lists: Stockdorf, Paris.
    D. Customs Confiscations: 2 instances: 1778, 1781.

426. *Mémoires de l'abbé Terray, contrôleur-général, contenant sa vie, son administration, ses intrigues et sa chûte.* 2 vols. [Jean-Baptiste-Louis Coquereau.] London, 1776. At least 1 other edition by 1777.
    A. STN
        Major Dealers: Buchet, Nîmes 26 (1);
        Charmet, Besançon 25 (1); Malherbe, Loudun 296 (8); Manoury,
        Caen 12 (1).   370 (14)
        Lorraine: Choppin, Bar-le-Duc 1 (1);
        Audéart, Lunéville 4 (1).
        Paris: Prévost 6 (1).
        Minor Dealers: Chevrier, Poitiers 6 (1);
        Sens, Toulouse 12 (1); Sombert, Châlons-sur-Marne 12 (1); Bonnard,
        Auxerre 3 (1); Habert, Bar-sur-Aube   107 (10)
        20 (1); Jarfaut, Melun 42 (3); Caldesaigues, Marseille 12 (2).

        Total: 477 (24)
    C. Police Confiscations: 2 of 10 lists: Moureau, Prot.

427. *Mémoires de Louis XV, roi de France et de Navarre, dans lesquels on donne une description impartiale de son caractère, de ses amours, de ses guerres, de la politique de sa cour, du génie et de l'habilité de ses ministres, généraux et favoris. Par un ancien*

secrétaire d'ambassade à la cour de France. Traduit de l'anglais. Rotterdam, 1775.

A. STN

Major Dealers: Blouet, Rennes 6 (1); Buchet, Nîmes 26 (1); Charmet, Besançon 28 (2); Letourmy, Orléans 25 (1); Manoury, Caen 75 (2); Mossy, Marseille 13 (1); Pavie, La Rochelle 24 (2); Rigaud, Pons, Montpellier 26 (1); Robert et Gauthier, Bourg-en-Bresse 12 (1).

Lorraine: Matthieu, Nancy 4 (1).

Colporteurs: Gilles 200 (1).

439 (15)

Total: 439 (15)

D. Customs Confiscations: 1 instance: 1778.

428. *Mémoires de Mademoiselle de Montpensier, fille de M. Gaston d'Orléans.* [Anne-Marie-Louise d'Orléans, duchesse de Montpensier.] Paris, 1718. At least 5 other editions by 1776.

A. STN

Major Dealers: Manoury, Caen 6 (1). } 6 (1)

Total: 6 (1)

D. Customs Confiscations: 1 instance: 1779.

429. *Mémoires de Mme la marquise de Pompadour où l'on découvre les motifs des guerres et des traités de paix, les ambassades, les négociations dans les différentes cours de l'Europe, les menées et les intrigues secrètes, le caractère des généraux, celui des ministres d'état, la cause de leur élévation et le sujet de leur disgrâce, et généralement tout ce qui s'est passé de plus remarquable à la cour de France pendant les vingt dernières années du règne de Louis XV, écrits par elle-même.* 2 vols. Liège, 1766. At least 5 other editions by 1776.

A. STN

Major Dealers: Blouet, Rennes 26 (2); Mauvelain, Troyes 7 (2); Mossy, Marseille 6 (1).

Lorraine: Bergue, Thionville 6 (1).

Paris: Prévost 2 (1).

continued

Colporteurs: Blaisot 6 (1); Planquais 6 ⎤ 65 (10)
(1); "Troisième" 6 (1). ⎦

Minor Dealers: Malassis, Nantes 2 (1); ⎫
Chevrier, Poitiers 4 (2). ⎬ 6 (3)
⎭

Total: 71 (13)

   B. Catalogues: 2 of 6 lists: (Grasset: Bern: "6 1.").
   C. Police Confiscations: 3 of 10 lists: Stockdorf, Prot, Paris.

430. *Mémoires de M. le comte de Saint-Germain, ministre et secrétaire d'état de la guerre, lieutenant-général des armées de France.* Claude-Louis, comte de St. Germain. En Suisse, 1779.
   A. STN

Major Dealers: Charmet, Besançon 52 ⎤
(2): Rigaud, Pons, Montpellier 12 ⎬ 64 (3)
(1). ⎦

Total: 64 (3)

431. *Mémoires d'une reine infortunée, entremêlés de lettres à plusieurs de ses parents et amies illustres, sur plusieurs sujets et en différentes occasions, traduits de l'anglais.* [Caroline-Mathilde, reine de Danemark?] London, 1776. (trans. from *Memoirs of an Unfortunate Queen.*) At least 2 other editions by 1782.
   A. STN

Major Dealers: Manoury, Caen 100 (1); ⎤
Mossy, Marseille 12 (1). ⎦ 112 (2)

Total: 112 (2)

432. *Mémoires d'un prisonnier d'état sur l'administration intérieure du château royal de Vincennes; pour servir de suite aux Mémoires sur la Bastille, publiés par M. Linguet.* London, 1783.
   D. Customs Confiscations: 1 instance: 1784.

Mémoires historiques de Maupeou. See #345, *Journal historique de la révolution . . .*

433. *Mémoires justificatifs de la comtesse de Valois de la Motte, écrits par elle-même.* London, 1789.
   D. Customs Confiscations: 4 instances: 1789 (4).

Mémoires militaires et politiques du général Lloyd. See #336, *Introduction à l'histoire de la guerre en Allemagne.*

434. **Mémoires philosophiques sur Dieu, l'homme et le monde.*
   B. Catalogues: 1 of 6 lists: (Bern: "12 1.").

435. *Mémoires pour servir à l'histoire de madame de Maintenon et à celle du siècle passé.* 6 vols. [Laurent Angliviel de La Beaumelle.] Amsterdam, 1755–56. At least 11 other editions by 1789; 1789 as *Mémoires et lettres . . .*

A. STN

Major Dealers: Charmet, Besançon 3 (1); Letourmy, Orléans 4 (1): Mauvelain, Troyes 1 (1); Mossy, Marseille 31 (2); Robert et Gauthier, Bourg-en-Bresse 3 (1).
Lorraine: Audéart, Lunéville 2 (1).
Paris: Desauges 25 (1). } 69 (8)

Total: 69 (8)

436. *Mémoires pour servir à l'histoire du siège de Gibraltar, par l'auteur des Batteries flottantes.* [Jean-Claude-Eléonore le Michaud d'Arçon.] Cadiz, 1783.

A. STN

Major Dealers: Mauvelain, Troyes 8 (2). } 8 (2)

Total: 8 (2)

437. *Mémoires secrets pour servir à l'histoire de Perse.* [Antoine Pecquet?, or François-Vincent Toussaint?] Amsterdam, 1745. At least 6 other editions by 1769; 1746 as *Anecdotes secrètes pour servir à l'histoire de la cour de Pékin* (Gay suggests this title is a different book, not a later edition).

A. STN (as *Anecdotes de Perse*)

Major Dealers: Manoury, Caen 12 (1). } 12 (1)

Total: 12 (1)

B. Catalogues: 1 of 6 lists: (Bern: "6 1.").

438. *Mémoires secrets pour servir à l'histoire de la république des lettres en France, depuis 1762 jusqu'à nos jours ou journal d'un observateur, par feu M. de Bachaumont.* 36 vols. [Louis Petit de Bachaumont, continued by Mathieu-François Pidansat de Mairobert, Barthélemy-François-Joseph Moufle d'Angerville, and others.] London, 1777–89.

A. STN

Major Dealers: Charmet, Besançon 6 (1); Manoury, Caen 70 (6);

continued

119

Mauvelain, Troyes 32 (10); Rigaud,
Pons, Montpellier 4 (2): Robert et
Gauthier, Bourg-en-Bresse 1 (1).   } 149   (24)
Lorraine: Bernard, Lunéville 3 (2): Bon-
thoux, Nancy 8 (1).
Paris: Desauges 25 (1).

Minor Dealers: Fontaine, Colmar 1 (1). }   1   (1)

                            Total: 150   (25)

  C. Police Confiscations: 1 of 10 lists: Paris.
  D. Customs Confiscations: 11 instances: 1783 (7), 1784
     (3), 1785.

439. *Mémoires sur la Bastille et sur la détention de M. Linguet, écrits
par lui-même.* Simon-Nicolas-Henri Linguet. London, 1783.
At least 1 other edition by 1784.
  A. STN

Major Dealers: Charmet, Besançon 13
(1); Manoury, Caen 25 (1);
Mauvelain, Troyes 33 (7); Mossy,   } 109   (11)
Marseille 25 (1); Robert et Gauthier,
Bourg-en-Bresse 13 (1).

Minor Dealers: Petit, Reims 52 (3); Waroquier, Soissons 2 (1).   } 54   (4)

                            Total: 163   (15)

440. *Mémoires sur les maisons de force du royaume de France.* Amsterdam, 1784.
  A. STN

Major Dealers: Mauvelain, Troyes 12
(2).   } 12   (2)

                            Total: 12   (2)

441. *Mémoires turcs, avec l'histoire galante de leur séjour en France,
par un auteur turc de toutes les académies mahométanes.* 2 vols.
[Claude Godard d'Aucour.] Paris, 1743. At least 18 other
editions by 1787.
  A. STN

Major Dealers: Letourmy, Orléans 22
(3); Mauvelain, Troyes 26 (2).
Lorraine: Choppin, Bar-le-Duc 1 (1);   } 59   (8)
L'Entretien, Lunéville 10 (2).

                            Total: 59   (8)

442. *Mémorial d'un mondain, par M. le comte Max. Lamberg.* 2 vols. Maximilien Joseph, Graf von Lamberg. London, 1774. At least 2 other editions by 1776.
    C. Police Confiscations: 1 of 10 lists: Desauges.

443. *Menagiana, ou les bons mots, les pensées critiques, historiques, morales et d'érudition de Ménage.* [Bernard de La Monnoye.] Paris, 1715. At least 2 other editions by 1762.
    A. STN
       Major Dealers: Mauvelain, Troyes 2 (2). }   2 (2)
                              Total: 2 (2)

444. *Méprise (la) d'Arras, par M. de Voltaire.* François-Marie Arouet de Voltaire. Lausanne, 1771. At least 4 other editions by 1773.
    C. Police Confiscations: 1 of 10 lists: Pilon.

445. *Mes Pensées.* [Laurent Angliviel de la Beaumelle.] Copenhagen, 1751. At least 6 other editions by 1773.
    C. Customs Confiscations: 1 instance: 1775.

Messaline. Tragédie. See #470, *Nouvelle (la) Messaline.*

446. **Meubles (les) vendus.*
    A. STN
       Minor Dealers: Chevrier, Poitiers 2 (1). }   2 (1)
                              Total: 2 (1)

447. *Militaire (le) philosophe ou difficultés sur la religion proposées au R. P. Malebranche, prêtre de l'Oratoire. Par un ancien officier.* [Robert Challe? Paul-Henri-Dietrich Thiry, baron d'Holbach, and Jacques-André Naigeon?] London, 1767. At least 4 other editions by 1776.
    A. STN
       Major Dealers: Blouet, Rennes 8 (2); Malherbe, Loudun 1 (1); Pavie, La Rochelle 14 (2); Robert et Gauthier, Bourg-en-Bresse 14 (2).
       Lorraine: Bertrand, Thionville 2 (1); Bergue, Thionville 6 (1): Audéart, Lunéville 2 (1).
       Lyon: Barret 6 (1).
       Colporteurs: Blaisot 6 (1); Planquais 6 (1); "Troisième" 1 (1); Gilles 4 (1).   70 (15)

Minor Dealers: Laisney, Beauvais 12 (1).}   12   (1)

Total: 82   (16)

B. Catalogues: 3 of 6 lists: (Grasset: "8°. 2 1."; Décombaz: "8°. Londres, 1770, 2 1. 10 s."; Bern: "5 1.").

C. Police Confiscations: 3 of 10 lists: Stockdorf, Pilon, Prot.

D. Customs Confiscations: 1 instance: 1772.

448. *Mœurs (les).* [François-Vincent Toussaint.] n.p., 1748. At least 5 other editions by 1771.

A. STN

   Major Dealers: Robert et Gauthier, Bourg-en-Bresse 6 (1). }   6   (1)

Total: 6   (1)

C. Police Confiscations: 3 of 10 lists: Jouy, et al., Prot, Paris.

449. **Moines (les) après le chien, en forme de dialogue.*

A. STN

   Major Dealers: Mauvelain, Troyes 12 (2). }   12   (2)

Total: 12   (2)

450. *Momus (le) français, ou aventures du duc de Roquelaure suivant les mémoires que l'auteur a trouvés dans le cabinet du maréchal d'H***, dont il était secrétaire; donné au public par le sieur L.R.* [Antoine, sieur de Le Roy.] Cologne, 1717. At least 26 other editions by 1789.

A. STN

   Major Dealers: Malherbe, Loudun 4 (1). }   4   (1)

Total: 4   (1)

451. *Monarque (le) accompli, ou prodiges de bonté, de savoir et de sagesse qui font l'éloge de Sa Majesté Impériale Joseph II.* 3 vols. [Joseph Lanjuinais.] Lausanne, 1774. At least 2 other editions by 1780.

A. STN

   Major Dealers: Blouet, Rennes 75 (3); Mossy, Marseille 8 (1); Pavie, La Rochelle 18 (2); Robert et Gauthier, Bourg-en-Bresse 6 (1).

   Lorraine: Chénoux, Lunéville 2 (1); Bergue, Thionville 6 (1); L'Entretien,

      124   (13)

continued

Lunéville 2 (1); Audéart, Lunéville 2
(1); Babin, Nancy 1 (1).
Lyon: Baritel 4 (1).
Minor Dealers: Chevrier, Poitiers 2 (1);
Cazin, Reims 76 (2): Sombert, Châ-
lons-sur-Marne 2 (1); Boisserand,
Roanne 6 (1).

86 (5)

Total: 210 (18)

C. Police Confiscations: 1 of 10 lists: Prot.
D. Customs Confiscations: 1 instance: 1776.

452. *Monde (le), son origine, et son antiquité, première partie.* [Jean-
Frédéric Bernard.] *Seconde partie: De l'Ame et de son immortalité.* [Jean-Baptiste de Mirabaud.] London, 1751. At least
1 other edition by 1778; includes *Troisième partie: Essai sur
la chronologie.* [Le Mascrier.]
A. STN
Major Dealers: Malherbe, Loudun 1 (1);
Robert et Gauthier, Bourg-en-Bresse
6 (1).

7 (2)

Total: 7 (2)

D. Customs Confiscations: 1 instance: 1785.

453. *Monialisme (le), histoire galante écrite par une ex-religieuse de
l'abbaye où se sont passées les aventures.* Rome, 1777.
A. STN
Lorraine: Gerlache, Metz 2 (2).
Paris: Prévost 6 (1); Lequay Morin 12
(2); Barré 2 (1); Védrène 6 (1).

28 (7)

Minor Dealers: Sens, Toulouse 6 (1);
Resplandy, Toulouse 13 (1); Bonnard, Auxerre 3 (1); Billault, Tours
13 (1); Caldesaigues, Marseille 4 (1).

39 (5)

Total: 67 (12)

B. Catalogues: 2 of 6 lists: (Nouffer; Chappuis et Didier: "2
vol. 12°. 1777, 15 s.").
C. Police Confiscations: 1 of 10 lists: Prot.

454. *Monsieur de Voltaire peint par lui-même ou lettres de cet écrivain
dans lesquelles on verra l'histoire de sa vie, de ses ouvrages, de
ses querelles, de ses correspondances et les principaux traits de son
caractère avec un grand nombre d'anecdotes, de remarques et*

de jugements littéraires. [Pub. by Laurent Angliviel de la Beaumelle.] Lausanne, 1766. At least 4 other editions by 1775.

D. Customs Confiscations: 2 instances: 1771, 1772.

455. *Monuments de la vie privée des douze Césars, d'après une suite de pierres gravées sous leurs règnes.* [Pierre-François Hugues d'Hancarville.] Capri, 1780. At least 3 other editions by 1786.

    A. STN

      Major Dealers: Charmet, Besançon 6 (2); Mauvelain, Troyes 3 (2); Mossy, Marseille 4 (1).

      Paris: Prévost 1 (1). }   14 (6)

                          Total: 14 (6)

456. *Monuments du culte secret des dames romaines, pour servir de suite aux Monuments de la vie privée des douze Césars.* [Pierre-François Hugues d'Hancarville.] Capri, 1784. At least 2 other editions by 1788.

    A. STN

      Major Dealers: Mauvelain, Troyes 3 (2). }   3 (2)

                          Total: 3 (2)

457. *Morale (la) des anciens philosophes par M. le marquis de ***.* Bern, 1770.

D. Customs Confiscations: 1 instance: 1771.

458. *Morale (la) universelle, ou les devoirs de l'homme fondés sur la nature.* 3 vols. [Paul-Henri-Dietrich Thiry, baron d'Holbach.] Amsterdam, 1776. At least 2 other editions in 1776.

    A. STN

      Major Dealers: Letourmy, Orléans 2 (1); Manoury, Caen 31 (2); Mossy, Marseille 6 (1).

      Lorraine: Chénoux, Lunéville 2 (1). }   41 (5)

      Minor Dealers: Chevrier, Poitiers 2 (1). }   2 (1)

                          Total: 43 (6)

C. Police Confiscations: 2 of 10 lists: Moureau, Prot.

459. *Moyen (le) de parvenir, œuvre contenant la raison de tout ce qui a été, est, et sera: avec démonstrations certaines et nécessaires, selon*

la rencontre des effets de la vertu. François Brouart, dit Béroalde de Verville?] n.p., 1610. At least 11 other 18th-century editions by 1786.

A. STN

Major Dealers: Charmet, Besançon 12 (1); Mauvelain, Troyes 3 (3).	}	15 (4)
Minor Dealers: Malassis, Nantes 4 (1). }		4 (1)
	Total:	19 (5)

B. Catalogues: 2 of 6 lists: (Décombaz: "12°. 2 vol. 1773, 3 l." Chappuis et Didier: "2 vol. 12°. 1777, 15 s.").

C. Police Confiscations: 1 of 10 lists: Jouy, et al.

D. Customs Confiscations: 4 instances: 1774, 1775, 1776, 1778.

460. *Muse (la) libertine ou œuvres posthumes de M. Dorat.* Claude-Joseph Dorat. n.p., 1783.

A. STN

Major Dealers: Mauvelain, Troyes 6 (1). }	6 (1)
Total:	6 (1)

461. *Muses (les) du foyer de l'Opéra. Choix de poésies libres, galantes et satiriques et autres, les plus agréables qui ont circulé depuis quelques années dans les sociétés galantes de Paris.* Au café du caveau, 1783.

A. STN

Major Dealers: Mauvelain, Troyes 40 (4).	}	40 (4)
	Total:	40 (4)

462. *Muses (les) en belle humeur, ou chansons et autres poésies joyeuses.* Villefranche, 1742. At least 1 other edition by 1779.

B. Catalogues: 1 of 6 lists: (Chappuis et Didier: "2 vol. 12°. 1779, 10 s.").

C. Police Confiscations: 1 of 10 lists: Paris.

D. Customs Confiscations: 1 instance: 1781.

463. *Mystères (les) du christianisme approfondis radicalement et reconnus physiquement vrais.* 2 vols. [Bebescourt.] London, 1771. At least 1 other edition by 1775.

A. STN

Major Dealers: Mauvelain, Troyes 1 (1); ⎤

continued

125

Robert et Gauthier, Bourg-en-Bresse 6 (1).	19	(3)
Paris: Desauges 12 (1).		
Minor Dealers: Chevrier, Poitiers 1 (1). }	1	(1)
Total:	20	(4)

B. Catalogues: 1 of 6 lists: (Bern: "24 1.").
C. Police Confiscations: 2 of 10 lists: Stockdorf, Pilon.
D. Customs Confiscations: 1 instance: 1779.

Mystères (les) plus secrètes des hautes grades de la franc-maçonne-rie. See #556, *Plus Secrètes Mystères (les)* . . .

464. *Nature (de la).* [Jean-Baptiste-René Robinet.] Amsterdam, 1761–63. At least 3 other editions by 1766.
   A. STN

Major Dealers: Blouet, Rennes 6 (1); Rigaud, Pons, Montpellier 2 (1).	20	(3)
Colporteurs: Gilles 12 (1).		
Minor Dealers: Lair, Blois 1 (1). }	1	(1)
Total:	21	(4)

   B. Catalogues: 1 of 6 lists: (Bern: "24 1.").
   C. Police Confiscations: 1 of 10 lists: Paris.
   D. Customs Confiscations: 4 instances: 1771 (2), 1772, 1775.

465. *Nature (de la) humaine, ou exposition des facultés, des actions et des passions de l'âme et de leurs causes, déduites d'après des prin-cipes qui ne sont communément ni reçus ni connus. Par Thomas Hobbes: ouvrage traduit de l'anglais.* [trans. by Paul-Henri-Die-trich Thiry, baron d'Holbach.] London, 1772. (trans. from *Human Nature: Or the Fundamental Elements of Policy* [1650] by Thomas Hobbes.) At least 1 other edition by 1787.
   A. STN

Major Dealers: Blouet, Rennes 4 (1). }	4	(1)
Total:	4	(1)

   B. Catalogues: 1 of 6 lists: (Bern: "4 1.").
   C. Police Confiscations: 3 of 10 lists: Stockdorf, Pilon, Prot.

466. *Nature (la) vengée, ou la réconciliation imprévue, par M. C**.* [Charles Compan.] Amsterdam and Paris, 1769.
   C. Police Confiscations: 1 of 10 lists: Prot.

467. *Nécessité (de la) du culte public parmi les chrétiens.* [Armand

Boisbeleau de la Chappelle.] Lausanne, 1746. At least 1 other edition by 1747.
B. Catalogues: 1 of 6 lists: (Bern: "5 1.").
C. Police Confiscations: 1 of 10 lists: Stockdorf.
D. Customs Confiscations: 1 instance: 1771.

468. *Nouveaux Mélanges philosophiques, historiques, critiques, etc., etc.* 3–19 vols. [François-Marie Arouet de Voltaire.] n.p., 1765–76.
A. STN

Major Dealers: Rigaud, Pons, Montpellier 2 (1). } 2 (1)

Total: 2 (1)

B. Catalogues: 1 of 6 lists: (Bern: "12 vol., 36 1.").
C. Police Confiscations: 3 of 10 lists: Pilon, Prot, Paris.
D. Customs Confiscations: 18 instances: 1771 (4), 1772 (3), 1773 (3), 1774 (4), 1775 (2), 1776, 1777.

Nouvelle Académie (la) des dames ou histoire de Mlle B*** D.C.D.L. See #294, *Histoire de Mademoiselle Brion, dite comtesse de Launay.*

469. *Nouvelle Marianne (la) ou les mémoires de la baronne de ***, écrits par elle-même.* [Claude-François Lambert.] The Hague, 1740. At least 5 other editions by 1772.
D. Customs Confiscations: 1 instance: 1779.

470. *Nouvelle Messaline (la), tragédie en un acte.* Charles-François Ragot de Grandval. Acône, Clitoris, 1752. At least 1 other edition by 1773 as *. . . par Pyron, dit Prépucius.*
A. STN

Major Dealers: Malherbe, Loudun 12
(1); Robert et Gauthier, Bourg-en-
Bresse 6 (1). } 20 (3)
Lorraine: Choppin, Bar-le-Duc 2 (1).
Minor Dealers: Jarfaut, Melun 4 (1). } 4 (1)

Total: 24 (4)

B. Catalogues: 1 of 6 lists: (Cailler).

471. *Nouvelles monacales, ou les aventures divertissantes de frère Maurice, publiées par le Sr. D***.* Cologne, 1763. At least 3 other editions by 1777; also as *Les Aventures monacales, ou la vie scandaleuse de frère Maurice, parmi les religieuses . . .*

A. STN

Major Dealers: Malherbe, Loudun 21 (1).

Minor Dealers: Jarfaut, Melun 4 (1).

$$\left.\begin{array}{l} \\ \\ \\ \end{array}\right\}$$

21	(1)
4	(1)
Total: 25	(2)

B. Catalogues: 2 of 6 lists: (Nouffer; Chappuis et Didier: "8°. 777 [sic], 7 s.").

472. *Nuit (la) et le moment ou les matinées de Cythère, dialogue.* [Claude-Prosper Jolyot de Crébillon, fils.] London, 1755. At least 11 other editions by 1786.

C. Police Confiscations: 3 of 10 lists: Jouy, et al., Prot, Paris.
D. Customs Confiscations: 1 instance: 1772.

473. *Nymphomanie (la) ou traité de la fureur utérine.* [J.-D.-T. de Bienville.] Amsterdam, 1771. At least 6 other editions by 1789.

A. STN

Minor Dealers: Waroquier, Soissons 4 (1).

$$\left.\begin{array}{l} \\ \\ \end{array}\right\}$$

4	(1)
Total: 4	(1)

474. *Observateur (l') anglais, ou correspondance secrète entre Milord All'Eye et Milord All'Ear.* 4 vols. [Mathieu-François Pidansat de Mairobert.] London, 1777–78. At least 2 other editions by 1784; also as *L'Espion anglais . . . ,* 10 vols.

A. STN

Major Dealers: Bergeret, Bordeaux 42 (3); Buchet, Nîmes 65 (3); Manoury, Caen 144 (8); Mauvelain, Troyes 33 (8); Mossy, Marseille 50 (1); Rigaud, Pons, Montpellier 4 (2); Robert et Gauthier, Bourg-en-Bresse 13 (1).
Lorraine: Carez, Toul 2 (1); Choppin, Bar-le-Duc 11 (4); Bernard, Lunéville 6 (1); Henry, Nancy 4 (1).
Paris: Desauges 13 (1); Prévost 1 (1).

$$\left.\begin{array}{l} \\ \\ \\ \\ \\ \\ \\ \\ \\ \end{array}\right\}$$

388 (35)

Minor Dealers: Petit, Reims 12 (3); Waroquier, Soissons 4 (3).

$$\left.\begin{array}{l} \\ \\ \end{array}\right\}$$

16	(6)
Total: 404	(41)

B. Catalogues: 1 of 6 lists: (Chappuis et Didier: "4 vol. gr. 12°. Holl. 1779, 7 1. 10 s.").

C. Police Confiscations: 1 of 10 lists: Paris.

D. Customs Confiscations: 5 instances: 1784 (2), 1785, 1786, 1787.

475. *Observations sur l'Histoire de la Bastille, publiée par M. Linguet, avec des remarques sur le caractère de l'auteur, suivies de quelques notes sur sa manière d'écrire l'histoire politique, civile et littéraire.* [Jean Dussaulx?] London, 1783.

A. STN

Major Dealers: Mauvelain, Troyes 18 (2).	18	(2)
Total:	18	(2)

476. *Odalisque (l'), ouvrage traduit du turc.* [André-Robert Andréa de Nerciat?, François-Marie Mayeur de Saint-Paul?, or Pigeon de Sainte-Paterne?] Constantinople, 1770. At least 2 other editions by 1787.

D. Customs Confiscations: 1 instance: 1785.

477. *Odazir ou le jeune syrien, roman philosophique, composé d'après les mémoires d'un turc par M. ***.* [Jean-Louis Carra.] The Hague, 1772. At least 1 other edition in 1772.

C. Police Confiscations: 1 of 10 lists: Pilon.

478. *Ode (l') sur l'anniversaire de la Saint-Barthélemy, pour l'année 1772.* [François-Marie Arouet de Voltaire.] n.p., n.d. (First appeared in *Nouveaux Mélanges,* 1772, as "Stances pour le 24 août 1772.")

A. STN

Minor Dealers: Chevrier, Poitiers 2 (1).	2	(1)
Total:	2	(1)

479. *Œufs rouges. Première partie. Sorbouet mourant à M. de Maupeou, chancelier de France.* [Jacques-Mathieu Augeard?, or Mathieu-François Pidansat de Mairobert?] n.p., 1772.

A. STN

Lorraine: Bergue, Thionville 20 (1); Matthieu, Nancy 4 (2). *Colporteurs:* Blaisot 6 (1); Planquais 6 (1).	36	(5)
Minor Dealers: Jarfaut, Melun 2 (1).	2	(1)
Total:	38	(6)

B. Catalogues: 1 of 6 lists: (Cailler).

480. *Œuvres.*[3] Bolingbroke (Henri Paulet de Saint-Jean, vicomte de). *Œuvres.* 3 vols. Geneva, 1760.

A. STN

Major Dealers: Blouet, Rennes 4 (1);
Malherbe, Loudun 7 (2).

11 (3)

Total: 11 (3)

481. *Œuvres.* Boulanger (Nicolas-Antoine). *Œuvres complètes.* 5 vols. Amsterdam, 1773–75. At least 1 other edition by 1778.

A. STN

Major Dealers: Mauvelain, Troyes 2 (2).
Lorraine: Bertrand, Thionville 1 (1).

3 (3)

Total: 3 (3)

C. Police Confiscations: 1 of 10 lists: Prot.
D. Customs Confiscations: 2 instances: 1779, n.d.

482. *Œuvres.* Brantôme (Pierre de Bourdeille, seigneur de Brantôme). *Œuvres du seigneur de Brantôme, avec des remarques historiques et critiques.* 15 vols. [ed. by Jacob Le Duchat, Antoine Lancelot, Prosper Marchand.] The Hague, 1740. At least 3 other editions by 1787.

D. Customs Confiscations: 1 instance: 1779.

483. *Œuvres.* Chevrier (François-Antoine). *Œuvres complètes de M. de Chevrier.* 3 vols. London, 1774.

A. STN

Major Dealers: Mauvelain, Troyes 6 (4). }

6 (4)

Total: 6 (4)

D. Customs Confiscations: 1 instance: 1778.

484. *Œuvres.* Crébillon, fils (Claude-Prosper Jolyot de). *Collection complète des œuvres de M. de Crébillon, fils.* 7 vols. London, 1772. At least 3 other editions by 1789.

A. STN

Major Dealers: Malherbe, Loudun 2 (1);
Manoury, Caen 9 (2); Mossy, Mar-

continued

[3]The titles, format, and number of volumes in eighteenth-century editions of collected works varied enormously; and in ordering copies, the booksellers often did not specify which edition they preferred. The following entries merely list the first editions and indicate the number of subsequent editions, without pretending to be comprehensive.

seille 3 (1); Letourmy, Orléans 1 (1).
Lorraine: Bertrand, Thionville 1 (1).
Paris: Desauges 13 (1); Prévost 1 (1).
Colporteurs: "Troisième" 2 (1).

32 (9)

Minor Dealers: Boisserand, Roanne 8
(3).

8 (3)

Total: 40 (12)

  B. Catalogues: 1 of 6 lists: (Décombaz: "8°. 7 vol. Londres, 1772, 12 l.").
  D. Customs Confiscations: 3 instances: 1774, 1775, 1785.

485. *Œuvres.* d'Argens (Jean-Baptiste de Boyer, marquis). *Œuvres de M. le marquis d'Argens, contenant les lettres juives, chinoises, cabalistiques et la philosophie du bon sens.* 24 vols. n.p., 1768.
  D. Customs Confiscations: 2 instances: 1771, 1768.

486. *Œuvres.* Diderot (Denis). *Œuvres philosophiques de M***.* 6 vols. Amsterdam, 1772. At least 1 other edition by 1773.
  A. STN
    Major Dealers: Letourmy, Orléans 2 (1);
      Malherbe, Loudun 21 (5); Robert et
      Gauthier, Bourg-en-Bresse 6 (1).
    Lorraine: Matthieu, Nancy 3 (1).
    Colporteurs: Planquais 1 (1).

33 (9)

Total: 33 (9)

  B. Catalogues: 1 of 6 lists: (Décombaz: "Œuvres philosophiques, littéraires & dramatiques de Mr. Diderot, 8°. 5 vol. Londres, 1773, 12 l.").
  C. Police Confiscations: 1 of 10 lists: Jouy, et al.
  D. Customs Confiscations: 5 instances: 1772, 1774, 1775, 1776, 1779.

487. *Œuvres.* Dorat (Claude-Joseph). *Œuvres complètes en vers et en prose par M. Dorat.* 2 vols. Paris, 1764–80. At least 2 other editions by 1776.
  D. Customs Confiscations: 1 instance: 1775.

488. *Œuvres.* Du Laurens (Henri-Joseph). *Œuvres diverses de l'A*** L***.* n.p., 1775–78.
  B. Catalogues: 1 of 6 lists: (Chappuis et Didier: "Oeuvres de l'abbé Laurent, contenant le Balay, la Chandelle d'Arras,

Imirce, l'Arretin moderne & le Compère Matthieu, ensemble 8 vol. 12°. Holl. 8 1.").

489. *Œuvres.* Fréret (Nicolas). *Œuvres complètes de M. Fréret.* 4 vols. London, 1775. At least 2 other editions by 1787.
   A. STN
   Major Dealers: Mauvelain, Troyes 15 (5); Robert et Gauthier, Bourg-en-Bresse 2 (1).
   Lorraine: Bertrand, Thionville 3 (2).
   Paris: Desauges 12 (1).
   Colporteurs: Gilles 4 (1).
   } 36 (10)

   Minor Dealers: Petit, Reims 1 (1). } 1 (1)
   Total: 37 (11)
   B. Catalogues: 1 of 6 lists: (Chappuis et Didier: "gr. 8°. Holl. 2 1. 10 s.").
   C. Police Confiscations: 1 of 10 lists: Prot.

490. *Œuvres.* Grécourt (Jean-Baptiste-Joseph Willart de). *Œuvres diverses de M. de Grécourt.* 2 vols. 1747. At least 7 other editions by 1782.
   A. STN
   Major Dealers: Letourmy, Orléans 2 (1); Mauvelain, Troyes 26 (2); Charmet, Besançon 6 (1).
   Lorraine: Carez, Toul 2 (1); Bertrand, Thionville 1 (1); L'Entretien, Lunéville 2 (1).
   Lyon: Cellier 4 (1).
   Paris: Prévost 4 (1); Védrène 4 (1).
   } 51 (10)

   Minor Dealers: Jarfaut, Melun 4 (1); Billault, Tours 1 (1). } 5 (2)
   Total: 56 (12)
   C. Police Confiscations: 2 of 10 lists: Pilon, Jouy, et al.
   D. Customs Confiscations: 4 instances: 1771, 1773, 1778, 1780.

491. *Œuvres.* Helvétius (Claude-Adrien). *Œuvres complètes de M. Helvétius.* 4 vols. Liège, 1774. At least 2 other editions by 1781.
   A. STN

Major Dealers: Letourmy, Orléans 12
(2); Malherbe, Loudun 4 (3);
Mauvelain, Troyes 3 (2).
Lorraine: Choppin, Bar-le-Duc 2 (1);
Bertrand, Thionville 1 (1); Bernard,
Lunéville 14 (3); L'Entretien, Luné-   } 99 (21)
ville 6 (1); d'Alancourt, Nancy 17
(3).
Paris: Cugnet 8 (2); Prévost 2 (1).
Colporteurs: Gilles 30 (2).
Minor Dealers: Bonnard, Auxerre 3 (1); }
Laisney, Beauvais 8 (2).   } 11 (3)

Total: 110 (24)

B. Catalogues: 1 of 6 lists: (Nouffer).
C. Police Confiscations: 3 of 10 lists: Prot, Desauges, Paris.
D. Customs Confiscations: 2 instances: 1778, 1779.

492. *Œuvres.* Hume (David). *Œuvres philosophiques de M. D. Hume.* 4 vols. (trans. by Jean-Baptiste Mérian.) Amsterdam, 1760.
C. Police Confiscations: 1 of 10 lists: Prot.
D. Customs Confiscations: 1 instance: 1771.

493. *Œuvres.* La Mettrie (Julien Offray de). *Œuvres philosophiques de M. de La Mettrie.* London, 1751. At least 3 other editions by 1774.
A. STN

Major Dealers: Blouet, Rennes 4 (1);
Charmet, Besançon 25 (1); Le-
tourmy, Orléans 11 (3); Mauvelain,
Troyes 8 (5); Robert et Gauthier,   }
Bourg-en-Bresse 12 (2).   } 86 (18)
Lorraine: Audéart, Lunéville 4 (2); Mat-
thieu, Nancy 1 (1).
Lyon: Flandin 15 (1); Cellier 2 (1).
Minor Dealers: Petit, Reims 1 (1); Bon- }
nard, Auxerre 3 (1).   } 4 (2)

Total: 90 (20)

B. Catalogues: 2 of 6 lists: (Décombaz: "12°. 4 vol. Berlin, 1775, 4 1. 10 s."; Bern: "9 1.").

C. Police Confiscations: 4 of 10 lists: Stockdorf, Pilon, Prot, Paris.

D. Customs Confiscations: 1 instance: 1775.

494. *Œuvres.* Piron (Alexis). *Œuvres d'Alexis Piron.* 3 vols. Paris, 1758. At least 3 other editions by 1782.

A. STN

Major Dealers: Letourmy, Orléans 9 (2); Manoury, Caen 18 (3); Rigaud, Pons, Montpellier 8 (2); Pavie, La Rochelle 1 (1).   40   (9)

Paris: Cugnet 4 (1).

Minor Dealers: Caldesaigues, Marseille 10 (1).   10   (1)

Total: 50   (10)

C. Police Confiscations: 1 of 10 lists: Desauges.

D. Customs Confiscations: 1 instance: 1780.

495. *Œuvres.* Rousseau (Jean-Jacques). *Œuvres diverses de M. J.-J. Rousseau.* 2 vols. Paris, 1756. At least 20 other editions by 1789; the number of volumes varies up to 38 (the Cazin edition).

A. STN

Major Dealers: Blouet, Rennes 2 (1); Buchet, Nîmes 2 (1); Letourmy, Orléans 9 (3); Mauvelain, Troyes 4 (4); Pavie, La Rochelle 1 (1); Manoury, Caen 15 (3); Mossy, Marseille 3 (1); Rigaud, Pons, Montpellier 23 (5).

Lorraine: Bernard, Lunéville 2 (1); Matthieu, Nancy 4 (3): d'Alancourt, Nancy 2 (1); Chénoux, Lunéville 12 (2); Choppin, Bar-le-Duc 6 (2); Gerlache, Metz 11 (3); Orbelin, Thionville 4 (2).   138   (41)

Paris: Prévost 5 (2): Desauges 8 (1); Cugnet 6 (1).

Colporteurs: Blaisot 3 (1); Planquais 2 (1); Gilles 14 (2).

Minor Dealers: Lair, Blois 1 (1); Laisney, Beauvais 30 (5); Habert, Bar-sur-Aube 4 (1); Boisserand, Roanne 2 (1); Malassis, Nantes 21 (3); Chevrier, Poitiers 26 (2); Petit, Reims 12 (1); Waroquier, Soissons 6 (3). } 102 (17)

Total: 240 (58)

B. Catalogues: 1 of 6 lists: (Décombaz: "8°. 11 vol. figur. 1775, 36 1.").

C. Police Confiscations: 1 of 10 lists: Prot.

D. Customs Confiscations: 11 instances: 1771, 1772 (2), 1773, 1774, 1780 (2), 1782, 1784, 1785, 1788.

496. *Œuvres posthumes de J.-J. Rousseau, ou recueil de pièces manuscrites pour servir de supplément aux éditions publiées pendant sa vie.* 11 vols. Geneva, 1782–83. At least 1 other edition by 1783.

A. STN

Major Dealers: Charmet, Besançon 8 (2): Mauvelain, Troyes 3 (2): Malherbe, Loudun 50 (1); Rigaud, Pons, Montpellier 1 (1); Robert et Gauthier, Bourg-en-Bresse 1 (1).
Lorraine: Carez, Toul 4 (1); Choppin, Bar-le-Duc 4 (2); Bonthoux, Nancy 7 (2).
Paris: Prévost 1 (1). } 79 (13)

Minor Dealers: Petit, Reims 28 (3). } 28 (3)

Total: 107 (16)

497. *Œuvres.* Shaftesbury (Anthony Ashley Cooper, 3rd Earl of). *Œuvres de milord comte de Shaftesbury, contenant ses caractéristiques, ses lettres et autres ouvrages, traduits de l'anglais en français sur la dernière édition.* 3 vols. [trans. by Denis Diderot.] Geneva, 1769.

C. Police Confiscations: 1 of 10 lists: Prot.

D. Customs Confiscations: 1 instance: 1771.

498. *Œuvres.* Voltaire (François-Marie Arouet de). *Œuvres de M.A. de V.* 3 vols. The Hague, 1728. At least 23 other editions

by 1789; the number of volumes varies up to 92 (the Kehl duodecimo edition).

A. STN

Major Dealers: Blouet, Rennes 1 (1); Malherbe, Loudun 2 (1); Manoury, Caen 7 (3); Mauvelain, Troyes 15 (6).

Lorraine: Chénoux, Lunéville 2 (1); Gerlache, Metz 9 (3); Bertrand, Thionville 5 (4); Bernard, Thionville 4 (2); L'Entretien, Lunéville 2 (1); Babin, Nancy 3 (1).

Paris: Prévost 2 (1).

52 (24)

Minor Dealers: Malassis, Nantes 1 (1); Laisney, Beauvais 5 (3); Lair, Blois 1 (1).

7 (5)

Total: 59 (29)

B. Catalogues: 1 of 6 lists: (Décombaz: "8°. 42 vol. Londres, 1770–75, 84 l.").

C. Police Confiscations: 1 of 10 lists: Prot.

D. Customs Confiscations: 41 instances: 1771 (3), 1772 (11), 1773 (15), 1774 (8), 1775, 1776, 1779 (2).

499. *Œuvres diverses de M. Abauzit, précédées de l'éloge de l'auteur.* 2 vols. [ed. by Jean-Pierre Béranger.] London, 1770–73.
C. Police Confiscations: 2 of 10 lists: Prot, Paris.

500. *Œuvres (les) galantes et amoureuses d'Ovide, traduction nouvelle en vers français.* 2 vols. [Jean Barrin.] Cythère, 1756. At least 1 other edition by 1770.
A. STN

Major Dealers: Malherbe, Loudun 2 (1). }   2 (1)

Total: 2 (1)

B. Catalogues: 2 of 6 lists: (Décombaz: "8°. 2 vol. fig. 1774, 3 l."; Bern: "4 l.").

501. *Œuvres (les) magiques de Henri-Corneille Agrippa, par P. d'Aban, latin et français, avec des secrets occultes.* Liège, 1547. [Caillet states that most dates of the complete works of Heinrich Cornelius Aggripa are apocryphal.]
C. Police Confiscations: 1 of 10 lists: Prot.

502. *Œuvres philosophiques et mathématiques de Mr. G. J. 'sGraves-
ande, rassemblées et publiées par Jean Nic. Seb. Allamand, qui y
a ajouté l'histoire de la vie et des écrits de l'auteur.* 2 vols. ed. by
Jean-Nicolas-Sébastien Allamand from works of Guillaume-
Jacob 'sGravesande. Amsterdam, 1774.
   C. Police Confiscations: 1 of 10 lists: Prot.

503. *Olinde, par l'auteur des Mémoires du vicomte de Barjac.* [Jean-
Pierre-Louis de La Roche du Maine, marquis de Luchet.]
London and Geneva, 1784. At least 3 other editions in 1784.
   A. STN

Major Dealers: Mauvelain, Troyes 19 (2) *Lorraine:* Bonthoux, Nancy 12 (1).	31 (3)
Total:	31 (3)

   D. Customs Confiscations: 1 instance: 1787.

504. *Opinion des anciens sur les juifs. Réflexions impartiales sur
l'Evangile, par feu M. de Mirabaud.* [Jean-Baptiste Mirabaud?,
or Paul-Henri-Dietrich Thiry, baron d'Holbach?, pub. by
Jacques-André Naigeon.] London, 1769. At least 1 other
edition by 1773; *Réflexions* also reprinted as *Examen critique
du Nouveau Testament, par M. Fréret,* 1777.
   A. STN

Major Dealers: Blouet, Rennes 4 (1); Mauvelain, Troyes 7 (2). *Lorraine:* Chénoux, Lunéville 4 (1). *Colporteurs:* Blaisot 6 (1).	21 (5)
Minor Dealers: Malassis, Nantes 2 (1); Chevrier, Poitiers 1 (1).	3 (2)
Total:	24 (7)

   B. Catalogues: 1 of 6 lists: (Bern: "4 1.").
   C. Police Confiscations: 3 of 10 lists: Stockdorf, Pilon, Prot.

505. **Oraison funèbre du vicaire savoyard.*
   A. STN

Major Dealers: Rigaud, Pons, Montpellier 12 (1).	12 (1)
Total:	12 (1)

506. *Orang-outang (l') d'Europe ou le polonais tel qu'il est; ouvrage*

méthodique qui a remporté un prix d'histoire naturelle en 1779.
[K'Morvand.] n.p., n.d.
D. Customs Confiscations: 1 instance: 1781.

Ordre (l') des francs-maçons trahi et le secret des Mopses révélé.
See #640, *Secrets (les) de l'ordre des francs-maçons dévoilés . . .*

507. *Origine (de l') des principes religieux.* [Jakob Heinrich Meister.] n.p., 1768.
    B. Catalogues: 1 of 6 lists: (Bern: "4 1.").
    D. Customs Confiscations: 1 instance: 1778.

508. *Ouvrages politiques et philosophiques d'un anonyme.* 3 vols. London, 1776.
    C. Police Confiscations: 1 of 10 lists: Prot.

509. *P. Adam (le) aux prises avec M. de Voltaire, ou les remontrances inutiles.* Antoine Adam. Ferney, 1777.
    A. STN
    Major Dealers: Mossy, Marseille 6 (1). }   6 (1)
                                                       Total: 6 (1)

510. *Paix (de la) perpétuelle, par le Docteur Goodheart.* [François-Marie Arouet de Voltaire.] n.p., n.d. (1769, according to Bengesco). At least 1 other undated edition.
    B. Catalogues: 2 of 6 lists: (Grasset; Bern: "2 1.").

511. **Pan et Syrinx.*
    D. Customs Confiscations: 1 instance: 1771.

512. *Papesse Jeanne (la), poème en dix chants.* [Charles Borde?] n.p., 1777. At least 1 other edition by 1778.
    A. STN
    Major Dealers: Mauvelain, Troyes 51 (6). }   51 (6)
                                                    Total: 51 (6)

513. *Parapilla, poème en cinq chants, traduit de l'italien.* [Charles Borde.] Florence, 1776. At least 4 other editions by 1784.
    A. STN
    Major Dealers: Mauvelain, Troyes 6 (1). }
    Lorraine: Carez, Toul 2 (1). }   8 (2)
                                                   Total: 8 (2)

514. *Parité de la vie et de la mort; Dieu nous a donné l'opinion et s'est réservé la science.* n.p., n.d. (1760?).

    C. Police Confiscations: 2 of 10 lists: Stockdorf, Manoury.

515. *Parnasse libertin, ou recueil de poésies libres.* Amsterdam, 1769. At least 5 other editions by 1783.

    A. STN

        Major Dealers: Charmet, Besançon 2 (1); Malherbe, Loudun 25 (1); Robert et Gauthier, Bourg-en-Bresse 12 (2).

        Lorraine: Chénoux, Lunéville 12 (2); Henry, Nancy 13 (1).

        Lyon: Jacquenod 6 (1).

        Paris: Barré 3 (1); Védrène 12 (1); Prévost 6 (1); Lequay Morin 12 (1).

        Colporteurs: "Troisième" 6 (1); Gilles 26 (1).

                          135 (14)

        Minor Dealers: Malassis, Nantes 6 (1); Chevrier, Poitiers 1 (1); Sens, Toulouse 12 (1); Resplandy, Toulouse 13 (1); Billault, Tours 2 (1).

                          34   (5)

                  Total: 169 (19)

    B. Catalogues: 2 of 6 lists: (Grasset; Décombaz: "8°. 1 1. 10 s.").

    C. Police Confiscations: 4 of 10 lists: Pilon, Jouy, et al., Prot, Paris.

    D. Customs Confiscations: 3 instances: 1778 (2), 1781.

516. *Partage (le) de la Pologne, en sept dialogues en forme de drame, ou conversation entre des personnages distingués, dans laquelle on fait parler les interlocuteurs, conformément à leurs principes et à leur conduite, par Gottlieb Panmouser; traduit de l'anglais par milady ***, duchesse de ***.* [trans. by Joseph-Mathias Gérard de Rayneval? from Lindsey?] London, 1775.

    A. STN

        Major Dealers: Letourmy, Orléans 6 (1). }   6 (1)

        Minor Dealers: Sens, Toulouse 6 (1); Bil-

continued

lault, Tours 3 (1); Caldesaigues, Mar-}   15   (3)
seille 6 (1).

Total: 21   (4)

   C. Police Confiscations: 1 of 10 lists: Prot.

517. *Passe-partout (le) de l'Eglise romaine. Ou histoire des tromperies des prêtres et des moines en Espagne, par Antoine Gavin. Traduit de l'anglais par M. Janiçon.* 3 vols. trans. by François-Michel Janiçon. London, 1726–27. (trans. from *A Master-Key to Popery* [1724] by Antonio Gavin.)

   A. STN

      Major Dealers: Malherbe, Loudun 1 (1).}   1   (1)

                                            Total: 1   (1)

518. **Passe-temps d'Antoinette.* (Probably *Les Passe-temps d'Antoinette et les amours du vizir de Vergennes.* London, 1783.)

   A. STN

      Major Dealers: Mauvelain, Troyes
        18 (2).   }   18   (2)

                                            Total: 18   (2)

519. *Passe-temps (le) agréable ou nouveaux choix de bons-mots, de pensées ingénieuses, de rencontres plaisantes et de gasconnades.* Rotterdam, 1709. At least 11 other editions by 1778.

   D. Customs Confiscations: 1 instance: 1779.

520. *Passe-temps (le) des mousequetaires, ou le temps perdu par M.D.B.****.* [Louis Desbiefs.] Berg-op-Zoom, 1755. At least 1 other edition by 1775.

   C. Police Confiscations: 1 of 10 lists: Jouy, et al.

521. *Passe-temps (le) du sexe.* Madrid, 1777. At least 1 other edition in 1777.

   A. STN

      Major Dealers: Malherbe, Loudun 12
        (1); Pavie, La Rochelle 8 (1). }   20   (2)

                                            Total: 20   (2)

522. **Passion (la) de Notre Seigneur en vers burlesques. Dédiée aux âmes dévotes.* Paris, 1649. (Attribution uncertain.)

   B. Catalogues: 1 of 6 lists: (Grasset: listed as "La Passion de notre Seigneur, 8°.").

523. *Pater (le) de JJR.
    D. Customs Confiscations: 1 instance: 1779.

524. Paysanne (la) parvenue ou les mémoires de madame la marquise
    de L.V. [Charles de Fieux, chevalier de Mouhy.] Paris, 1735.
    At least 18 other editions by 1788.
    D. Customs Confiscations: 1 instance: 1779.

525. Paysan (le) perverti, ou les dangers de la ville, histoire récente mise
    au jour d'après les véritables lettres des personnages par N.E.R. de
    la Bretonne. 4 vols. Nicolas-Edmé Restif de la Bretonne. The
    Hague, 1776 (actually 1775, according to Martin-Mylne-
    Frautschi). At least 9 other editions by 1789.
    A. STN
        Major Dealers: Letourmy, Orléans 5 (2);
            Malherbe, Loudun 188 (4);
            Manoury, Caen 12 (1).
        Lorraine: Choppin, Bar-le-Duc 1 (1);
            Gerlache, Metz 11 (4); Bernard,   233   (18)
            Lunéville 6 (3); L'Entretien, Luné-
            ville 6 (1).
        Paris: Prévost 4 (2).
        Minor Dealers: Jarfaut, Melun 6 (1).   6   (1)
                                    Total: 239   (19)
    D. Customs Confiscations: 2 instances: 1777, 1778.

526. Pensées de Pascal. [ed. by Jean-Antoine-Nicolas de Caritat,
    marquis de Condorcet.] London, 1776. (Original edition,
    1672.)
    D. Customs Confiscations: 1 instance: 1777.

527. Pensées libres sur la religion, l'église et sur le bonheur de la nation.
    Traduites de l'anglais du docteur B.M. 2 vols. [trans. by Ber-
    nard de Mondeville.] The Hague, 1723. (trans. from Free
    Thoughts on Religion, the Church and National Happiness
    [1720] by Justus van Effen.) At least 2 other editions by
    1772.
    C. Police Confiscations: 1 of 10 lists: Prot.

528. Pensées nouvelles et philosophiques. Amsterdam, 1777.
    A. STN
        Lorraine: Bernard, Lunéville 2 (1).   2   (1)

Minor Dealers: Bonnard, Auxerre 6 (1). }
                                           6   (1)
                              Total: 8   (2)

529. *Pensées philosophiques.* [Denis Diderot.] The Hague, 1746. At least 5 other editions by 1777.

    A. STN

        Minor Dealers: Chevrier, Poitiers 1 (1). }   1   (1)
                              Total: 1   (1)

    B. Catalogues: 2 of 6 lists: (Décombaz: " ... sur divers sujets, 12°. La Haye, 1761. 15 s."; Bern: "4 1.").

    C. Police Confiscations: 2 of 10 lists: Stockdorf, Pilon.

    D. Customs Confiscations: 1 instance: 1775.

530. *Pensées (les) philosophiques de M. de Voltaire, ou tableau encyclopédique des connaissances humaines, contenant l'esprit, principes, maximes, caractères, portraits, tirés des ouvrages de ce célèbre auteur et rangés suivant l'ordre des matières.* 2 vols. n.p., 1766.

    D. Customs Confiscations: 2 instances: 1771, 1779.

531. *Pensées secrètes et observations critiques attribuées à feu M. de S.-H.* [Hyacinthe Cordonnier, dit Thémiseul de Saint-Hyacinthe.] London, 1735.

    A. STN

        Major Dealers: Mauvelain, Troyes 7 (2). }   7   (2)
        Minor Dealers: Chevrier, Poitiers 1 (1). }   1   (1)
                              Total: 8   (3)

    B. Catalogues: 1 of 6 lists: (Bern: "6 1.").

    C. Police Confiscations: 2 of 10 lists: Pilon, Prot.

532. *Pensées sur l'interprétation de la nature.* [Denis Diderot.] n.p., 1754. (First edition was entitled *De l'Interprétation de la nature* [1753], according to Cioranescu).

    A. STN

        Minor Dealers: Chevrier, Poitiers 1 (1). }   1   (1)
                              Total: 1   (1)

    B. Catalogues: 1 of 6 lists: (Bern: "30 s.").

    C. Police Confiscations: 3 of 10 lists: Stockdorf, Pilon, Prot.

    D. Customs Confiscations: 1 instance: 1775.

533. *Pensées théologiques relatives aux erreurs du temps.* [Nicolas Jamin.] Paris, 1769. At least 2 other editions by 1778.

    D. Customs Confiscations: 2 instances: 1779, 1780.

534. **Père (le) français ou l'espion d'une nouvelle espèce.*
    D. Customs Confiscations: 1 instance: 1781.

    Petit Albert. See #641, *Secrets merveilleux* . . .

535. *Petit Code (le) de la raison humaine, ou exposition succincte de ce que la raison dicte à tous les hommes pour éclairer leur conduite et assurer leur bonheur, par M.B.D.* [Jacques Barbeu du Bourg.] London, 1774. At least 1 other edition by 1782.
    C. Police Confiscations: 1 of 10 lists: Prot.
    D. Customs Confiscations: 1 instance: 1774.

536. *Petit-fils (le) d'Hercule.* n.p., 1701 (actually 1784, according to Martin-Mylne-Frautschi). At least 2 other editions by 1788; 1787 as *Le Lutteur ou le petit-fils* . . .
    A. STN
      Major Dealers: Mauvelain, Troyes 38 (3).

38	(3)
Total: 38	(3)

537. *Petits Soupers (les) et les nuits de l'hôtel Bouill-n. Lettre de milord comte de ****** à milord ****** au sujet des récréations de M. de C-stri-s, ou de la danse de l'ours; anecdote singulière d'un cocher qui s'est pendu à l'hôtel Bouill-n, le 31 décembre 1778, à l'occasion de la danse de l'ours.* [Anne-Gédéon La Fitte, marquis de Pellepore.] Bouillon, 1783.
    A. STN
      Major Dealers: Mauvelain, Troyes 18 (2).

18	(2)
Total: 18	(2)

538. *Petit Tableau (le) de Paris.* [Jean-Pierre-Louis de La Roche du Maine, marquis de Luchet?, or Claude-Carloman de Rulhière?] n.p., 1783.
    A. STN
      Major Dealers: Mauvelain, Troyes 18 (3).

18	(3)
Total: 18	(3)

    D. Customs Confiscations: 1 instance: 1786.

539. *Philadelphien (le) à Genève, ou lettres d'un Américain sur la dernière révolution de Genève, sa constitution nouvelle, l'émigration en Irlande, etc., pouvant servir de tableau politique de Genève*

jusqu'en 1784. Jacques-Pierre Brissot de Warville. Dublin, 1783.

A. STN

Major Dealers: Mauvelain, Troyes 12 (2).	12	(2)
Total:	12	(2)

540. *Philosophe (le) du Valais, ou correspondance philosophique, avec des observations de l'éditeur.* 2 vols. [Gabriel Gauchet?] Paris, 1772.

B. Catalogues: 1 of 6 lists: (Bern: "6 1.").

541. *Philosophe (le) ignorant.* [François-Marie Arouet de Voltaire.] n.p., 1766. At least 7 other editions by 1767.

A. STN

Major Dealers: Charmet, Besançon 6 (1).	6	(1)
Total:	6	(1)

B. Catalogues: 3 of 6 lists: (Grasset; Décombaz: "8°. 1766, 15 s."; Bern: "40 s.").

C. Police Confiscations: 2 of 10 lists: Stockdorf, Pilon.

D. Customs Confiscations: 1 instance: 1779.

542. *Philosophie (de la) de la nature.* 3 vols. [Jean-Baptiste-Claude Isoard, dit Delisle de Sales.] Amsterdam, 1769. At least 3 other editions by 1777.

A. STN

Major Dealers: Letourmy, Orléans 14 (3); Mauvelain, Troyes 2 (2); Pavie, La Rochelle 6 (1); Rigaud, Pons, Montpellier 17 (3). *Lorraine:* Choppin, Bar-le-Duc 6 (2). *Colporteurs:* Gilles 4 (1).	49	(12)
Minor Dealers: Lair, Blois 1 (1).	1	(1)
Total:	50	(13)

B. Catalogues: 1 of 6 lists: (Bern: "9 1.").

D. Customs Confiscations: 3 instances: 1779, 1781, n.d.

543. *Philosophie (la) de l'histoire, par feu M. l'abbé Bazin.* [François-Marie Arouet de Voltaire.] Amsterdam, 1765. At least 3 other editions by 1769.

A. STN

Major Dealers: Bergeret, Bordeaux 4
   (1); Blouet, Rennes 6 (1); Malherbe,
   Loudun 2 (1).
Colporteurs: Planquais 2 (1).

14 (4)

Minor Dealers: Waroquier, Soissons
   1 (1).

1 (1)

Total: 15 (5)

B. Catalogues: 3 of 6 lists: (Grasset; Décombaz: "8°. 1765,
   2 1."; Bern: "6 1.").
D. Customs Confiscations: 1 instance: 1771.

544. *Philosophie du bon sens ou réflexions philosophiques sur l'incerti-*
   tude des connaissances humaines, à l'usage des cavaliers et du beau
   sexe par M. le marquis d'Argens. 2 vols. [Jean-Baptiste de
   Boyer, marquis d'Argens.] London, 1737. At least 3 other
   editions by 1768.
   C. Police Confiscations: 2 of 10 lists: Prot, Paris.
   D. Customs Confiscations: 3 instances: 1771, 1779, 1780.

545. *Pièces curieuses et intéressantes concernant la famille Calas, qui*
   ont été fournies par M. de Voltaire. François-Marie Arouet de
   Voltaire. Lausanne, 1768.
   A. STN

   Major Dealers: Letourmy, Orléans 2 (1).
   Lorraine: Gay, Lunéville 4 (1).

6 (2)

   Minor Dealers: Sens, Toulouse 11 (2);
      Caldesaigues, Marseille 2 (1).

13 (3)

Total: 19 (5)

546. *Pièces détachées, relatives au clergé séculier et régulier.* 3 vols. [ed.
   by François-Jacques-Maximilien de Chastenet, marquis de
   Puységur.] Amsterdam, 1771.
   A. STN

   Major Dealers: Mauvelain, Troyes 7 (2).

7 (2)

   Minor Dealers: Malassis, Nantes 2 (1).

2 (1)

Total: 9 (3)

   C. Police Confiscations: 1 of 10 lists: Pilon.

547. *Pièces échappées du portefeuille de M. de Voltaire, comte de Tour-*
   nay. Lausanne, 1759.

A. STN

    Major Dealers: Robert et Gauthier,
      Bourg-en-Bresse 18 (2).

    Lorraine: Bergue, Thionville 10 (1);
      Audéart, Lunéville 4 (1).

                                        32   (4)

    Minor Dealers: Boisserand, Roanne
      6 (1).   6   (1)

                            Total: 38   (5)

Pièces fugitives en vers et en prose. See #565, *Portefeuille (le) trouvé* . . .

548. *Pièces heureusement échappées de la France, par M. D***, avocat à Rouen.* London, 1775.

   A. STN

    Major Dealers: Charmet, Besançon 45
      (2); Pavie, La Rochelle 4 (1).   49   (3)

    Minor Dealers: Sens, Toulouse 1 (1);
      Sombert, Châlons-sur-Marne 2 (1);
      Fontaine, Colmar 17 (2); Billault,   22   (5)
      Tours 2 (1).

                            Total: 71   (8)

549. *Pièces libres de M. Ferrand, et poésies de quelques autres auteurs sur divers sujets.* [ed. by Antoine Ferrand?] London, 1738. At least 5 other editions by 1762. (Contains works by Legrand, Voltaire, and others.)

   B. Catalogues: 1 of 6 lists: (Bern: "3 1.").

   C. Police Confiscations: 2 of 10 lists: Stockdorf, Paris.

550. *Pièces philosophiques contenant i° "Parité de la vie et de la mort," ii° "Dialogues sur l'âme," iii° "Brunus redivivus, ou traité des erreurs populaires, ouvrage critique, historique et philosophique, imité de Pompance."* [trans. by Paul-Henri-Dietrich Thiry, baron d'Holbach, with notes by Jacques-André Naigeon.] (trans. from works by John Toland.) Amsterdam, 1768–71.

   A. STN

    Major Dealers: Blouet, Rennes 12 (1);
      Malherbe, Loudun 1 (1); Mauvelain,   20   (4)
      Troyes 7 (2).

    Minor Dealers: Chevrier, Poitiers 1 (1).   1   (1)

                            Total: 21   (5)

B. Catalogues: 1 of 6 lists: (Bern: "5 1.").

C. Police Confiscations: 2 of 10 lists; Stockdorf, Prot.

551. *Plaisirs (des) de la volupté.* (Possibly *Le Plaisir et la volupté, conte allégorique.*) [Madeleine d'Arsant, madame de Puisieux.] Paphos, 1752. At least 1 other edition by 1755.

D. Customs Confiscations: 1 instance: 1779.

552. *Plaisirs (les) de l'amour ou recueil de contes, histoires et poèmes galants de La Fontaine, Dorat, Gresset, etc.* 3 vols. Chez Apollon, au Montparnasse, 1782.

D. Customs Confiscations: 1 instance: 1784.

553. *Plaisirs (les) de tous les siècles et de tous les âges.* London, 1785.

A. STN

Major Dealers: Manoury, Caen 100 (1). }	100	(1)
Total:	100	(1)

C. Police Confiscations: 1 of 10 lists: Prot.

554. *Plaisirs (les) du cloître, comédie en trois actes et en vers libres, par de M.D.L.C.A.P. . . . .* n.p., 1773.

A. STN

Major Dealers: Pavie, La Rochelle 8 (1). }	8	(1)
Total:	8	(1)

555. *Plaisirs (les) secrets d'Angélique ou ses voyages au bout du monde.* [abbé Delsue?, or abbé de la Suze?, or abbé Delrue?] London, 1751. At least 1 other edition by 1755; also as *Voyages d'Angélique.*

A. STN

Major Dealers: Malherbe, Loudun 1 (1); Robert et Gauthier, Bourg-en-Bresse 4 (1). }	5	(2)
Total:	5	(2)

556. *Plus Secrets Mystères (les) des hauts grades de la maçonnerie dévoilés, ou le vrai Rose-Croix; traduit de l'anglais, suivi du Noachite traduit de l'allemand.* [trans. by Bérage?, ed. by Karl-Friedrich Koeppen.] Jerusalem, 1766. At least 5 other editions by 1786.

A. STN

Major Dealers: Blouet, Rennes 6 (1); Charmet, Besançon 6 (1); Manoury,

continued

Caen 92 (5); Mossy, Marseille 92 (4); Rigaud, Pons, Montpellier 16 (4); Robert et Gauthier, Bourg-en-Bresse 3 (1); Malherbe, Loudun 6 (1); Letourmy, Orléans 8 (1); Bergeret, Bordeaux 13 (2).	290	(29)
Lorraine: Carez, Toul 4 (1); Choppin, Bar-le-Duc 2 (1); Bernard, Lunéville 2 (1); Matthieu, Nancy 2 (1); d'Alancourt, Nancy 26 (3).		
Paris: Prévost 12 (2).		
Minor Dealers: Cazin, Reims 6 (1); Sens, Toulouse 6 (1); Sombert, Châlons-sur-Marne 6 (1); Bonnard, Auxerre 10 (3); Caldesaigues, Marseille 3 (1).	31	(7)
Total:	321	(36)

Poème sur la guerre civile de Genève. See #278, *Guerre (la) civile de Genève* . . .

557. *Poésies de la Lane et du marquis du Montplaisir.* [ed. by Charles-Hugues Le Febvre de Saint-Marc.] Amsterdam, 1759.
    D. Customs Confiscations: 1 instance: 1780.

558. *Poésies (les) gaillardes, galantes et amoureuses de ce temps.* 2 vols. [ed. by Guillaume Colletet?] n.p., n.d. (c. 1650, according to Gay).
    A. STN

Major Dealers: Blouet, Rennes 6 (1).	16	(5)
Lorraine: Audéart, Lunéville 4 (1).		
Colporteurs: Blaisot 2 (1); Planquais 2 (1); "Troisième" 2 (1).		
Total:	16	(5)

559. *Point (le) d'appui entre les principales puissances de l'Europe ou tableau militaire, politique, critique, impartial des troubles des temps présents, avec figures en taille douce.* 5 vols. [François-Antoine Chevrier.] Liège, 1759.
    B. Catalogues: 1 of 6 lists: (Grasset: "Point d'Appui ou Hist.

Pol. de la dern. guerre entre les Puissances de l'Europe avec les Plans des Siéges [sic] & Batailles, 8°. 5 vol. fig.").

560. *Politique (la) naturelle. Ou discours sur les vrais principes du gouvernement par un ancien magistrat.* 2 vols. [Paul-Henri-Dietrich, baron d'Holbach?] London, 1773. At least 2 other editions by 1774.

    A. STN

Major Dealers: Charmet, Besançon 12 (1); Malherbe, Loudun 20 (1). *Lorraine:* Audéart, Lunéville 4 (1). *Colporteurs:* Gilles 30 (2).	}	66 (5)
Minor Dealers: Malassis, Nantes 6 (10). }		6 (1)
	Total:	72 (6)

    B. Catalogues: 1 of 6 lists: (Décombaz: "8°. 2 vol. Londres, 1773, 6 l.").

    C. Police Confiscations: 1 of 10 lists: Prot.

561. *Pornographe (le), ou idées d'un honnête-homme sur un projet de règlement pour les prostituées, propre à prévenir les malheurs qu'occasionne le publicisme des femmes, avec des notes historiques et justificatives.* [Nicolas-Edmé Restif de la Bretonne.] London and The Hague, 1769. At least 5 other editions by 1786.

    D. Customs Confiscations: 1 instance: 1774.

562. *Portefeuille d'un exempt de police.* London, 1785.

    D. Customs Confiscations: 1 instance: 1786.

563. *Portefeuille (le) de madame Gourdan, dite la Comtesse, pour servir à l'histoire des moeurs du siècle et principalement de celles de Paris.* [Charles Théveneau de Morande.] Spa, 1783. At least 3 other editions by 1785; also as *Correspondance de Madame Gourdan . . .*

    A. STN

Major Dealers: Mauvelain, Troyes 44 (5).	}	44 (5)
	Total:	44 (5)

564. *Portefeuille (le) d'un philosophe, ou mélange de pièces philosophiques, politiques, critiques, satiriques et galantes.* 6 vols. [Henri-Joseph Du Laurens.] Cologne, 1770.

    A. STN

Major Dealers: Charmet, Besançon 6
(1); Mauvelain, Troyes 7 (2); Robert ⎫
et Gauthier, Bourg-en-Bresse 6 (1). ⎬ 25 (5)
Colporteurs: Blaisot 6 (1).   ⎭

Minor Dealers: Malassis, Nantes 3 (1). }   3 (1)

                       Total: 28 (6)

  C. Police Confiscations: 3 of 10 lists: Stockdorf, Pilon, Paris.

  D. Customs Confiscations: 1 instance: 1774.

565. *Portefeuille (le) trouvé, ou tablettes d'un curieux contenant une quantité de pièces fugitives de M. de Voltaire qui ne sont dans aucune de ses éditions.* 2 vols. [Pub. by Pierre Louis d'Aquin de Château-Lyon.] Geneva, 1757.

  A. STN

Major Dealers: Rigaud, Pons, Montpel- ⎫
lier 20 (1); Robert et Gauthier,   ⎬ 32 (2)
Bourg-en-Bresse 12 (1).   ⎭

                       Total: 32 (2)

  B. Catalogues: 1 of 6 lists: (Bern: "6 vol., 15 1.").

Portier (le) des Chartreux. See #287 *Histoire de dom B . . .*

566. *Postillon de Versailles.* Versailles, n.d. (c. 1781, according to NUC).

  D. Customs Confiscations: 1 instance: 1781.

567. *Pot (le) aux roses, ou correspondance secrète et familière de l'honorable Thomas Boot, cordonnier royal, avec Sa Majesté George III, roi de la Grande Bretagne et ses ministres les Lords Stormont, Sandwich, Germaine, et North, sur les affaires présentes de l'Europe.* London, 1781.

  A. STN

Major Dealers: Mauvelain, Troyes 6 (1). }   6 (1)

                       Total: 6 (1)

568. *Pot-pourri (le), étrennes aux gens de lettres.* [Jacques-Pierre Brissot de Warville.] London, 1777.

  A. STN

Major Dealers: Mauvelain, Troyes 6 (1). }   6 (1)

                       Total: 6 (1)

569. *Précis des arguments contre les matérialistes, avec de nouvelles réflexions sur la nature de nos connaissances, l'existence de Dieu,*

l'immatérialité et l'immortalité et de l'âme. Isaac Pinto. The Hague, 1774. At least 1 other edition by 1775.

   C. Police Confiscations: 1 of 10 lists: Prot (listed as *Précis des arguments pour les matérialistes*).

570. *Précis du siècle de Louis XV par M. de Voltaire, servant de suit au Siècle de Louis XIV du même auteur.* 2 vols. François-Marie Arouet de Voltaire. Geneva, 1769. At least 11 other editions by 1785.

   B. Catalogues: 1 of 6 lists: (Grasset: "8°. 2 vol.").

Précis historique de la vie de madame la comtesse du Barry. See 269, *Gazette (la) de Cythère, ou aventures galantes et récentes . . .*

Prêtres (les) démasqués, ou des iniquités du clergé chrétien. Ouvrage traduit de l'anglais. See #213, *Esprit (l') du clergé . . .*

571. *Princesse (la) de Babylone.* [François-Marie Arouet de Voltaire.] Geneva, 1768. At least 8 other editions by 1772; also as *Voyages et aventures d'une princesse babylonienne.*
   A. STN

Minor Dealers: Chevrier, Poitiers 1 (1). }	1	(1)
Total:	1	(1)

   B. Catalogues: 2 of 6 lists: (Décombaz: "8°. 1768. 15 s."; Bern: "30 s.").
   C. Police Confiscations: 2 of 10 lists: Stockdorf, Pilon.
   D. Customs Confiscations: 2 instances: 1771, 1778.

572. *Principes de la législation universelle.* [Georg Ludwig Schmid.] Amsterdam, 1776.
   C. Police Confiscations: 1 of 10 lists: Prot.

573. *Principes de la philosophie morale, ou essai de M. S*** sur le mérite et la vertu, avec des réflexions.* [trans. by Denis Diderot.] (trans. from *An Inquiry Concerning Virtue, or Merit* [1711] by Anthony Ashley Cooper, 3rd Earl of Shaftesbury.) Amsterdam, 1745. At least 1 other edition by 1751.
   A. STN

Major Dealers: Letourmy, Orléans 10 (2). }	10	(2)
Total:	10	(2)

574. *Principes (les) de la révolution justifiés dans un sermon prêché à Cambridge le 29 mai 1776, par Richard Wattson, suivi d'un*

extrait du pamphlet américain, intitulé le "Common-sense."
n.p., n.d.
A. STN

> *Major Dealers:* Charmet, Besançon 12
> (1); Rigaud, Pons, Montpellier 6 (1). ⎱   18   (2)
>
>   Total: 18   (2)

Principes du droit politique. See 124, *Contrat (du) social . . .*

Principes du gouvernement français, démontrés par la raison et par les faits. See #718, *Vrais Principes (les) . . .*

575. *Prix de la justice et de l'humanité, par l'auteur de la Henriade, avec son portrait.* [François-Marie Arouet de Voltaire.] Ferney, 1778. At least 3 other editions in 1778.
    C. Police Confiscations: 1 of 10 lists: Desauges.

576. *Problème historique: qui des jésuites ou de Luther et Calvin ont le plus nui à l'Eglise chrétienne?* 2 vols. [abbé Mesnier.] Avignon, 1757. At least 1 other edition by 1763.
    A. STN

    > *Major Dealers:* Blouet, Rennes 2 (1);
    > Buchet, Nîmes 3 (1); Letourmy,
    > Orléans 1 (1).   ⎱   8   (4)
    > *Lorraine:* d'Alancourt, Nancy 2 (1). ⎰
    >
    >   Total: 8   (4)

577. *Procès (le) des trois rois: Louis XVI de France-Bourbon, Charles III d'Espagne-Bourbon, et Georges III d'Hanovre, fabricant de boutons, plaidé aux tribunaux des puissances européennes; par appendice l'Appel au pape, traduit de l'anglais.* [Simon-Nicolas-Henri Linguet?, or Bouffonidor, pseud. of Ange Goudar?] London, 1780.
    D. Customs Confiscations: 2 instances: 1781 (2).

578. *Profession (la) de foi des théistes, par le comte Da . . . au R.D. Traduit de l'allemand.* [François-Marie Arouet de Voltaire.] n.p., n.d. (1768, according to Bengesco).
    A. STN

    > *Major Dealers:* Blouet, Rennes 4 (1);
    > Letourmy, Orléans 6 (1); Malherbe,
    > Loudun 12 (1).

continued

Lorraine: Bergue, Thionville 6 (1);   60   (8)
    Audéart, Lunéville 26 (3).
Paris: Prévost 6 (1).
Minor Dealers: Billault, Tours 1 (1). }   1   (1)
                 Total: 61   (9)

B. Catalogues: 3 of 6 lists: (Grasset: "8°. 8 s."; Décombaz; Bern: "3 1.").

579. *Progrès (les) de la raison dans la recherche du vrai. Ouvrage post-hume de M. Helvétius.* Claude-Adrien Helvétius. (London, 1775.

A. STN

    Major Dealers: Malherbe, Loudun 6 (1). }   6   (1)
                 Total: 6   (1)

C. Police Confiscations: 1 of 10 lists: Prot.

580. *Projet d'une réforme à faire en Italie, ou moyens de corriger les abus les plus dangereux et de réformer les lois les plus pernicieuses établies en Italie, ouvrage traduit de l'italien de Carlo Ant. Pilati.* [trans. by Jean Manzon.] Amsterdam, 1769. (trans. from *Di Una Riforma d'Italia* [1767] by Carlo Antonio Pilati de Tassulo.)

B. Catalogues: 1 of 6 lists: (Bern: "4 1.").

C. Police Confiscations: 2 of 10 lists: Stockdorf, Prot.

581. *Projet pour rendre la paix perpétuelle en Europe et générale entre toutes les puissances de l'Europe.* [Charles-Irène Castel de Saint-Pierre.] Utrecht, 1713 and 1716. At least 1 other edition by 1717 as *Projet d'une paix perpétuelle et générale . . .*

A. STN

    Colporteurs: Blaisot 6 (1).   }   6   (1)
                 Total: 6   (1)

582. **Provision pour le couvent.* Estampes.

D. Customs Confiscations: 1 instance: 1771.

583. *Pucelle (la) d'Orléans, poème héroï-comique.* François-Marie Arouet de Voltaire. Paris, 1755. At least 35 other editions by 1789.

A. STN

    Major Dealers: Blouet, Rennes 18 (3);
       Charmet, Besançon 75 (3); Le-

continued

tourmy, Orléans 17 (4); Malherbe,
Loudun 77 (3); Robert et Gauthier,
Bourg-en-Bresse 12 (2).

Lorraine: Bertrand, Thionville 8 (1);
Bergue, Thionville 25 (1); Orbelin,
Thionville 6 (1).

Paris: Prévost 8 (1); Barré 3 (1).

Colporteurs: Blaisot 6 (1); Planquais 10
(2); "Troisième" 2 (1); Gilles 102 (2).

369 (26)

Minor Dealers: Chevrier, Poitiers 15
(4); Petit, Reims 2 (1); Sens, Toulouse 12 (1); Sombert, Châlons-sur-
Marne 6 (1); Bonnard, Auxerre 6
(2); Habert, Bar-sur-Aube 10 (1); Billault, Tours 2 (1); Caldesaigues, Marseille 14 (2).

67 (13)

Total: 436 (39)

B. Catalogues: 5 of 6 lists: (Décombaz: ". . . en 18 chants
. . . 8°. Londres, 1774, 2 1." and ". . . en 21 chants, 8°.
fig. Londres, 1774, 6 1."; Cailler; Nouffer; Chappuis et
Didier: ". . . en 22 chants, nouv. édit. augm. de variantes,
belle édition, gr. 12°. avec 21 nouvelles planches très-
bien gravées dans un mois."; Bern: "8°. avec figures, 12
1.", "12° avec figures, 9 1.", "16°. avec figures, 24 1.",
"16°. sans figures, 5 1.", "32°. sans figures, 5 1.").

C. Police Confiscations: 5 of 10 lists: Stockdorf, Moureau,
Prot, Paris, Versailles.

D. Customs Confiscations: 18 instances: 1772 (2) 1773 (2),
1774 (2), 1775 (3), 1776, 1777 (2), 1778 (3), 1779,
1781, 1783.

584. *Putain (la) errante, ou dialogue de Madeleine et de Julie, par P.
Arétin, fidèlement traduit en français par N. Lampsaque, 1760.*
(trans. from *La Puttane errante* [1540] by Niccolò Franco?)
At least 9 other editions by 1788; also in *Le Cabinet d'amour
et de Vénus* and as *Histoire et vie de l'Arétin ou entretiens de
Magdelon et de Julie.*

A. STN

Major Dealers: Buchet, Nîmes 26 (1);
Charmet, Besançon 31 (2); Le-

continued

tourmy, Orléans 20 (2); Malherbe,
Loudun 12 (1); Pavie, La Rochelle
36 (2).

Lorraine: Choppin, Bar-le-Duc 6 (2); } 179 (18)
Bertrand, Thionville 9 (3); Audéart,
Lunéville 19 (2).

Paris: Prévost 2 (1); Barré 6 (1);
Lequay Morin 12 (1).

Minor Dealers: Malassis, Nantes 3 (1);
Sens, Toulouse 12 (1); Resplandy,
Toulouse 13 (1); Sombert, Châlons-
sur-Marne 6 (1); Bonnard, Auxerre 4 } 82 (9)
(1); Billault, Tours 26 (2); Caldesaigues, Marseille 18 (2).

Total: 261 (27)

B. Catalogues: 2 of 6 lists: (Décombaz: "8°. *Lampsaque,*
1760, 3 1." and as "*Histoire et vie d'Arretin,* 8°. fig. 1774,
1 1."; Cailler: *Putain errante* as "12°. 1777" and as "*His-*
toire et vie de L'Arretin. 8°. fig. 1775").
C. Police Confiscations: 1 of 10 lists: Paris.
D. Customs Confiscations: 3 instances: 1778, 1784, 1786.

585. **Putain (la) parvenue.* (Identified in a margin note, presum-
ably by a police official, as "La Putain parvenue ou histoire
de la comtesse du Barry avec figures comme Le Portier.")
B. Catalogues: 1 of 6 lists: (Bern).

586. *Pyrrhonisme (le) de l'Eglise romaine, ou lettres du*
P.H.B.D.R.A.P. à M*** avec les réponses. [Boullier.] Amster-
dam, 1757.
A. STN
Major Dealers: Blouet, Rennes 4 (1); } 11 (3)
Mauvelain, Troyes 7 (2).
Minor Dealers: Chevrier, Poitiers 1 (1). } 1 (1)
Total: 12 (4)
C. Police Confiscations: 2 of 10 lists: Pilon, Prot.

587. *Questions (les) de Zapata, traduites par le sieur Tamponet, doc-*
teur de Sorbonne. [François-Marie Arouet de Voltaire.] Leipzig, 1766 (actually 1767, according to Bengesco). At least 2
other editions in 1767.

A. STN
Major Dealers: Blouet, Rennes 6 (1).
Lorraine: Bergue, Thionville 6 (1); Gay,
Lunéville 12 (1); Audéart, Lunéville
44 (6).
Colporteurs: Blaisot 6 (2); Planquais 2
(1); Gilles 12 (1).

$\left. \right\}$ 88 (13)

Total: 88 (13)

B. Catalogues: 2 of 6 lists: (Grasset: "8°. 8 s."; Bern: "30 s.").

588. *Questions sur l'Encyclopédie par des amateurs.* 9 vols. [François-Marie Arouet de Voltaire.] n.p., 1770–72. At least 4 other editions by 1779.

A. STN
Major Dealers: Blouet, Rennes 4 (1);
Buchet, Nîmes 8 (2); Charmet,
Besançon 18 (3); Letourmy, Orléans
14 (2); Malherbe, Loudun 39 (7);
Mossy, Marseille 6 (1); Rigaud, Pons,
Montpellier 70 (4); Robert et Gau-
thier, Bourg-en-Bresse 1 (1); Pavie,
La Rochelle 2 (1).
Lorraine: Chénoux, Lunéville 18 (4);
Sandré, Lunéville 2 (1); Augé, Luné-
ville 12 (3); Gerlache, Metz 40 (2);
Bertrand, Thionville 4 (3); Bergue,
Thionville 12 (1); Orbelin, Thion-
ville 2 (1); Gay, Lunéville 36 (4);
Audéart, Lunéville 9 (4); Matthieu,
Nancy 13 (2); Bonthoux, Nancy 4
(2); Babin, Nancy 2 (1).
Colporteurs: Blaisot 2 (1); Planquais 4
(1); Gilles 16 (2).

$\left. \right\}$ 338 (54)

Minor Dealers: Malassis, Nantes 25 (2);
Chevrier, Poitiers 19 (2); Cazin,
Reims 16 (2); Laisney, Beauvais 27
(2); Lair, Blois 1 (1).

$\left. \right\}$ 88 (9)

Total: 426 (63)

B. Catalogues: 3 of 6 lists: (Grasset; Décombaz: "8°. 9 vol.
1772, 18 l."; Bern: "27 l.").

C. Police Confiscations: 3 of 10 lists: Pilon, Prot, Paris.

D. Customs Confiscations: 41 instances: 1771 (7), 1772 (12), 1773 (7), 1774 (4), 1775 (4), 1776 (2), 1777, 1779 (2), 1782, 1786.

589. *Questions sur les miracles à M. Claparède, professeur de théologie à Genève, ou extrait de diverses lettres de M. de Voltaire, avec les réponses par M. Needham, de la Société Royale des Sciences.* [François-Marie Arouet de Voltaire.] London, 1769. At least 2 other editions in 1769. (An abridged edition of a series of letters published in 1765 under various titles, including *Lettres sur les miracles* and *Collection des lettres sur les miracles . . .*)

A. STN

Major Dealers: Blouet, Rennes 2 (1); Mauvelain, Troyes 8 (3).	}	10	(4)
Minor Dealers: Chevrier, Poitiers 1 (1). }		1	(1)
	Total:	11	(5)

B. Catalogues: 1 of 6 lists: (Bern: "5 1.").

C. Police Confiscations: 3 of 10 lists: Stockdorf, Pilon, Prot.

590. *Quinze Joies (les) de mariage, ouvrage très-ancien, auquel on a joint le Blason des fausses amours, le Loyer des folles amours, et le Triomphe des muses contre l'amour. Le tout enrichi de remarques et de diverses leçons.* [ed. by François de Rosset, with *remarques* by J. Le Duchat; *Quinze Joyes* attributed to Antoine de La Sale, c. 1470–80; *Loyer* attributed to Guillaume Cretin.] The Hague, 1726. At least 1 other edition by 1734.

A. STN

Minor Dealers: Chevrier, Poitiers 2 (1). }		2	(1)
	Total:	2	(1)

Raison (la) par alphabet. See #153, *Dictionnaire philosophique portatif.*

591. **Rapport de l'homme avec la nature.*

A. STN

Major Dealers: Pavie, La Rochelle 10 (2).	}	10	(2)
	Total:	10	(2)

592. **Recherches philosophiques de Collin sur la liberté des actions humaines.* (Probably *Recherches philosophiques sur la liberté de l'homme* in *Recueil de diverses pièces sur la philosophie, la religion*

naturelle, l'histoire, les mathématiques, etc., par Leibniz, Clarke, Newton et autres auteurs célèbres.) 2 vols. [ed. by Pierre Des Maizeaux.] Amsterdam, 1720. (Includes a translation of Anthony Collins's *A Philosophical Inquiry Concerning Human Liberty* [1717] with a commentary by Samuel Clark.) At least 1 other edition by 1740.
C. Police Confiscations: 1 of 10 lists: Stockdorf.

593. *Recherches philosophiques sur les Américains, ou mémoires inté-ressants pour servir à l'histoire de l'espèce humaine par M. de P****. 2 vols. [Cornelius de Pauw.] Berlin, 1768–69. At least 13 other editions by 1777.
A. STN

Major Dealers: Bergeret, Bordeaux 6 (1); Charmet, Besançon 30 (5).
Lorraine: Carez, Toul 2 (1); Chénoux, Lunéville 50 (1); Bernard, Lunéville 7 (2); L'Entretien, Lunéville 3 (2). ⎫ 117 (15)
Lyon: Baritel 12 (1).
Paris: Cugnet 4 (1); Prévost 3 (1). ⎭

Minor Dealers: Jarfaut, Melun 6 (1); Boisserand, Roanne 6 (2); Malassis, Nantes 2 (1); Resplandy, Toulouse 13 (1); Sombert, Châlons-sur-Marne ⎬ 49 (10) 2 (1); Bonnard, Auxerre 6 (2); Lais-ney, Beauvais 12 (1); Caldesaigues, Marseille 2 (1). ⎭

Total: 166 (25)

C. Police Confiscations: 5 of 10 lists: Stockdorf, Pilon, Jouy, et al., Prot, Desauges.
D. Customs Confiscations: 10 instances: 1771 (2), 1772, 1773, 1775 (2), 1776 (2), 1779 (2).

594. *Recherches philosophiques sur les Egyptiens et les Chinois par M. de P****. 2 vols. [Cornelius de Pauw.] Berlin, 1773. At least 1 other edition by 1774.
A. STN

Major Dealers: Blouet, Rennes 2 (1); Charmet, Besançon 2 (1); Robert et Gauthier, Bourg-en-Bresse 2 (1).

continued

158

Lorraine: Carez, Toul 2 (1); Chénoux, Lunéville 12 (1); Bernard, Lunéville 4 (2); L'Entretien, Lunéville 3 (2). } 60 (13)
Paris: Cugnet 5 (2); Prévost 3 (1).
Colporteurs: Gilles 25 (1).

Minor Dealers: Sombert, Châlons-sur-Marne 2 (1); Boisserand, Roanne 2 (1); Caldesaigues, Marseille 2 (1). } 6 (3)

Total: 66 (16)

B. Catalogues: 1 of 6 lists: (Grasset: "12°. 2 vol. avec une carte géographique").
C. Police Confiscations: 4 of 10 lists: Pilon, Jouy, et al., Prot, Desauges.
D. Customs Confiscations: 2 instances: 1773, 1774.

595. *Recherches sur l'entendement humain d'après les principes du sens commun.* 2 vols. (trans. from *An Inquiry into the Human Mind, or the Principles of Common Sense* [1764] by Thomas Reid.) Amsterdam, 1768.
B. Catalogues: 1 of 6 lists: (Bern: "5 1.").
C. Police Confiscations: 1 of 10 lists: Stockdorf.

596. **Recherches sur les causes de phénomènes.*
D. Customs Confiscations: 1 instance: 1779.

597. **Recherches sur les finances.*
D. Customs Confiscations: 1 instance: 1778.

598. *Recherches sur les miracles, par l'auteur de l'Examen des apologistes de la religion chrétienne.* [Jean Lévesque de Burigny?] London, 1773.
A. STN
Major Dealers: Manoury, Caen 25 (1). } 25 (1)
Total: 25 (1)
B. Catalogues: 1 of 6 lists: (Bern: "4 1.").
C. Police Confiscations: 2 of 10 lists: Stockdorf, Pilon.

599. *Recherches sur l'origine de l'esclavage religieux et politique du peuple en France.* [François-René-Jean de Pommereul.] London, 1781. At least 1 other edition by 1783.
A. STN
Minor Dealers: Petit, Reims 6 (1). } 6 (1)
Total: 6 (1)

600. *Recherches sur l'origine du despotisme oriental. Ouvrage posthume de Mr. B.I.D.P.E.C.* [Nicolas-Antoine Boulanger?, ed. by Paul-Henri-Dietrich Thiry, baron d'Holbach.] n.p., 1761. At least 8 other editions by 1777.
   A. STN
      Major Dealers: Blouet, Rennes 4 (1); Malherbe, Loudun 1 (1); Pavie, La Rochelle 8 (1); Robert et Gauthier, Bourg-en-Bresse 6 (1).
      Lorraine: Bergue, Thionville 6 (1).
      Colporteurs: Planquais 6 (1). } 31 (6)
      Minor Dealers: Chevrier, Poitiers 1 (1). } 1 (1)
                                        Total: 32 (7)
   B. Catalogues: 3 of 6 lists: (Grasset; Décombaz: "12°. 1761, 2 l."; Bern: "6 l.").
   C. Police Confiscations: 3 of 10 lists: Pilon, Prot, Paris.
   D. Customs Confiscations: 5 instances: 1771, 1774, 1779, 1786, n.d.

601. *Recueil de comédies et de quelques chansons gaillardes. Imprimé pour ce monde.* n.p., 1775.
   A. STN
      Major Dealers: Charmet, Besançon 12 (1); Letourmy, Orléans 66 (6); Malherbe, Loudun 152 (4); Pavie, La Rochelle 18 (2); Robert et Gauthier, Bourg-en-Bresse 6 (1).
      Lorraine: L'Entretien, Lunéville 2 (1); Audéart, Lunéville 14 (3).
      Lyon: Flandin 12 (1); Cellier 4 (1).
      Paris: Prévost 3 (1); Barré 6 (1); Védrène 12 (1). } 306 (23)
      Minor Dealers: Malassis, Nantes 3 (1); Sens, Toulouse 12 (1); Resplandy, Toulouse 13 (1); Billault, Tours 13 (1). } 41 (4)
                                        Total: 347 (27)
   B. Catalogues: 2 of 6 lists: (Grasset; Décombaz: "12°. 1773, 1 l. 5 s.").
   C. Police Confiscations: 2 of 10 lists: Prot, Paris.
   D. Customs Confiscations: 3 instances: 1774, 1781 (2).

602. *Recueil de pièces fugitives en prose et en vers, accompagnées de notes critiques et impartiales par M. de V.* [François-Marie Arouet de Voltaire.] n.p., 1740. At least 5 other editions by 1744.
   A. STN
   > *Major Dealers:* Letourmy, Orléans 4 (1);
   >   Mossy, Marseille 24 (2); Rigaud,
   >   Pons, Montpellier 24 (2).
   > *Lorraine:* Bertrand, Thionville 4 (1);   72   (9)
   >   Bergue, Thionville 6 (1); Orbelin,
   >   Thionville 6 (1).
   > *Colporteurs:* Blaisot 4 (1).
   > *Minor Dealers:* Sens, Toulouse 2 (1).   2   (1)
   >   Total: 74   (10)

   C. Police Confiscations: 1 of 10 lists: Prot.

   Recueil de pièces sur le clergé régulier et séculier. See #330, *Imposture (de l') sacerdotale* . . .

   Recueil de toutes les pièces intéressantes publiées en France, relativement aux troubles des parlements . . . See #96, *Code (le) français* . . .

603. *Recueil des chansons des francs-maçons.* n.p., 1742.
   A. STN
   > *Major Dealers:* Malherbe, Loudon 4 (1).   4   (1)
   >   Total: 4   (1)

604. *Recueil des poésies de M. B***.* Geneva, 1756.
   A. STN
   > *Minor Dealers:* Chevrier, Poitiers 1 (1).   1   (1)
   >   Total: 1   (1)

   B. Catalogues: 1 of 6 lists: (Bern: "4 1.").

605. *Recueil des réclamations, remontrances, lettres, arrêtés, et protestations des parlements, cours des aides, chambres des comptes, bailliages, présidiaux, élections, au sujet de l'édit de décembre 1770, l'érection des conseils supérieurs, la suppression des parlements, etc.* 2 vols. Amsterdam, 1775.
   A. STN
   > *Major Dealers:* Mauvelain, Troyes 3 (2);   6   (3)
   >   Rigaud, Pons, Montpellier 3 (1).
   >   Total: 6   (3)

606. *Recueil des romans de M. de Voltaire.* François-Marie Arouet de Voltaire. n.p., 1764. At least 10 other editions by 1789; also as *Romans et contes philosophiques par M. de Voltaire.*
   A. STN

Major Dealers: Bergeret, Bordeaux 4 (1); Buchet, Nîmes 6 (1); Charmet, Besançon 6 (1). *Lyon:* Baritel 12 (1). *Colporteurs:* Gilles 12 (1).	40	(5)
Total:	40	(5)

   B. Catalogues: 2 of 6 lists: (Grasset; Décombaz: "8°. 2 vol. Londres, 1773, 4 1.").
   D. Customs Confiscations: 3 instances: 1774 (2), 1778.

607. *Recueil intéressant sur l'affaire de la mutilation du crucifix d'Abbéville, arrivé le 9 août 1765, et sur la mort du chevalier de La Barre, pour servir de supplément aux cause célèbres.* [ed. by L. A. Devérité.] London, 1773. At least 1 other edition by 1776.
   C. Police Confiscations: 1 of 10 lists: Paris.

608. *Recueil nécessaire avec l'Evangile de la raison.* 2 vols. [François-Marie Arouet de Voltaire.] London, 1768 (first published in 1766, according to Bengesco). At least 1 other edition by 1776.
   A. STN

Major Dealers: Blouet, Rennes 6 (1); Malherbe, Loudun 1 (1). *Lorraine:* Sandré, Lunéville 6 (1).	13	(3)
Minor Dealers: Chevrier, Poitiers 1 (1).	1	(1)
Total:	14	(4)

   B. Catalogues: 2 of 6 lists: (Décombaz: "contenant: 'Analyse de la religion chrétienne; Vicaire savoyard; Catéchisme de l'honnête homme; Sermon des cinquante; Examen de Bolingbrocke,' &c. 8°. 1765, 4 1. 10 s."; Bern: "12 1.").
   C. Police Confiscations: 3 of 10 lists: Stockdorf, Pilon, Prot.

609. *Recueil philosophique, ou mélange de pièces sur la religion et la morale, par différents auteurs.* 2 vols. [ed. by Jacques-André Naigeon.] Amsterdam, 1770.
   A. STN

Major Dealers: Blouet, Rennes 14 (2). }   14   (2)

Minor Dealers: Chevrier, Poitiers 1 (1). }   1   (1)

Total: 15   (3)

  B. Catalogues: 1 of 6 lists: (Bern: "6 1.").

  C. Police Confiscations: 3 of 10 lists: Stockdorf, Pilon, Prot.

610. *Réflexions d'un citoyen catholique sur les lois de France relatives aux protestants.* [Jean-Antoine-Nicolas de Caritat, marquis de Condorcet.] n.p., 1778.

  A. STN

    Major Dealers: Letourmy, Orléans 2 (1); Malherbe, Loudun 13 (1); Manoury, Caen 12 (1); Rigaud, Pons, Montpellier 12 (1).   39   (4)

Total: 39   (4)

611. *Réflexions d'un fossoyeur et d'un curé sur les cimetières de la ville de Lyon.* [Rast de Maupas?] Lyon, 1777.

  B. Catalogues: 1 of 6 lists: (Nouffer).

612. *Réflexions impartiales sur l'Evangile par feu M. de Mirabaud.* [Jean-Baptiste de Mirabaud?] London, 1769. Republished as *Examen critique du Nouveau Testament.* London, 1777.

  A. STN

    Lorraine: Chénoux, Lunéville 1 (1). }   1   (1)

    Minor Dealers: Malassis, Nantes 2 (1). }   2   (1)

Total: 3   (2)

  B. Catalogues: 1 of 6 lists: (Bern: "4 1.").

  C. Police Confiscations: 2 of 10 lists: Stockdorf, Manoury.

  D. Customs Confiscations: 1 instance: 1779.

613. *Réflexions philosophiques sur le Système de la nature.* 2 vols. [Holland] Neuchâtel, 1773.

  C. Police Confiscations: 2 of 10 lists: Pilon, Prot.

614. *Réflexions politiques sur la Pologne ou lettre d'un patriote modéré à son ami, avec plusieurs autres lettres et un coup d'œil sur les vues secrètes que peuvent avoir les puissances de l'Europe par rapport à la situation actuelle de la Pologne, le 10 juin 1770.* [Pyrrhys de Varville?] London, 1772.

  C. Police Confiscations: 1 of 10 lists: Pilon.

615. *Réflexions sur la désertion et sur la peine des déserteurs, en forme de lettre à monseigneur le duc de Choiseul . . . par M. de ***.* [César-François de Flavigny.] En France, 1768.
   D. Customs Confiscations: 1 instance: 1772.

616. *Réforme (de la) politique des juifs, par M. C. G. Dohm, conseiller de guerre du roi de Prusse, traduit d'allemand.* [trans. by Jean Bernoully.] (trans. from Christian Wilhelm von Dohm.) Dessau, 1782.
   D. Customs Confiscations: 1 instance: 1784.

617. **Relation de la bataille de Suffrens.*
   D. Customs Confiscations: 1 instance: 1783.

618. *Relation de la mort du chevalier de La Barre, par M. Cass***, avocat au conseil du Roi, à M. le marquis de Beccaria.* [François-Marie Arouet de Voltaire.] n.p., 1766. At least 1 other edition by 1768.
   A. STN
   Major Dealers: Mauvelain, Troyes 7 (2). }   7   (2)
                      Total: 7   (2)
   B. Catalogues: 1 of 6 lists: (Grasset: "8°. 6 s.").

619. *Relation du bannissement des jésuites de la Chine par l'auteur du Compère Mathieu.* [François-Marie Arouet de Voltaire.] Amsterdam, 1768. At least 1 other undated edition.
   B. Catalogues: 4 of 6 lists: (Grasset: "8°. 6 s."; Décombaz: "8°. 1769, 10 s."; Cailler; Bern: "1 l." and "12 s.").
   C. Police Confiscations: 2 of 10 lists: Stockdorf, Pilon.

   Religieuse (la) en chemise. See #697, Vénus dans le cloître . . .

620. *Religieuse (la) intéressée et amoureuse avec l'histoire du comte de Clare.* [Madame de Tenain?] Cologne, 1695. At least 12 other editions by 1776.
   C. Police Confiscations: 1 of 10 lists: Paris.

621. *Religion (la) naturelle, poème en quatre parties, au roi de Prusse. Par M.V.***.* [François-Marie Arouet de Voltaire.] Geneva, 1756.
   B. Catalogues: 1 of 6 lists: (Bern: "20 s.").
   C. Police Confiscations: 1 of 10 lists: Jouy, et al.

622. *Remarques historiques et anecdotes sur le château de la Bastille.* [Brossais du Perray.] n.p., 1774.

A. STN

Major Dealers: Mauvelain, Troyes
12 (2).

$\left.\begin{array}{l} \\ \\ \end{array}\right\}$ 12 (2)

Total: 12 (2)

D. Customs Confiscations: 2 instances: 1784 (2).

623. *Remarques sur les erreurs de l'Histoire philosophique et politique de M. G. Th. Raynal, par rapport aux affaires de l'Amérique septentrionale, par M. Thomas Paine. Traduites de l'anglais et augmentées d'une préface et de quelques notes par A.-M. Cerisier.* trans. by Antoine-Marie Cerisier. (trans. from *Letter Addressed to the Abbé Raynal on the Affairs of North America. In Which the Mistakes in the Abbé's Account of the Revolution in America Are Corrected and Cleared Up* [1782] by Thomas Paine.) Amsterdam, 1783.
D. Customs Confiscations: 1 instance: 1786.

624. *Remontrances du corps des pasteurs du Gévaudan à Antoine-Jean Rustan, pasteur suisse à Londres.* [François-Marie Arouet de Voltaire.] Amsterdam, 1768.
A. STN

Major Dealers: Robert et Gauthier,
Bourg-en-Bresse 4 (1).
Colporteurs: Blaisot 4 (1); "Troisième"
1 (1).

$\left.\begin{array}{l} \\ \\ \\ \\ \end{array}\right\}$ 9 (3)

Total: 9 (3)

B. Catalogues: 1 of 6 lists: (Grasset: "8°. 5 s.").

625. *Remontrances du Père Adam à Voltaire pour être mises à la suite de sa confession.* Antoine Adam. n.p., 1775.
A. STN

Minor Dealers: Fontaine Colmar 26 (1). $\}$ 26 (1)

Total: 26 (1)

626. *Rendez à César ce qui appartient à César; introduction à une nouvelle histoire des papes.* n.p., 1783.
A. STN

Major Dealers: Mauvelain, Troyes
12 (2).

$\left.\begin{array}{l} \\ \\ \end{array}\right\}$ 12 (2)

Total: 12 (2)

627. **Réponses aux lettres de Mad. de Pompadour.* (Probably *Lettres de Mme la marquise de Pompadour depuis 1746 jusqu'en 1762*

inclusivement.) 2 vols. [François, marquis de Barbé-Marbois?, or Claude-Prosper Jolyot de Crébillon, fils?] London, 1771. At least 4 other editions by 1776, including a 4-vol. edition published in 1774 as *Lettres et réponses écrites à Madame la marquise de Pompadour depuis 1753 jusqu'à 1762 inclusivement.*
B. Catalogues: 1 of 6 lists: (Bern: "40 s.").

628. *Représentations à M. le lieutenant-général de police de Paris sur les courtisanes à la mode et les demoiselles du bon ton.* [Denis-Laurian Turmeau de la Morandière.] n.p., 1760. At least 1 other edition by 1762.
B. Catalogues: 1 of 6 lists: (Décombaz: "8°. 1772, 1 1. 10 s.").
C. Police Confiscations: 1 of 10 lists: Paris.

629. *République (la) des philosophes, ou histoire des ajaciens, ouvrage posthume de M. de Fontenelle.* Bernard Le Bouvier de Fontenelle. Geneva, 1768.
A. STN (listed as *République des incrédules.*)
     Major Dealers: Mauvelain, Troyes 7 (2). }   7   (2)
     Total: 7   (2)
B. Catalogues: 1 of 6 lists: (Bern: "3 1.").
C. Police Confiscations: 1 of 10 lists: Stockdorf.

630. *Requête à tous les magistrats du royaume, composée par trois avocats d'un parlement.* [François-Marie Arouet de Voltaire.] n.p., 1769.
B. Catalogues: 1 of 6 lists: (Bern).

631. *Requête au conseil du roi, par M. Linguet, avocat. Contre les arrêts du parlement de Paris, des 29 mars et 4 février 1775.* Simon-Nicolas-Henri Linguet. Amsterdam, 1776.
A. STN
     Major Dealers: Letourmy, Orléans 25 (1); Manoury, Caen 149 (4); Mauvelain, Troyes 1 (1); Pavie, La Rochelle 12 (1); Rigaud, Pons, Montpellier 48 (3).   252   (13)
     Lorraine: Choppin, Bar-le-Duc 2 (1).
     Lyon: Cellier 12 (1).
     Paris: Lequay Morin 3 (1).

Minor Dealers: Sens, Toulouse 40 (2); Resplandy, Toulouse 20 (1); Jarfaut, Melun 6 (1). } 66 (4)

Total: 318 (17)

D. Customs Confiscations: 1 instance (listed as *Requête de Linguet.)*, 1778.

632. **Requête au roi pour la suppression des moines.*
A. STN
Major Dealers: Mauvelain, Troyes 12 (2). } 12 (2)

Total: 12 (2)

Rétablissement (du) des jésuites en France, par M. S***, ancien magistrat. See #361, *Lettre sur le rappel des jésuites en France.*

633. **Rhétorique d'un homme d'esprit.*
B. Catalogues: 1 of 6 lists: (Bern: "2 1.").

634. *Roger Bontemps en belle humeur par le duc de Roquelaure.* Cologne, 1670. At least 10 other editions by 1776.
C. Customs Confiscations: 1 instance: 1779.

Romans et contes philosophiques par M. de Voltaire. See #606, *Recueil des romans de M. de Voltaire.*

635. *Rosette, ou la fille du monde philosophe.* Rotterdam, 1767.
B. Catalogues: 1 of 6 lists: (Décombaz: "12°. 2 part. Rotterdam, 1767, 1 1. 10 s.").

636. *Rousseau juge de Jean-Jacques. Dialogues.* [Jean-Jacques Rousseau.] London, 1780. At least 6 other editions by 1782.
C. Police Confiscations: 1 of 10 lists: Desauges.

637. *Saül, tragédie tirée de l'Ecriture Sainte par M. de V . . .* [François-Marie Arouet de Voltaire.] n.p., 1755 (actually 1763, according to Bengesco). At least 7 other editions by 1768.
A. STN
Major Dealers: Bergeret, Bordeaux 6 (1); Blouet, Rennes 12 (1). } 18 (2)

Total: 18 (2)

B. Catalogues: 3 of 6 lists: (Grasset; Chappuis et Didier: "gr. 12°. 1778, 8 s." [bound with *David*]; Bern: "30 s.").
C. Police Confiscations: 2 of 10 lists: Stockdorf, Pilon.

638. *Saxe (la) galante.* 2 vols. [Karl-Ludwig, Freiherr von Pöllnitz.] Amsterdam, 1734. At least 9 other editions by 1763.
   A. STN
   Major Dealers: Pavie, La Rochelle 2 (1). }   2   (1)
                                     Total: 2   (1)
   B. Catalogues: 1 of 6 lists: (Décombaz: "8°. Amsterdam, 1763, 1 1. 10 s.").

639. **Science du bordel.*
   A. STN
   Major Dealers: Robert et Gauthier,
       Bourg-en-Bresse 4 (1).   }   4   (1)
                              Total: 4   (1)

640. *Secrets (les) de l'ordre des francs-maçons dévoilés et mis au jour par M***.* [Gabriel-Louis-Calabre Pérau.] Amsterdam, 1745.
   A. STN
   Major Dealers: Bergeret, Bordeaux 7
       (1); Mossy, Marseille 27 (1); Robert   }   37   (3)
       et Gauthier, Bourg-en-Bresse 3 (1).
   Minor Dealers: Bonnard, Auxerre 3 (1). }   3   (1)
                                   Total: 40   (4)
   D. Police Confiscations: 3 instances: 1776 (2), 1779.

641. *Secrets merveilleux de la magie naturelle et cabalistique du Petit-Albert, traduit sur l'original latin.* (trans. from *Alberti Parvi. Lucii libellus de mirabilibus naturae arcanus.*) Lyon, 1706. At least 5 other editions by 1752.[4]
   A. STN
   Major Dealers: Malherbe, Loudun 20
       (1); Charmet, Besançon 6 (1).
   Lorraine: Bertrand, Thionville 6 (1);   }   44   (6)
       Audéart, Lunéville 2 (1).
   Paris: Prévost 10 (2).
   Minor Dealers: Sombert, Châlons-sur-
       Marne 12 (1); Bonnard, Auxerre 9
       (2); Jarfaut, Melun 6 (1); Calde-   }   31   (5)
       saigues, Marseille 4 (1).
                                   Total: 75   (11)

[4] Not to be confused with *Les Admirables Secrets d'Albert le Grand . . .* or a legal book entitled *L'Albert moderne . . .* (See Caillet, pp. 20–21, and *Mercure de France*, February 1769, pp. 115–117.)

B. Catalogues: 1 of 6 lists: (Cailler).

642. *Sermon des cinquante.* [François-Marie Arouet de Voltaire.] n.p., 1749 (actually c. 1762, according to Bengesco).
   A. STN
   Major Dealers: Mauvelain Troyes 9 (3). }   9 (3)
   Total: 9 (3)

643. *Sermon du papa Nicolas Charisteski, prononcé dans l'Eglise de Sainte-Toleranski, village de Lithuanie, le jour de Sainte Epiphanie.* [François-Marie Arouet de Voltaire.] n.p., n.d. (1771, according to Bengesco).
   A. STN
   Major Dealers: Blouet Rennes 6 (1). }   6 (1)
   Total: 6 (1)
   B. Catalogues: 1 of 6 lists: (Grasset).

644. *Sermon du Rabin Akib, prononcé à Smyrne le 20 novembre 1761. Traduit de l'hébreu.* [François-Marie Arouet de Voltaire.] n.p., n.d. (1761, according to Bengesco). At least 1 other undated edition.
   C. Police Confiscations: 1 of 10 lists: Pilon.

645. *Sermons prêchés à Toulouse devant Messieurs du parlement et du capitoulat par le R.P. Apompée de Tragopone.* Eleutheropolis, 1772.
   B. Catalogues: 2 of 6 lists: (Décombaz: "12°. Eleutheropolis, 1772, 3 1. 10 s."; Bern: "6 1.").
   C. Police Confiscations: 3 of 10 lists: Stockdorf, Pilon, Prot.

Siège de Cythère. See #304, *Histoire du siège de Cythère.*

646. *Singularités (les) de la nature, par un académicien de Londres, de Bologne, de Pétersbourg, de Berlin, etc.* [François-Marie Arouet de Voltaire.] Basel, 1768. At least 6 other editions by 1772.
   A. STN
   Major Dealers: Blouet, Rennes 4 (1). }
   Lorraine: Bergue, Thionville 6 (1). }   10 (2)
   Total: 10 (2)
   B. Catalogues: 2 of 6 lists: (Grasset; Décombaz: "8°. Basle, 1768, 15 s.").
   D. Customs Confiscations: 1 instance: 1779.

647. *Soirées (les) de quelques religieuses de l'abbaye de ***.* Geneva, 1786.

A. STN
   Major Dealers: Charmet, Besançon
   2 (1). } 2 (1)

   Total: 2 (1)

648. *Soirées (les) du Palais-Royal ou les veillées d'une jolie femme,
   contenant quatre lettres à une amie, avec la Conversation des ch-
   aises du Palais-Royal.* [Jean-Auguste Jullien, dit Desboulmiers.] Sous l'arbre de Cracovie, 1762.
   C. Police Confiscations: 1 of 10 lists: Prot.

649. *Soldat (le) citoyen, ou vues patriotiques sur la manière la plus
   avantageuse de pourvoir à la défense du royaume.* [Jacques-
   Antoine-Hippolyte de Guibert?] Dans le pays de la liberté,
   1780. At least 1 other edition by 1781.
   D. Customs Confiscations: 1 instance: 1781.

650. *Sonnettes (les) ou mémoires de monsieur le marquis D***.* [Jean-
   Baptiste Guiard de Servigné.] n.p., 1749. At least 6 other
   editions by 1781; 1776 as *Le Carillon de Cythère.*
   A. STN
      Major Dealers: Robert et Gauthier,
      Bourg-en-Bresse 4 (1). } 4 (1)

      Total: 4 (1)

651. *Sopha (le), conte moral.* 2 vols. [Claude-Prosper Jolyot de
   Crébillon, fils.] Gaznah, 1742. At least 21 other editions by
   1789.
   B. Catalogues: 1 of 6 lists: (Décombaz: "12°. 2 vol. fig.
      1773, 2 1."; Bern: "avec figures, 4 1.").
   C. Police Confiscations: 2 of 10 lists: Jouy, et al., Paris.
   D. Customs Confiscations: 3 instances: 1774, 1775, 1781.

652. *Soupé (le) des petits-maîtres, ouvrage moral.* [Jean-François Cail-
   hava de L'Estendoux.] London, n.d. (c. 1770, according to
   Gay). At least 6 other editions by 1782.
   A. STN
      Major Dealers: Mauvelain, Troyes 6 (1). } 6 (1)
      Total: 6 (1)

653. *Soupers (les) de Daphné et les dortoirs de Lacédémone. Anecdotes
   grecques, ou fragments historiques publiés pour la première fois et
   traduits sur la version arabe imprimée à Constantinople, l'an de*

l'hégire 1110 et de notre ère 1731. [Anne-Gabriel Meusnier de Querlon.] Oxfort [sic], 1740. At least 1 other edition by 1746.

A. STN

Major Dealers: Mauvelain, Troyes 12 (2).	}	12	(2)
Total:		12	(2)

654. *Souvenirs (les) de Mme de Caylus.* [pub. by François-Marie Arouet de Voltaire.] Amsterdam, 1770.

C. Police Confiscations: 1 of 10 lists: Prot.

D. Customs Confiscations: 1 instance: 1771.

655. *Superstitieux (le), comédie en trois actes en vers par le sieur R . . .* Jean-Antoine Romangnesi. Paris, 1740.

A. STN

Major Dealers: Pavie, La Rochelle 12 (2).	}	12	(2)
Total:		12	(2)

656. *Supplément au Roman comique, ou mémoires pour servir à la vie de Jean Monnet, ci-devant Directeur de l'Opéra-Comique à Paris, de l'Opéra de Lyon et d'une Comédie française à Londres. Ecrits par lui-même.* 2 vols. [Jean Monnet.] London, 1772. At least 3 other editions by 1777; also as *Mémoires . . .*

A. STN

Lorraine: Chénoux, Lunéville 26 (2); Augé, Lunéville 2 (1).	}	53	(4)
Lyon: Barret 25 (1).			
Total:		53	(4)

657. **Supplément aux Poésies gaillardes.*

A. STN

Major Dealers: Robert et Gauthier, Bourg-en-Bresse 12 (1).	}	12	(1)
Total:		12	(1)

Supplément de l'abbé Raynal. See #663, *Tableau de l'Europe . . .*

658. *Système de la nature, ou des lois du monde physique et du monde moral, par M. Mirabaud.* 2 vols. [Paul-Henri-Dietrich Thiry, baron d'Holbach?, and/or Denis Diderot?] London, 1770. At least 12 other editions by 1781.

171

A. STN

    Major Dealers: Blouet, Rennes 25 (1);
      Charmet, Besançon 12 (1); Le-
      tourmy, Orléans 11 (3); Malherbe,
      Loudun 167 (7); Manoury, Caen 12
      (1); Pavie, La Rochelle 16 (3);
      Rigaud, Pons, Montpellier 43 (13);
      Robert et Gauthier, Bourg-en-Bresse
      24 (2).

    Lorraine: Chénoux, Lunéville 12 (1);
      Augé, Lunéville 18 (4); Bertrand,
      Thionville 3 (2); Bergue, Thionville
      12 (1); Orbelin, Thionville 10 (2);
      L'Entretien, Lunéville 2 (1); Gay,
      Lunéville 20 (3); Audéart, Lunéville
      25 (7); Matthieu, Nancy 60 (9); Bon-
      thoux, Nancy 5 (3).

    Lyon: Cellier 2 (1); Jacquenod 6 (1);
      Barret 61 (3).

    Paris: Barré 3 (1); Prévost 8 (2):
      Védrène 12 (1).

    Colporteurs: Blaisot 12 (1); Planquais 7
      (2); "Troisième" 6 (1); Gilles 106 (3).

                        700   (80)

    Minor Dealers: Malassis, Nantes 3 (1);
      Chevrier, Poitiers 7 (3); Petit, Reims
      1 (1); Sens, Toulouse 4 (1); Lair,
      Blois 2 (2); Resplandy, Toulouse 13
      (1); Bonnard, Auxerre 4 (2); Laisney,
      Beauvais 27 (2); Habert, Bar-sur-
      Aube 4 (1); Jarfaut, Melun 2 (1); Bil-
      lault, Tours 1 (1).

                        68   (16)

                  Total: 768 (96)

B. Catalogues: 4 of 6 lists: (Grasset; Décombaz: "8°. 2 vol.
   Londres, 1774, 8 1." and "8°. 2 vol. Hollande, 1770, 12
   1."; Chappuis et Didier: "2 part. gr. 8°. Holl. 1777, 4 1.";
   Bern: "15 1.").

C. Police Confiscations: 3 of 10 lists: Stockdorf, Pilon, Prot.

D. Customs Confiscations: 8 instances: 1771 (2), 1774,
   1778, 1779 (2), 1783, 1786.

659. *Système (le) des anciens et des modernes, concilié par l'exposition des sentiments différents de quelques théologiens sur l'état des âmes séparées des corps. En quatorze lettres. Nouvelle édition.* [Marie Huber.] Amsterdam, 1733.
C. Police Confiscations: 1 of 10 lists: Prot.

660. **Système féodal ou essai sur le système féodal.*
A. STN
Major Dealers: Pavie, La Rochelle 12 (1).

$$\left.\begin{array}{c} 12 \quad (1) \end{array}\right\}$$

Total: 12 (1)

661. *Système général de la philosophie de Descartes et de Newton.* 4 vols. [Aimé-Henri Paulian.] Avignon, 1769.
C. Police Confiscations: 1 of 10 lists: Prot.

662. *Système social. Ou principes naturels de la morale et de la politique, avec un examen de l'influence du gouvernement sur les mœurs.* 3 vols. [Paul-Henri-Dietrich Thiry, baron d'Holbach.] London, 1773. At least 3 other editions by 1774.
A. STN
Major Dealers: Charmet, Besançon 6 (1); Letourmy, Orléans 4 (1); Malherbe, Loudun 14 (3); Mauvelain, Troyes 4 (3).
Lorraine: Chénoux, Lunéville 6 (1); Bertrand, Thionville 6 (3); Audéart, Lunéville 10 (2); Matthieu, Nancy 14 (3); Babin, Nancy 1 (1).
Lyon: Flandin 6 (1); Cellier 2 (1).
Paris: Barré 6 (1); Prévost 2 (1).
Colporteurs: Planquais 6 (1); "Troisième" 4 (1); Gilles 102 (2).

193 (26)

Minor Dealers: Malassis, Nantes 2 (1); Chevrier, Poitiers 6 (1); Sens, Toulouse 4 (1); Bonnard, Auxerre 6 (2); Billault, Tours 1 (1).

19 (6)

Total: 212 (32)

B. Catalogues: 3 of 6 lists: (Grasset: "8°. 3 vol. 4 1."; Décombaz: "8°. 3 vol. Londres, 1774, 5 1."; Bern: "8°. 3 vols. 12 1.").

173

C. Police Confiscations: 4 of 10 lists: Stockdorf, Pilon, Prot, Desauges.

D. Customs Confiscations: 4 instances: 1773 (3), 1783.

Tableau de l'amour conjugal. See #271, *Génération (la) de l'homme, ou le tableau de l'amour conjugal . . .*

663. *Tableau de l'Europe, pour servir de supplément à l'Histoire philosophique.* [re-ed. by Alexandre Deleyre.] Maestricht, 1774.

A. STN

Major Dealers: Manoury, Caen 12 (1). }   12 (1)

Total: 12 (1)

C. Police Confiscations: 1 of 10 lists: Versailles.

D. Customs Confiscations: 1 instance: 1786.

664. *Tableau de Paris.* 2 vols. [Louis-Sébastien Mercier.] Hamburg-Neuchâtel, 1781. At least 1 other edition by 1782–88; with supplements, up to 12 vols.

A. STN

Major Dealers: Bergeret, Bordeaux 63 (3); Charmet, Besançon 42 (3); Manoury, Caen 150 (3); Mauvelain, Troyes 12 (5); Mossy, Marseille 118 (6); Rigaud, Pons, Montpellier 22 (3); Robert et Gauthier, Bourg-en-Bresse 28 (3).   612 (33)

Lorraine: Carez, Toul 6 (1); Choppin, Bar-le-Duc 6 (2).

Lyon: Jacquenod 2 (1).

Paris: Desauges 150 (2); Cugnet 13 (1).

Minor Dealers: Petit, Reims 32 (3); Waroquier, Soissons 45 (4).   77 (7)

Total: 689 (40)

D. Customs Confiscations: 10 instances: 1781, 1782, 1783, 1784 (6), 1785.

665. *Tableau de Spa.* (Possibly *Les Amusements de Spa.*) 2 vols. [Jean-Philippe de Limbourg.] Amsterdam, 1763. At least 1 other edition by 1781.

D. Customs Confiscations: 1 instance: 1786.

666. *Tableau des saints, ou examen de l'esprit, de la conduite, des maximes et du mérite des personnages que le christianisme révère et*

propose pour modèles. 2 vols. [Paul-Henri-Dietrich Thiry, baron d'Holbach.] London, 1770.

A. STN

Major Dealers: Blouet, Rennes 4 (1); Malherbe, Loudun 4 (1).	8	(2)
Minor Dealers: Chevrier, Poitiers 1 (1).	1	(1)
Total:	9	(3)

B. Catalogues: 1 of 6 lists: (Bern: "6 1.").

C. Police Confiscations: 2 of 10 lists: Stockdorf, Pilon.

667. *Tableau philosophique du genre humain depuis l'origine du monde jusqu'à Constantin. Traduit de l'anglais.* 3 vols. [Charles Borde.] London, 1767. At least 1 other edition by 1770.

A. STN

Minor Dealers: Malassis, Nantes 1 (1); Chevrier, Poitiers 1 (1).	2	(2)
Total:	2	(2)

B. Catalogues: 1 of 6 lists: (Bern: "5 1.").

C. Police Confiscations: 3 of 10 lists: Stockdorf, Pilon, Prot.

668. *Tanzaî et Néadarné, histoire japonaise.* 2 vols. [Claude-Prosper Jolyot de Crébillon, fils.] Pékin, 1734. At least 22 other editions by 1786; also as *L'Ecumoire, histoire japonaise.*

A. STN

Major Dealers: Mauvelain, Troyes 3 (1).	3	(1)
Total:	3	(1)

B. Catalogues: 1 of 6 lists: (Décombaz: "12°. 2 vol. 1771, 2 1.").

C. Police Confiscations: 1 of 10 lists: Jouy, et al.

D. Customs Confiscations: 2 instances: 1774, 1779.

669. *Taureau (le) blanc. Traduit du syriaque par Dom Calmet.* (also as . . . par Mamaki.) [François-Marie Arouet de Voltaire.] Memphis, 1774. At least 5 other editions in 1774.

A. STN

Major Dealers: Malherbe, Loudun 12 (1); Mauvelain, Troyes 7 (2). *Lorraine:* Bertrand, Thionville 10 (2); Audéart, Lunéville 26 (2). *Paris:* Prévost 6 (1).	65	(10)

continued

Colporteurs: Planquais 2 (1); "Troisième" 2 (1).

Minor Dealers: Malassis, Nantes 3 (1). }   3   (1)

Total: 68 (11)

  B. Catalogues: 2 of 6 lists: (Décombaz: "8°. 1774, 15 s.";
    Cailler).
  C. Police Confiscations: 1 of 10 lists: Prot.
  D. Customs Confiscations: 2 instances: 1774, 1776.

670. *Temple du bonheur.* (Possibly *Le Temple du bonheur, ou recueil
des plus excellents traités sur le bonheur, extraits des meilleurs
auteurs anciens et modernes.* 3 vols. Bouillon, 1769. At least 1
other edition by 1770.)
  D. Customs Confiscations: 1 instance: 1775.

671. *Testament de Jean Meslier.* [Jean Meslier and François-Marie
Arouet de Voltaire.] n.p., n.d. (Geneva, 1762, according to
Bengesco).
  A. STN

    Major Dealers: Mauvelain, Troyes 6 (1). }   6   (1)

Total: 6 (1)

672. *Testament politique de M. de V*** trouvé parmi ses papiers après
sa mort.* [Jean-Henri Marchand.] n.p., n.d. (1762, according
to Cioranescu.) At least 3 other editions by 1778.
  B. Catalogues: 1 of 6 lists: (Grasset).
  D. Customs Confiscations: 1 instance: 1774.

673. *Théâtre gaillard.* 2 vols. Glasgow, 1776. At least 2 other editions by 1788.
  A. STN

    Minor Dealers: Malassis, Nantes 2 (1). }   2   (1)

Total: 2 (1)

  D. Customs Confiscations: 1 instance: 1784.

674. *Théisme (le), essai philosophique.* 2 vols. [Charles Elie, marquis
de Ferrières.] London, 1773. At least 1 other edition by
1785.
  A. STN

    Major Dealers: Bergeret, Bordeaux 10
    (2); Robert et Gauthier, Bourg-en-
    Bresse 4 (1).

continued

Lorraine: Bergue, Thionville 6 (1);   }   46   (6)
    Chénoux, Lunéville 24 (1).
Colporteurs: "Troisième" 2 (1).

                                  Total: 46   (6)

  C. Police Confiscations: 1 of 10 lists: Prot.

675. *Thémidore.* [Claude Godard d'Aucour.] The Hague, 1744. At least 15 other editions by 1785.

  A. STN
      Lorraine: L'Entretien, Lunéville 6 (1).   }   6   (1)
      Minor Dealers: Jarfaut, Melun 4 (1).   }   4   (1)
                               Total: 10   (2)

  B. Catalogues: 1 of 6 lists: (Bern: "3 1.").
  C. Police Confiscations: 3 of 10 lists: Prot, Desauges, Paris.
  D. Customs Confiscations: 2 instances: 1772, 1774.

676. *Théologie portative ou dictionnaire abrégé de la religion chré-tienne. Par M. l'abbé Bernier, licencié en théologie.* [Paul-Henri-Dietrich Thiry, baron d'Holbach.] London, 1768. At least 6 other editions by 1785.

  A. STN
      Major Dealers: Bergeret, Bordeaux 6 (1); Blouet, Rennes 28 (2); Mal-herbe, Loudun 10 (1); Mauvelain Troyes 36 (5); Pavie, La Rochelle 24 (1).
      Lorraine: Bergue, Thionville 6 (1); Audéart, Lunéville 6 (2).   }   140   (18)
      Paris: Prévost 6 (1).
      Colporteurs: Blaisot 4 (1); Planquais 6 (1); "Troisième" 2 (1); Gilles 6 (1).

      Minor Dealers: Malassis, Nantes 1 (1); Chevrier, Poitiers 1 (1); Sens, Tou-louse 2 (1); Jarfaut, Melun 2 (1); Bil-lault, Tours 13 (1); Caldesaigues, Marseille 4 (1).   }   23   (6)

                                 Total: 163   (24)

  B. Catalogues: 5 of 6 lists: (Grasset: "8°. 2 1."; Décombaz; Cailler; Chappuis et Didier: "8°. 15 s."; Bern: "6 1.").
  C. Police Confiscations: 2 of 10 lists: Stockdorf, Prot.
  D. Customs Confiscations: 1 instance: 1771.

677. *Théorie des lois criminelles.* Jacques-Pierre Brissot de Warville. Berlin, 1781.

A. STN

Major Dealers: Charmet, Besançon 6 (1); Mossy, Marseille 31 (2).	37	(3)
Minor Dealers: Petit, Reims 2 (1).	2	(1)
Total:	39	(4)

678. *Thérèse philosophe, ou mémoires pour servir à l'histoire du P. Dirrag et de Mlle Eradice.* 2 vols. [X. d'Arles de Montigny?, or Jean-Baptiste de Boyer, marquis d'Argens?] n.p., n.d. (1748, according to Martin-Mylne-Frautschi). At least 15 other editions by 1785.

A. STN

Major Dealers: Bergerct, Bordeaux 12 (2); Blouet, Rennes 43 (4); Letourmy, Orléans 4 (1); Malherbe, Loudun 52 (1); Pavie, La Rochelle 14 (2); Robert et Gauthier, Bourg-en-Bresse 6 (1).

Lorraine: Sandré, Lunéville 2 (1); Bertrand, Thionville 6 (1); Bergue, Thionville 50 (1); Orbelin, Thionville 6 (1); Gay, Lunéville 4 (1); Audéart, Lunéville 2 (1).

Colporteurs: Blaisot 12 (1); Planquais 4 (1); "Troisième" 10 (1); Gilles 104 (2).

331 (22)

Minor Dealers: Malassis, Nantes 1 (1); Chevrier, Poitiers 1 (1); Petit, Reims 2 (1); Laisney, Beauvais 1 (1); Habert, Bar-sur-Aube 4 (1); Caldesaigues, Marseille 25 (1).

34 (6)

Total: 365 (28)

B. Catalogues: 3 of 6 lists: (Grasset: "8°. 2 part. fig."; Décombaz: "8°. fig. 1774, 7 1. 10 s." and "8°. fig. Hollande, 1774, 9 1."; Bern: "belles estampes, 18 1.").

C. Police Confiscations: 6 of 10 lists: Stockdorf, Pilon, Manoury, Prot, Paris, Versailles.

D. Customs Confiscations: 12 instances: 1771 (2), 1772, 1773, 1774 (2), 1778 (2), 1779, 1781, 1784, 1786.

679. *Timée de Locres en grec et en français avec des dissertations sur les principales questions de la métaphysique, de la physique, & de la morale des anciens; qui peuvent servir de suite et de conclusion à la Philosophie du bon sens, par Mr. le marquis d'Argens.* Jean Baptiste de Boyer, marquis d'Argens. Berlin, 1763.
    A. STN
       Major Dealers: Blouet, Rennes 2 (1).   }   2   (1)
                                              Total: 2   (1)

680. *Tocsin des rois, aux souverains de l'Europe, par M. de Voltaire.* [François-Marie Arouet de Voltaire.] n.p., 1772.
    B. Catalogues: 2 of 6 lists: (Grasset: "8°. 2 l."; Bern: "6 s.").

681. *Tolérance (de la) dans la religion ou de la liberté de conscience. Par Crellius. L'Intolérance convaincue de crime et de folie. Ouvrage traduit de l'anglais.* [Paul-Henri-Dietrich Thiry, baron d'Holbach.] London, 1769.
    B. Catalogues: 1 of 6 lists: (Bern: "50 s.").
    C. Police Confiscations: 2 of 10 lists: Pilon, Prot.

    Tolérance (la), tragédie par Voltaire. See #277, *Guèbres (les)*
    Tourière (la) des Carmélites. See #290, *Histoire de la tourière des Carmélites.*

682. *Traité de la morale des pères de l'Eglise, où en défendant un article de la préface sur Puffendorf, contre l'Apologie de la morale des Pères du P. Ceillier, on fait diverses réflexions sur plusieurs matières importantes. Par Jean Barbeyrac.* Jean Barbeyrac. Amsterdam, 1728.
    C. Police Confiscations: 1 of 10 lists: Prot.

683. *Traité de la nature et du gouvernement de l'Eglise.* 3 vols. [Jacques Tailhé.] Bern, 1768.
    A. STN
       Major Dealers: Bergeret, Bordeaux 13 }   15   (2)
       (1); Pavie, La Rochelle 2 (1).   ─────────
                                              Total: 15   (2)

684. *Traité de l'infini créé, avec l'explication de la possibilité de la transsubstantiation. Traité de la confession et de la communion, par le P. Malebranche.* [Henri, comte de Boulainvilliers?] Amsterdam, 1769.
    B. Catalogues: 1 of 6 lists: (Bern: "5 l.").

C. Police Confiscations: 1 of 10 lists: Stockdorf.

D. Customs Confiscations: 1 instance: 1771.

685. *Traité des délits et des peines traduit de l'italien, d'après la troi-sième édition.* trans. by André Morellet. Lausanne, 1766. (trans. from *Dei Delitti et delle pene* [1764] by César Bone-sana, marquis de Beccaria.)

A. STN

Major Dealers: Buchet, Nîmes 19 (2); Charmet, Besançon 6 (1); Letourmy, Orléans 3 (1); Robert et Gauthier, Bourg-en-Bresse 2 (1). *Lyon:* Flandin 6 (1). *Paris:* Barré 6 (1); Prévost 9 (2); Védrène 12 (1).	63	(10)
Minor Dealers: Sens, Toulouse 13 (2); Bonnard, Auxerre 7 (2); Calde-saigues, Marseille 6 (1).	26	(5)
Total:	89	(15)

D. Customs Confiscations: 1 instance: 1778.

686. *Traité des droits du génie, dans lequel on examine si la connais-sance de la vérité est avantageuse aux hommes et possible au philo-sophe.* [Seguier de Saint-Brisson.] Karlsruhe, 1769.

A. STN

Major Dealers: Blouet, Rennes 2 (1).	2	(1)
Total:	2	(1)

687. *Traité des erreurs populaires sur la santé.* [P. T. de Bienville.] The Hague, 1775. At least 1 other edition by 1776.

D. Customs Confiscations: 1 instance: 1778.

688. *Traité des lois civiles par M. de P. de T.* 2 vols. Carlo Antonio Pilati de Tassulo. The Hague, 1774.

C. Police Confiscations: 1 of 10 lists: Prot.

689. *Traité des trois imposteurs.* [Jan Vroesen?] Yverdon, 1768. Originally printed from an MS treatise with revisions by Jean Aymon and Jean Rousset in *La Vie et l'esprit de M. Benoît Spinoza,* 1719. At least 5 editions between 1768 and 1780.

A. STN

Major Dealers: Bergeret, Bordeaux 6

continued

180

(1); Blouet, Rennes 9 (2); Charmet,
Besançon 6 (1); Malherbe, Loudun 1
(1); Mauvelain, Troyes 6 (1); Letourmy, Orléans 13 (4).

Lorraine: Gerlache, Metz 6 (1); Bergue,
Thionville 6 (1); Audéart, Lunéville
12 (4).

} 88 (21)

Paris: Barré 6 (1); Prévost 3 (1);
Védrène 6 (1).

Colporteurs: Blaisot 6 (1); "Troisième" 2
(1).

Minor Dealers: Malassis, Nantes 2 (1);
Sens, Toulouse 6 (1); Resplandy,
Toulouse 6 (1); Sombert, Châlons-
sur-Marne 6 (1); Billault, Tours 13
(1); Caldesaigues, Marseille 12 (2).

} 45 (7)

Total: 133 (28)

B. Catalogues: 3 of 6 lists: (Grasset: "8°. 1 1."; Chappuis et
Didier: "8°. 12 s."; Bern: "4 1.")

C. Police Confiscations: 2 of 10 lists: Stockdorf, Pilon.

D. Customs Confiscations: 3 instances: 1773, 1781, 1786.

690. *Traité du mariage et de sa législation, par M.P.D.T.* Carlo
Antonio Pilati de Tassulo. The Hague, 1776.

C. Police Confiscations: 1 of 10 lists: Prot.

691. *Traité sur la tolérance.* [François-Marie Arouet de Voltaire.]
n.p., 1763. At least 2 other editions by 1765.

B. Catalogues: 3 of 6 lists: (Grasset; Décombaz: "8°. 1773,
2 1."; Bern: "60 s.").

C. Police Confiscations: Stockdorf, Pilon.

D. Customs Confiscations: 2 instances: 1778, 1779.

692. *Trois Epîtres (les).* [François-Marie Arouet de Voltaire.] n.p.,
n.d. (Contains *L'Epître à Boileau* [1769], *L'Epître à l'auteur du
nouveau livre des trois imposteurs* [1769], and *L'Epître à Saint-
Lambert* [1769].)

A. STN

Major Dealers: Blouet, Rennes 6 (1).
Lorraine: Bergue, Thionville 6 (1);
Audéart, Lunéville 2 (1).

}

continued

181

Colporteurs: Planquais 1 (1); "Troisième" 2 (1). }   17 (5)

Total: 17 (5)

B. Catalogues: 2 of 6 lists: (Grasset: "8°. 2 s."; Bern).

693. *Trois Voluptés (les).* n.p., 1746.
    B. Catalogues: 1 of 6 lists: (Bern: "20 s.").

694. *Trop est trop. Capitulation de la France avec ses moines et religieux de toutes livrées, avec la revue générale de leurs patriarches.*
[Jean-Henri Maubert de Gouvest.] The Hague, 1767.
    C. Police Confiscations: 1 of 10 lists: Paris.

695. *Utile Emploi (l') des religieux et des communalistes, ou mémoire
politique à l'avantage des habitants de la campagne.* [Joachim
Faiguet de Villeneuve.] Amsterdam, 1770.
    A. STN

      Major Dealers: Blouet, Rennes 3 (1). }   3 (1)

Total: 3 (1)

696. *Van Espen, Supplementum et vita.* (Probably *Supplementum
ad varias collectiones operum clar. viri. Z. B. van Espen.* Zeger
Bernard Van Espen. Paris, 1768. At least 1 other edition by
1769. [Weller cites a *Vie de M. Z. B. Van Espen par D. de
Bellegarde.* Louvain, 1767.])
    D. Customs Confiscations: 1 instance: 1771.

697. *Vénus dans le cloître, ou la religieuse en chemise.* [Jean Barrin?,
or François de Chavigny de La Bretonnière?] Cologne, 1683
(c. 1682, according to Gay). At least 22 other editions by
1782; also as *Les Délices du cloître, ou la religieuse éclairée, La
Religieuse en chemise, ou la nonne éclairée,* and *La Nonne éclairée,
ou les délices du cloître.*
    A. STN

      Major Dealers: Blouet, Rennes 2 (2);
        Charmet, Besançon 12 (1); Le-
        tourmy, Orléans 14 (2); Malherbe,
        Loudun 12 (1); Pavie, La Rochelle 24
        (2).
      Lorraine: Choppin, Bar-le-Duc 2 (1);   94 (13)
        Bertrand, Thionville 6 (1).
      Paris: Barré 6 (1); Prévost 4 (1);
        Lequay Morin 12 (1).

Minor Dealers: Chevrier, Poitiers 1 (1);
Sens, Toulouse 12 (1); Resplandy,
Toulouse 13 (1); Bonnard, Auxerre } 52 (6)
3 (1); Billault, Tours 13 (1); Caldesaigues, Marseille 10 (1).

Total: 146 (19)

B. Catalogues: 3 of 6 lists: (Cailler; Chappuis et Didier:
"nouv. & jolie édit. 8°. fig. 1779, 18 s."; Bern: "3 l.").

C. Police Confiscations: 3 of 10 lists: Stockdorf, Manoury,
Prot.

D. Customs Confiscations: 3 instances: 1775, 1777, 1781.

698. *Vénus physique.* [Pierre-Louis Moreau de Maupertius.] n.p.,
1745. At least 3 other editions by 1780.
A. STN

Major Dealers: Robert et Gauthier, } 6 (1)
Bourg-en-Bresse 6 (1).

Total: 6 (1)

C. Police Confiscations: 1 of 10 lists: Prot.

D. Customs Confiscations: 1 instance: 1781.

699. **Véritable Arétin.*
A. STN

Lorraine: Bertrand, Thionville 3 (1). } 3 (1)

Total: 3 (1)

700. *Véritable Grimoire avec un recueil de secret magique.* n.p., n.d.
D. Customs Confiscations: 1 instance: 1777.

701. *Vérité (de la) ou méditations sur tous les moyens de parvenir à
la vérité dans toutes les connaissances humaines.* Jacques-Pierre
Brissot de Warville. Neuchâtel, 1782.
A. STN

Major Dealers: Bergeret, Bordeaux 14 } 52 (4)
(2); Mossy, Marseille 38 (2).

Total: 52 (4)

Vérité (la) des mystères du christianisme See #463, *Mystères
(les) du christianisme . . .*

702. *Vérité rendue sensible à Louis XVI par un admirateur de M.
Necker.* 2 vols. London, 1782.
D. Customs Confiscations: 1 instance: 1782.

703. *Vicaire savoyard, tiré d'Emile.* [Jean-Jacques Rousseau.] n.p., n.d.
   D. Customs Confiscations: 1 instance: 1771.

704. *Vicomte (le) de Barjac, ou mémoires pour servir à l'histoire de ce siècle.* 2 vols. [Jean-Pierre-Louis de La Roche du Maine, marquis de Luchet.] Dublin, 1764. At least 3 other editions in 1784.
   A. STN
      Major Dealers: Charmet, Besançon 2
         (1); Mauvelain, Troyes 25 (3).   40 (5)
      Lorraine: Bonthoux, Nancy 13 (1).
                                       Total: 40 (5)
   D. Customs Confiscations: 1 instance: 1784.

705. **Vie d'Antoinette.*
   A. STN
      Major Dealers: Mauvelain, Troyes 8 (3). }   8 (3)
                                       Total: 8 (3)

706. *Vie d'Appolonius de Thyane, par Philostrate, avec les commentaires donnés en anglais par Charles Blount.* 4 vols. [Herbert de Cherbury, trans. by Giovanni Francesco Mario Melchior Salvemini di Castiglione (Castillon).] Berlin, 1774. At least 1 other edition by 1779.
   C. Police Confiscations: 1 of 10 lists: Prot.

   Vie de l'Arétin. See #584, *Putain (la) errante . . .*

707. *Vie de Louis depuis son avènement à la couronne jusqu'au 24 août 1774 exclusivement, jour à jamais mémorable pour la France, en forme de drame ou conversations intéressantes entre trois personnes distinguées, et ornée de plusieurs anecdotes secrètes.* [Prince de Buriabled, pseud. of John Paul Jones.] London, 1774.
   A. STN
      Major Dealers: Pavie, La Rochelle 12
         (1).   12 (1)
                                       Total: 12 (1)
   C. Police Confiscations: 1 of 10 lists: Prot.

708. *Vie de Madame la comtesse du Barry, suivie de ses correspondances épistolaires et de ses intrigues galantes et politiques.* n.p., n.d.

C. Police Confiscations: 4 of 10 lists: Manoury, Pilon, Prot, Lyon.

Vieillard (le) du mont Caucase. See #90, *Chrétien (un) contre six juifs.*

709. *Vie privée de Louis XV, ou principaux événements, particularités et anecdotes de son règne.* 4 vols. [Barthélemy-François-Joseph Moufle d'Angerville?, or Arnoux Laffrey?] London, 1781. At least 3 other editions by 1785.
   A. STN

Major Dealers: Charmet, Besançon 104 (4); Mauvelain, Troyes 12 (6); Robert et Gauthier, Bourg-en-Bresse 50 (1). *Lorraine:* Carez, Toul 6 (1); Choppin, Bar-le-Duc 6 (1); Bernard, Lunéville 1 (1). *Paris:* Cugnet 13 (1); Prévost 2 (1).	194 (16)
Minor Dealers: Petit, Reims 4 (1).	4 (1)
Total:	198 (17)

   D. Customs Confiscations: 6 instances: 1781 (2), 1782 (3), 1785.

710. *Vie (la) privée d'un prince célèbre, ou détails des loisirs du prince Henri de Prusse dans sa retraite de Reinsberg.* [Louis Bernard, baron Guyton de Morveau.] Veropolis, 1784.
   A. STN

Lorraine: Bonthoux, Nancy 13 (1).	13 (1)
Total:	13 (1)

711. *Vie (la) privée du roi de Prusse ou mémoires pour servir à la vie de M. de Voltaire, écrits par lui-même.* [François-Marie Arouet de Voltaire.] Amsterdam, 1784. Also as *Mémoires de M. de Voltaire, écrits par lui-même* (1784).
   A. STN

Lorraine: Bonthoux, Nancy 26 (1).	26 (1)
Total:	26 (1)

712. *Vie privée, ou apologie du très sérénissime prince Mgr. le duc de Chartres, contre un libelle diffamatoire écrit en 1781, mais qui n'a point paru à cause des menaces que nous avons faites à l'auteur*

de le déceler. Par une société des amis du prince. [Charles Théveneau de Morande.] London, 1784.

A. STN

> *Major Dealers:* Mauvelain, Troyes 12
> (2); Pavie, La Rochelle 50 (1).

62 (3)

Total: 62 (3)

D. Customs Confiscations: 1 instance: 1784.

713. *Vie (la) voluptueuse entre les Capucins et les nonnes, dévoilée par
la confession d'un frère de cet ordre.* Cologne, 1755. At least 8
other editions by 1779; several editions carry a note: *"Augmentée d'un poème héroï-comique sur leurs barbes et de plusieurs
autres pièces relatives à cet ordre."*

A. STN

> *Lorraine:* Choppin, Bar-le-Duc 2 (1).
> *Lyon:* Jacquenod 6 (1).
> *Paris:* Lequay Morin 12 (1); Prévost 2
> (1); Védrène 12 (1).

34 (5)

> *Minor Dealers:* Sens, Toulouse 12 (1);
> Resplandy, Toulouse 13 (1); Som-
> bert, Châlons-sur-Marne 6 (1); Bil-
> lault, Tours 2 (1).

33 (4)

Total: 67 (9)

B. Catalogues: 2 of 6 lists: (Décombaz; Cailler).

C. Customs Confiscations: 1 instance: 1778.

714. *Voltaire aux Champs-Elysées, oraison funèbre, histoire, satire,
etc., etc., etc. Le tout à volonté. Mis au jour par M. Abr.
Chaumeix.* [Abraham-Joseph Chaumeix.] Trévoux, 1773.

C. Police Confiscations: 1 of 10 lists: Pilon.

715. *Voix (la) du curé sur le procès des serfs du mont Jura.* [François-
Marie Arouet de Voltaire.] n.p., n.d. (1772, according to
Bengesco).

A. STN

> *Major Dealers:* Charmet, Besançon 12
> (1); Manoury, Caen 12 (1); Rigaud,
> Pons, Montpellier 6 (1).

30 (3)

> *Minor Dealers:* Laisney, Beauvais 6 (1).

6 (1)

Total: 36 (4)

B. Catalogues: 1 of 6 lists: (Grasset: "8°. 2 s.").

716. *Voyages et aventures de Jacques Massé.* [Simon Tyssot de Patot.] Bordeaux, 1710. At least 4 other editions by 1760.
   A. STN
      Colporteurs: "Troisième" 4 (1). } $\qquad \underline{4 \quad (1)}$
      Total: 4 (1)
   B. Catalogues: 1 of 6 lists: (Décombaz: "8°. 2 vol. 1760, 3 1.").

Vraie Religion (la). See #244, *Examen de la religion dont on cherche l'éclaircissement de bonne foi* . . .

717. *Vrai Sens (le) du Système de la nature, ouvrage posthume de M. Helvétius.* [Claude-Adrien Helvétius?, or Paul-Henri-Dietrich Thiry, baron d'Holbach?] London, 1774.
   A. STN
      Major Dealers: Malherbe, Loudun 10 (1); Robert et Gauthier, Bourg-en-Bresse 12 (1). } 22 (2)
      Total: $\overline{22 \quad (2)}$
   B. Catalogues: 1 of 6 lists: (Décombaz: "8°. Londres, 1774, 1 1. 10 s.").
   C. Police Confiscations: 2 of 10 lists: Prot, Versailles.
   D. Customs Confiscations: 1 instance: 1774.

718. *Vrais Principes (les) du gouvernement français démontrés par la raison et par les faits, par un français.* Pierre-Louis-Claude Gin. Geneva, 1777. At least 2 other editions by 1787.
   A. STN
      Major Dealers: Charmet, Besançon 6 (1); Letourmy, Orléans 8 (2); Malherbe, Loudun 10 (1); Mossy, Marseille 19 (2).
      Paris: Barré 25 (1); Lequay Morin 3 (1). } 71 (8)
      Minor Dealers: Bonnard, Auxerre 8 (2); Laisney, Beauvais 13 (1); Jarfaut, Melun 4 (1). } 25 (4)
      Total: $\overline{96 \quad (12)}$
   B. Catalogues: 1 of 6 lists (Nouffer).

719. *Yeux (les), le nez et les tétons, ouvrages curieux, galants et badins, composés pour le divertissement d'une dame de qualité par J. P. N.*

du C., dit V. [Jean-Pierre-Nicolas du Commun, dit Véron.] Cologne, 1775.

    B. Catalogues: 1 of 6 lists: (Bern: "4 1.").

    C. Police Confiscations: 2 of 10 lists: Prot, Paris.

    D. Customs Confiscations: 1 instance: 1773.

720. *Zinzolin (le) jeu frivole et morale.* [Pierre-Joseph-François Luneau de Boisjermain?, or Charles-François Toustaint de Limésy?] Amsterdam, 1769.

    C. Police Confiscations: 1 of 10 lists: Pilon.

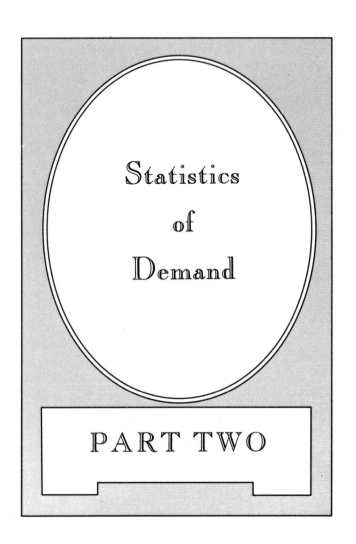

Statistics

of

Demand

PART TWO

Best-Sellers

THE FOLLOWING LIST shows the seventy-four books most in demand according to orders placed by booksellers, both major and minor dealers, with the STN. As explained in the Introduction, it provides a rough indication of the relative demand for books that sold best within the general corpus of forbidden literature; but it does not show the absolute number of copies in circulation. Instead, it is based on samples taken from the correspondence of sixty-three booksellers. Their orders, 3,266 in all, cover 28,212 books.

The list includes several elements that can be used to correct for biases inherent in the data. Titles published by the STN are set off with an asterisk, because they were ordered more often than books that the STN kept in its general stock or procured from allied publisher-wholesalers by means of exchanges. The list includes the number of orders, set in parentheses, as well as the number of copies ordered. And it indicates whether the books also appeared in soundings taken in three other sources, which are always indicated by the same letters:

A: Orders placed with the STN.

B: Catalogues of forbidden books sold by other publishers.

C: Inventories made by the police after raids on bookstores.

D: Registers of books confiscated in the Paris Customs.

By weighing all these elements, one can determine aberrations and inconsistencies in the data.

For example, two works that appear in the middle of the list seem to have been equally in demand: *Histoire de dom B . . ., portier des Chartreux,* thirty-fifth on the list, a book from the STN's general stock, and *Dissertation sur l'établissement de l'abbaye de St. Claude,* thirty-sixth, a book published by the STN itself. The STN sold 190 copies of each—quite a lot, given the scale of the sample and the conservative character of ordering by eighteenth-century booksellers. But the STN received twenty orders for *Histoire de dom B . . .* and only eight for the *Dissertation.* Moreover, if one studies the sales pattern of each book from the bibliography listed above, it becomes clear that *Histoire de dom B . . .* sold everywhere in France, whereas the *Dissertation* sold primarily in Franche-Comté and Bresse, where readers were interested in a scandal related to the seigneurial dues collected by the abbey of Saint-Claude.

The STN had published the *Dissertation,* which was actually a polemical tract by Charles-Gabriel-Frédéric Christin, a Comtois lawyer, in 1772, hoping to capitalize on the scandal. The same calculation led two booksellers of the area to speculate on unusually large orders: Charmet of Besançon sent for 50 copies, and Robert et Gauthier of Bourg-en-Bresse for 100. But neither of them repeated their initial order, and Charmet later complained that the book sold badly. Furthermore, the *Dissertation* does not show up in any of the other sources, whereas *Histoire de dom B . . .* appears in five of the six publishers' catalogues, is listed in five of the ten inventories of police raids, and was confiscated twice in the Paris Customs. It went through at least nineteen editions between 1745 and 1789. And the STN sold it regularly and in small quantities to a wide variety of booksellers, including Robert et Gauthier in Bourg-en-Bresse, who ordered a total of thirty-six copies on three occasions. In short, all the supplementary evidence indicates that *Histoire de dom B . . .* really was a best-seller and that the *Dissertation* really was not.

It is important to take all these elements into account in estimating the demand for the books on the list. Any work that appears in only one source is not likely to have been much in demand; any that appears prominently in three or four of the sources probably was a best-seller. In fact, there is a great deal of overlap in lists drawn up from all four inquiries. Of the 74 titles at the top of the STN list, 36 (47%) appear in the other three, and an additional 12 (16%) appear in two of them. One can judge the extent of the overlapping as opposed to the incidence of works that appear in only one source by the following table:

A	189	(works that appear only in the STN list)
AB	32	
ABC	46	
ABCD	85	(works that appear in all four sources)
ABD	12	
AC	23	
ACD	25	
AD	45	
B	50	(works that appear only in the catalogues)
BC	22	
BCD	9	
BD	5	
C	78	(works that appear only in the police inventories)
CD	12	
D	87	(works that appear only in the Customs confiscations)
	720	Total

The table shows, on the one hand, that quite a few books appear in only one source and therefore were probably marginal in the pattern of demand. On the other hand, it points to a core of 85 works, those mentioned in all four sources, at the heart of the market. If, in addition to those 85, one also includes works that appear in two sources as well as in the orders to the STN (i.e., ABC, ABD, and ACD), the number of core works increases by 83, to a total of 168. In contrast, only nine books appeared in three of the sources (BCD) without figuring among the orders to the STN. It follows that very few works for which there was a strong demand escaped the soundings in the papers of the STN.

BEST-SELLERS
Total Orders (Major and Minor Dealers)

Title [Author]	Books	Orders	Sources†
1. *An (l') 2440...* [Mercier]	1,394	(124)	ABCD
2. *Anecdotes sur Mme la comtesse du Barry.* [Pidansat de Mairobert?]	1,071	(52)	ACD
3. **Système de la nature...* [d'Holbach]	768	(96)	ABCD
4. **Tableau de Paris...* [Mercier]	689	(40)	AD
5. **Histoire philosophique...* [Raynal]	620	(89)	ABCD
6. *Journal historique ... par M. de Maupeou...* [Pidansat de Mairobert and Moufle d'Angerville]	561	(46)	ACD
7. *Arrétin (l').* [Du Laurens]	512	(29)	ABCD
8. *Lettre philosophique...* Anon.	496	(38)	ABCD
9. *Mémoires de l'abbé Terray...* [Coquereau]	477	(24)	AC
10. *Pucelle (la) d'Orléans...* [Voltaire]	436	(39)	ABCD
11. **Questions sur l'Encyclopédie...* [Voltaire]	426	(63)	ABCD
12. *Mémoires de Louis XV...* Anon.	419	(14)	AD
13. **Observateur (l') anglais...* [Pidansat de Mairobert]	404	(41)	ABCD
14. *Fille (la) de joie...* [trans. by Lambert? or Fougeret de Monbron?]	372	(30)	ABCD
15. *Thérèse philosophe...* [d'Arles de Montigny? or d'Argens?]	365	(28)	ABCD
16. *Recueil de comédies et ... chansons gaillardes...* Anon.	347	(27)	ABCD
17. **Essai philosophique sur le monachisme ...* [Linguet]	335	(19)	A
18. *Histoire critique de Jésus-Christ ...* [d'Holbach]	327	(36)	ABCD
19. *Plus Secrets Mystères (les) ... de la maçonnerie...* [trans. by Bérage?, ed. by Koeppen]	321	(36)	A
20. **Requête au conseil du roi ...* [Linguet]	318	(17)	AD
21. *Putain (la) errante...* [Niccolò Franco?]	261	(27)	ABCD

* An STN edition

† A = STN; B = Catalogues; C = Police confiscations; D = Customs confiscations.

Title [Author]	Books	Orders	Sources†
22. *Christianisme (le) dévoilé . . .* [d'Holbach]	259	(31)	ABCD
23. *OEuvres.* Rousseau	240	(58)	ABCD
24. *Paysan (le) perverti. . .* [Restif de la Bretonne]	239	(19)	AD
25. *Ecole (l') des filles. . .* [Milot]	223	(16)	ABCD
26. *Bon-Sens (le). . .* [d'Holbach]	220	(16)	ABCD
27. *Lettre de M. Linguet à M. le comte de Vergennes. . .* [Linguet]	216	(4)	A
28. *Homme (de l'). . .* [Helvétius]	215	(21)	ABCD
29. *Système social. . .* [d'Holbach]	212	(32)	ABCD
30. *Monarque (le) accompli . . .* [Lanjuinais]	210	(18)	ACD
31. *Dictionnaire philosophique portatif . . .* [Voltaire]	204	(27)	ABCD
32. *Vie privée de Louis XV. . .* [Moufle d'Angerville? or Laffrey?]	198	(17)	AD
33. *Lyre (la) gaillarde. . .* Anon.	197	(14)	ABCD
34. *Lauriers (les) ecclésiastiques. . .* [Rochette de La Morlière]	191	(22)	ABC
35. *Histoire de dom B. . . , portier des Chartreux. . .* [Gervaise de Latouche? or Nourry?]	190	(20)	ABCD
36. **Dissertation sur l'établissement de l'abbaye de St. Claude. . .* [Christin]	190	(8)	A
37. *Correspondance secrète et familière de M. de Maupeou. . .* [Pidansat de Mairobert]	189	(22)	ACD
38. *Antiquité (l') et perpétuité de la religion protestante. . .* [Renoult]	180	(5)	A
39. *Fastes (les) de Louis XV. . .* [Goudar]	175	(7)	AD
40. *Recherches philosophiques sur les Américains. . .* [de Pauw]	169	(25)	ACD
41. *Parnasse libertin. . .* Anon.	169	(19)	ABCD
42. *Académie (l') des dames. . .* [Nicolas]	168	(18)	ABCD
43. *Théologie portative. . .* [d'Holbach]	163	(24)	ABCD
44. *Mémoires sur la Bastille. . .* [Linguet]	163	(15)	A
45. *Adoption (l') ou la maçonnerie des dames . . .* [Saint-Victor?]	161	(21)	A
46. **Commentaire historique sur les oeuvres de l'auteur de la Henriade. . .* [Voltaire]	160	(25)	A
47. *Epîtres, satires, contes, odes et pièces fugitives. . .* [Voltaire]	160	(22)	ABCD

Title [Author]	Books	Orders	Sources†
48. *Compère (le) Mathieu*. . . [Du Laurens]	154	(16)	ABCD
49. *Mémoires secrets*. . . [Bachaumont and others]	150	(25)	ACD
50. *Examen important de Milord Bolingbroke* . . . [Voltaire]	146	(21)	ABCD
51. *Vénus dans le cloître*. . . [Barrin]	146	(19)	ABCD
52. *Chrétien (un) contre six juifs.* [Voltaire]	146	(6)	AB
53. *Gazetier (le) cuirassé*. . . [Théveneau de Morande]	135	(13)	ABCD
54. *Législation (de la)*. . . [Bonnot de Mably]	134	(16)	A
55. *Traité des trois imposteurs.* [Vroes?]	133	(28)	ABCD
56. *Fille (la) naturelle.* [Restif de la Bretonne]	132	(16)	AD
57. *Confessions (les) de J.-J. Rousseau.* [Rousseau]	132	(10)	AD
58. *Contagion (la) sacrée*. . . [d'Holbach?, trans.]	131	(17)	ABC
59. *Histoire de Jenni*. . . [Voltaire]	129	(15)	ABD
60. *Essai sur le despotisme.* [Mirabeau]	127	(16)	AC
61. *Cruauté (de la) religieuse.* [d'Holbach, trans.]	124	(15)	ABC
62. *Examen critique des apologistes de la religion chrétienne*. . . [Lévesque de Burigny?]	123	(19)	ABCD
63. *Lettre de Thrasibule à Leucippe*. . . [Fréret? or d'Holbach? or Naigeon?]	122	(12)	ABC
64. *Chandelle (la) d'Arras*. . . [Du Laurens]	121	(13)	ABCD
65. *Contes de Boccace.* [Boccaccio]	115	(12)	AD
66. *Mémoires d'une reine infortunée*. . . [Caroline-Mathilde, reine de Danemark?]	112	(2)	A
67. *Œuvres.* Helvétius	110	(24)	ABCD
68. *Espion (l') dévalisé.* [Baudouin de Guémadeuc]	110	(13)	AC
69. *Lettres chinoises, indiennes et tartares* . . . [Voltaire]	109	(13)	A
70. *Mémoires authentiques de Mme la comtesse du Barry*. . .	109	(6)	ABCD
71. *OEuvres posthumes de J.-J. Rousseau* . . .	107	(16)	A
72. *Devoirs (les), statuts ou règlements généraux des F.·. M.·.* . . . . Anon.	106	(18)	A

Title [Author]	Books	Orders	Sources†
73. *Eloge historique de la raison...* [Voltaire]	106	(11)	A
74. *Contes et nouvelles en vers de M. de la Fontaine.* [La Fontaine]	103	(23)	ABCD

Best-Selling
Authors

THE FOLLOWING LIST shows which authors were most in demand according to the total number of books by them that were ordered from the STN. Voltaire and d'Holbach lead the list, not only because they wrote individual best-sellers like *La Pucelle d'Orléans* and *Système de la nature,* but also because they were so prolific. Voltaire produced 68 and d'Holbach (with his collaborators) 33 of the 457 forbidden books sold by the STN. By comparison, all the other authors wrote (or collaborated on) a relatively small number of books: nine in the case of Diderot; eight in the case of Morande; seven in the case of d'Argens, Du Laurens, Pidansat de Mairobert, and Rousseau; six in the case of Helvétius, Mercier, Mirabeau, and Naigeon. A few belong to the list of best-selling authors even though they produced only one best-seller: Raynal, Coquereau, Bérage, Milot, Lanjuinais, and Moufle d'Angerville.

The list provides only a suggestive ranking of authors, however, because most illegal books were published anonymously and many were written by several authors. The Holbachean works pose special problems of attribution. D'Holbach himself acted only as editor, translator, or co-author in the production of at least twenty-five of them. If one counted collaborations and doubtful cases and also tabulated the same title after the name of more than one of its authors, the list would look quite different: Diderot would be ninth, Naigeon twenty-first, and Fréret twenty-seventh. But it seemed preferable to count each title only once and to group the Holbachean works in one entry, as "d'Holbach and collaborators." The same considerations apply to Pidansat de Mairobert, who worked with several other authors in compiling multi-volume publications like *Mémoires secrets pour servir à l'histoire de la république des lettres en France* (36 volumes) and *Journal historique de la révolution opérée dans la constitution de la monarchie française par M. de Maupeou* (7 volumes). If those works were attributed to Mairobert's closest collaborator, Moufle d'Angerville, as well as to Mairobert, Moufle would be seventh on the list.

Finally, it should be remembered that works printed by the STN weighed more heavily in its trade than works from its general stock. That tendency reinforced the position on the list of Voltaire, d'Holbach, Mercier, and Raynal; but it was mitigated by several factors, especially the practice of swapping a large proportion of new editions. In fact, the STN's sales did not excessively favor its own publications. It sold far more copies of Mercier's *L'An 2440,* which it did not print, than of his *Jezennemours,* which it did. So the list of best-selling authors should not be read as a precise ranking of their appeal to the reading public; but it does provide a rough indication of the writers whose works were most in demand.

Authors by Number of Books Ordered

1.	Voltaire, François-Marie Arouet de	3,545
2.	D'Holbach, Paul-Henri-Dietrich Thiry, baron de (and collaborators)	2,903
3.	Pidansat de Mairobert, Matthieu-François (and collaborators)	2,425
4.	Mercier, Louis-Sébastien	2,199
5.	Théveneau de Morande, Charles	1,360
6.	Linguet, Simon-Nicolas-Henri	1,038
7.	Du Laurens, Henri-Joseph	866
8.	Raynal, Guillaume-Thomas-François[1]	620
9.	Rousseau, Jean-Jacques	505
10.	Helvétius, Claude-Adrien	486
11.	Coquereau, Jean-Baptiste-Louis[2]	477

[1] One title—*Histoire philosophique . . . deux Indes.*
[2] One title—*Mémoires de l'abbé Terrai.*

12. Argens, Jean-Baptiste de Boyer, marquis d'[3]   457
13. Fougeret de Monbron, Charles-Louis[4]   409
14. Restif de la Bretonne, Nicolas-Edmé   371
15. Bérage-Koeppen, Karl-Friedrich[5]   321
16. Mirabeau, Honoré-Gabriel Riqueti, comte de   312
17. Franco, Niccolò[6]   261
18. de Pauw, Cornelius   235
19. Milot (or Mililot)[7]   223
20. Goudar, Ange   214
21. Lanjuinais, Joseph[8]   210
22. Moufle d'Angerville, Barthélemy-François-Joseph[9]   198
23. Rochette de la Morlière, Charles-Jacques-Louis-Auguste 197

[3] Includes *Thérèse philosophe* (365 books, 28 orders), which is also attributed to d'Arles de Montigny. D'Argens, however, has six other titles attributed to him, so he is not disproportionately high on the list.

[4] Includes *La Fille de joie*, his translation of *Memoirs of a Woman of Pleasure* by John Cleland. This translation has also been attributed to a certain Lambert.

[5] One title—*Les Plus Secrets Mystères des hauts grades de la maçonnerie dévoilés, ou le vrai Rose-Croix; traduit de l'anglais, suivi du Noachite traduit de l'allemand*. By usage, the translator is cited as "Bérage" (e.g., Barbier and Caillet). Fesch gives Koeppen as the editor, without citing any original English or German works.

[6] One title—*Putain (la) errante*. The authorship of this work is uncertain.

[7] One title—*Ecole des filles*.

[8] One title—*Monarque accompli*.

[9] One title—*Vie privée de Louis XV*, attributed to both Moufle d'Angerville and Arnoux Laffrey (198 books, 17 orders).

Genres

THE FOLLOWING TABLES indicate which genres of forbidden literature were most favored in the orders received by the STN. Like any other classification scheme, the one used here has certain arbitrary characteristics. The choice of categories and subcategories cannot do justice to the rich profusion of themes treated in the literature as a whole; and the subject matter of a single work may be so varied as to defy classification under one rubric. But after a great deal of experimentation, the categories used below seemed quite appropriate. They respect the three main areas defined as taboo in the legislation on the book trade under the Old Regime: literature that offended the church, the state, and general standards of morality. At the same time, they leave room for forbidden books whose subjects were either highly specialized—illegal treatises on occultism and Freemasonry, for example—or extremely general, like Voltaire's *Dictionnaire philosophique,* Mercier's *Tableau de Paris,* and Raynal's *Histoire philosophique.* The first two have been classified in a separate category, "Other," and the third in an omnibus subcategory, "General Social and Cultural Criticism," under "Philosophy." As philosophy in the late eighteenth century connoted a general critical stance toward the world rather than an academic discipline, this procedure seemed to correspond best to contemporary attitudes.

The greatest difficulty occurred in classifying books that were both anti-clerical and obscene, such as *Histoire de dom B . . . , por-*

tier des Chartreux. I placed them in a special subcategory of works attacking religion, "Irreligious Ribaldry, Pornography," but they could go just as well in the general category of books treating sex. If they were to be shifted to that category, the percentage of obscene or pornographic works would go up from 12.9 percent to 20.9 percent of the whole.

The subcategories of works on politics and current events also posed a problem, because the divisions between them are particularly blurred. The *Journal historique de la révolution opérée dans la constitution de la monarchie française par M. de Maupeou,* classified with "Libels, Court Satire," could also be considered one of the "Topical Works" or even one of the *"Chroniques Scandaleuses."* I considered it worthwhile to sort the vast area of political writing into subdivisions, and I found it possible to group together works with strong family resemblances. But I acknowledge the subjective element in those judgments. Others might choose differently; and to help them do so, I have listed the main titles as I have classified them. By reworking this material, it should be possible to see other patterns within the general corpus of literature treated as illegal in the eighteenth century.

General Pattern of Demand by Genres

Category and Subcategory		Number of Titles	Per-centage	Number of Copies Ordered	Per-centage
I.	RELIGION				
	A. Treatises	45	9.8%	2,810	10.0%
	B. Satire, Polemics	81	17.7	3,212	11.4
	C. Irreligious Ribaldry, Pornography	18	3.9	2,260	8.0
	Subtotals	144	31.5*	8,282	29.4
II.	PHILOSOPHY				
	A. Treatises	31	6.8	723	2.6
	B. Collected Works, Compilations	28	6.1	1,583	5.6
	C. Satire, Polemics	9	2.0	242	0.9

*Rounding creates the discrepancy in the subtotals of percentages.

Category and Subcategory		Number of Titles	Per-centage	Number of Copies Ordered	Per-centage
D. General Social, Cultural Criticism		33	7.2	4,515	16.0
	Subtotals:	101	22.1	7,063	25.1*
III. POLITICS, CURRENT EVENTS					
A. Treatises		20	4.4	986	3.5
B. Topical Works		50	10.9	2,213	7.8
C. Libels, Court Satire		45	9.8	4,085	14.5
D. *Chroniques Scandaleuses*		17	3.7	1,051	3.7
	Subtotals:	132	28.9*	8,335	29.5
IV. SEX		64	14.0	3,654	12.9
V. OTHER					
A. Occultism		2	0.4	111	0.4
B. Freemasonry		6	1.3	639	2.3
	Subtotals:	8	1.7	750	2.7
VI. UNCLASSIFIED		8	1.8	128	0.5
	Totals:	457	100.0%	28,212	100.0%

Most Frequently Ordered Titles in Each Category and Subcategory

I. RELIGION

A. Treatises
1. *Système de la nature.* [d'Holbach] — 768
2. *Histoire critique de Jésus-Christ. . .* [d'Holbach] — 327
3. *Christianisme (le) dévoilé. . .* [d'Holbach] — 259
4. *Bon-Sens (le). . .* [d'Holbach] — 220
5. *Contagion (la) sacrée. . .* [trans. by d'Holbach?] — 131
6. *Cruauté (de la) religieuse.* [trans. by d'Holbach] — 124
7. *Examen critique des apologistes de la religion chrétienne. . .* [Lévesque de Burigny?] — 123
8. *Lettre de Thrasibule à Leucippe. . .* [Fréret, d'Holbach, or Naigeon?] — 122

9. *Lettre d'un théologien à l'auteur du Dictionnaire des trois siècles littéraires.* [Condorcet]   90

10. *Militaire (le) philosophe...* [d'Holbach and Naigeon]   82

B. Satire, Polemics

1. *Essai philosophique sur le monachisme...* [Linguet]   335

2. *Dissertation sur l'établissement de l'abbaye de St. Claude...* [Christin]   190

3. *Antiquité (l') et perpétuité de la religion protestante...* Renoult   180

4. *Théologie portative...* [d'Holbach]   163

5. *Compère Mathieu...* [Du Laurens]   154

6. *Chrétien (un) contre six juifs.* [Voltaire]   146

7. *Examen important de Milord Bolingbroke...* [Voltaire]   146

8. *Traité des trois imposteurs.* [Vroes?]   133

9. *Histoire de Jenni...* [Voltaire]   129

10. *Dialogue entre un évêque et un curé...* [Guidi]   100

C. Irreligious Ribaldry, Pornography

1. *Arrétin (l').* [Du Laurens]   512

2. *Lettre philosophique...* Anon.   496

3. *Pucelle (la) d'Orléans...* Voltaire   436

4. *Lauriers (les) ecclésiastiques...* [Rochette de La Morlière]   191

5. *Histoire de dom B..., portier des Chartreux...* [Gervaise de Latouche or Nourry?]   190

6. *Chandelle (la) d'Arras...* [Du Laurens]   121

7. *Monialisme (le)...* Anon.   67

8. *Vie (la) voluptueuse entre les Capucins et les nonnes...* Anon.   67

9. *Histoire de la tourière des Carmélites...* [Meusnier de Querlon]   64

10. *Nouvelles monacales...* Anon.   25

II. PHILOSOPHY

A. Treatises

1. *Homme (de l')...* [Helvétius]   215

2. *Bonheur (le)...* Helvétius   78

3. *Félicité (de la) publique...* [Chastellux]   63

4. *Esprit (de l').* [Helvétius]   55

5. *Vérité (de la)*. . . Brissot de Warville   52

6. *Philosophie (de la) de la nature*. [Delisle de Sales]   50

7. *Morale (la) universelle*. . . [d'Holbach]   43

8. *Manuel du philosophe*. . . Anon.   22

9. *Nature (de la)*. [Robinet]   21

10. *Antiquité dévoilée*. . . [d'Holbach]   18

B. Collected Works, Compilations
    1. *Œuvres*. Rousseau   240

    2. *Commentaire historique sur les oeuvres de l'auteur de la Henriade*. . . [Voltaire]   160

    3. *Epîtres, satires, contes, odes et pièces fugitives*. . . [Voltaire]   160

    4. *Œuvres*. Helvétius   110

    5. *Œuvres posthumes de J.-J. Rousseau*. . .   107

    6. *Eloge historique de la raison*. . . [Voltaire]   106

    7. *Œuvres*. La Mettrie   90

    8. *Evangile (l') du jour*. [Voltaire]   76

    9. *Choses (les) utiles et agréables*. [Voltaire]   63

    10. *Œuvres*. Voltaire   59

C. Satire, Polemics
    1. *A.B.C. (l'), dialogue curieux*. . . [Voltaire]   62

    2. *Concubitus sine Lucina, ou le plaisir sans peine*. . . [Richard Roe.] (trans. by Meusnier de Querlon? or de Combes?)   62

    3. *Pièces échappées du portefeuille de M. de Voltaire, comte de Tournay*. Anon.   38

    4. *Remontrances du Père Adam à Voltaire*. . . Antoine Adam   26

    5. *Dialogue de Pégase et du vieillard*. [Voltaire]   20

    6. *Philosophie (la) de l'histoire*. . . [Voltaire]   20

    7. *Etrennes aux désoeuvrés ou lettre d'un Quaker à ses fréres*. . . Lewis Penn   7

    8. *Philosophe (le) ignorant*. [Voltaire]   6

    9. *Pot-pourri (le), étrennes aux gens de lettres*. [Brissot de Warville]   6

D. General Social, Cultural Criticism
    1. *An (l') deux mille quatre cent quarante*. . . [Mercier]   1,394

    2. *Tableau de Paris*. [Mercier]   689

    3. *Histoire philosophique et politique des établisse-*

ments et du commerce des Européens dans les deux
Indes. [Raynal]   620

4. *Questions sur l'Encyclopédie par des amateurs.*
[Voltaire]   426

5. *Paysan (le) perverti.* . . Restif de la Bretonne   239

6. *Dictionnaire philosophique portatif.* [Voltaire]   204

7. *Recherches philosophiques sur les Américains.* . .
[de Pauw]   169

8. *Confessions (les) de J.-J. Rousseau.* Rousseau   132

9. *Lettres chinoises, indiennes et tartares.* . . [Vol-
taire]   109

10. *Recherches philosophiques sur les Egyptiens* . . . [de
Pauw]   66

11. *Lettres chinoises, ou correspondance philosophique*
. . . [d'Argens]   66

III. POLITICS, CURRENT EVENTS

A. Treatises
    1. *Système social.* . . [d'Holbach]   212
    2. *Législation (de la).* . . Mably   134
    3. *Essai sur le despotisme.* [comte de Mirabeau]   127
    4. *Vrais Principes (les) du gouvernement français.* . .
    Gin   96
    5. *Traité des délits et des peines.* . . (Beccaria, trans.
    by Morellet)   89
    6. *Maximes du droit public français.* . . [Mey]   75
    7. *Politique (la) naturelle.* . . [d'Holbach?]   72
    8. *Théorie des lois criminelles.* Brissot de Warville   39
    9. *Bibliothèque philosophique du législateur.* . . Bris-
    sot de Warville, ed.   38
    10. *Recherches sur l'origine du despotisme oriental.* . .
    [Boulanger?, ed. by d'Holbach]   32

B. Topical Works
    1. *Requête au conseil du roi.* . . Linguet   318
    2. *Lettre de M. Linguet à M. le comte de Vergennes*
    . . . Linguet   216
    3. *Monarque (le) accompli.* . . [Lanjuinais]   210
    4. *Mémoires sur la Bastille.* . . Linguet   163
    5. *Mémoires d'une reine infortunée.* . . [Caroline-
    Mathilde, reine de Danemark?]   112

6. *Lettres (des) de cachet et des prisons d'Etat...* [comte de Mirabeau] 96

7. *Ami (l') des lois.* [Martin de Marivaux] 73

8. *Pièces heureusement échappées de la France...* Anon. 71

9. *Fragments sur l'Inde et sur le général Lalli.* [Voltaire] 69

10. *Mémoires de M. le comte de Saint-Germain...* Claude-Louis, comte de St.-Germain 64

C. Libels, Court Satire
  1. *Anecdotes sur Mme la comtesse du Barry.* [Pidansat de Mairobert? or Théveneau de Morande?] 1,071

  2. *Journal historique de la révolution opérée... par M. de Maupeou...* [Pidansat de Mairobert and Moufle d'Angerville] 561

  3. *Mémoires de l'abbé Terray...* [Coquereau] 477

  4. *Mémoires de Louis XV...* Anon. 419

  5. *Vie privée de Louis XV...* [Moufle d'Angerville or Laffrey?] 198

  6. *Correspondance secrète et familière de M. de Maupeou...* [Pidansat de Mairobert.] 189

  7. *Fastes (les) de Louis XV...* [Ange Goudar] 175

  8. *Gazetier (le) cuirassé...* [Théveneau de Morande] 135

  9. *Mémoires authentiques de Mme la comtesse du Barry...* Anon. 109

  10. *Mémoires de Mme la marquise de Pompadour...* Anon. 71

D. Chroniques Scandaleuses
  1. *Observateur (l') anglais...* [Pidansat de Mairobert] 404

  2. *Mémoires secrets...* [Petit de Bachaumont, continued by Pidansat de Mairobert, Moufle d'Angerville, and others] 150

  3. *Espion (l') dévalisé.* [Baudouin de Guémadeuc] 110

  4. *Gazette de Cythère...* [Bernard] 100

  5. *Chronique (la) scandaleuse...* [Imbert de Bourdeaux] 71

  6. *Mémoires pour servir à l'histoire de madame de Maintenon...* [Angliviel de La Beaumelle] 69

7. *Portefeuille (le) de Madame Gourdan. . .* [Théveneau de Morande]   44

8. *Anecdotes du XVIIIe siècle.* [Imbert de Bourdeaux]   31

9. *Espion (l') chinois. . .* [Ange Goudar]   26

10. *Espion (l') français à Londres. . .* [Ange Goudar]   13

VI. SEX

1. *Fille (la) de joie. . .* (Cleland, trans. by Lambert? or Fougeret de Monbron?)   372

2. *Thérèse philosophe. . .* [d'Arles de Montigny? or d'Argens?]   365

3. *Recueil de comédies. . . chansons gaillardes . . .* Anon.   347

4. *Putain (la) errante. . .* [Niccolò Franco?]   261

5. *Ecole (l') des filles. . .* [Milot]   223

6. *Lyre (la) gaillarde. . .* Anon.   197

7. *Parnasse libertin. . .* Anon.   169

8. *Académie (l') des dames. . .* [Nicolas]   168

9. *Vénus dans le cloître. . .* [Barrin]   146

10. *Fille (la) naturelle.* [Restif de la Bretonne]   132

V. OTHER

A. Occultism

1. *Secrets merveilleux de la magie. . . du Petit-Albert . . .* Anon.   75

2. *Admirables (les) Secrets d'Albert le Grand. . .* Anon.   36

B. Freemasonry

1. *Plus Secrets Mystères (les) des hauts grades de la maçonnerie dévoilés. . .* [trans. by Bérage?, ed. by Koeppen]   321

2. *Adoption (l') ou la maçonnerie des dames en trois grades.* [Guillemain de Saint-Victor?]   161

3. *Devoirs (les), statuts ou règlements généraux des F∴ M∴ . . .*   106

4. *Secrets (les) de l'ordre des francs-maçons dévoilés. . .* [Pérau]   40

5. *Essais sur les mystères et le véritable objet de la confrérie des francs-maçons.* [Koeppen]   7

6. *Recueil des chansons des francs-maçons.* Anon.   4

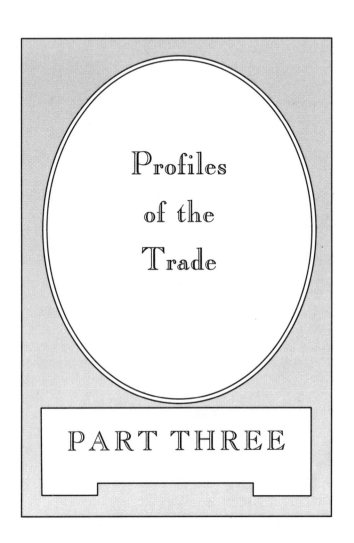

Profiles
of the
Trade

PART THREE

THE FOLLOWING STATISTICS provide a picture of the trade in forbidden literature as it was conducted by booksellers scattered across the map of France. As explained in chapter 2 of *The Forbidden Best-Sellers,* the first set concerns twelve "major dealers"—booksellers who ordered regularly from the STN. By identifying all the forbidden books in their orders and compiling statistics from them, one can form a general idea of their businesses and create a best-seller list for each of them. In each case, the first figure in the right-hand column represents the total number of copies per title and the figure in parentheses represents the total number of orders. The numbers are relatively small, because booksellers could not return unsold copies to their suppliers. Therefore, in calculating demand, they tended to be conservative; and in fact they often arranged sales with their clients before ordering the books from publishers or wholesalers.

The second set of statistics concerns orders from Lorraine, Lyon, and Paris, which have been grouped so as to form a general picture of the illegal trade in each of those large markets. It is followed by similar composite statistics drawn from the orders of four peddlers *(colporteurs* or *marchands forains),* who hawked books through Normandy, the Loire country, and the Ile de France. One of them placed his orders through Malherbe, a dealer in Loudun, and appears in Malherbe's correspondence only as "un troisième."

The final set of statistics concerns seventeen "minor dealers" or booksellers who ordered only occasionally from the STN. Their orders were not frequent or extensive enough to furnish profiles of their individual businesses. But by combining them, one can form a general picture of casual ordering from the STN; and by comparing that picture with the orders from the "major dealers" (the last set of statistics), one can confirm that the general pattern is basically the same. Of course, each business had a character of its own. The orders include a few works with largely local appeal, such as Jean-Baptiste Renoult's *L'Antiquité et perpétuité de la religion protestante,* which sold well in Nîmes, where Protestants made up an important part of the reading public. But there are not many regional differences in the sales patterns. While providing pictures of individual businesses, the statistics show that the same general corpus of forbidden books penetrated every corner of the kingdom.

Booksellers by Location

Major Dealers:

Bergeret, Bordeaux
Blouet, Rennes
Buchet, Nîmes
Charmet, Besançon
Letourmy, Orléans
Malherbe, Loudun
Manoury, Caen
Mauvelain, Troyes
Mossy, Marseille
Pavie, La Rochelle
Rigaud, Pons, Montpellier
Robert et Gauthier, Bourg-en-Bresse

Lorraine:

Audéart, Lunéville
Augé, Lunéville
Babin, Nancy
Bergue, Thionville
Bernard, Lunéville
Bertrand, Thionville
Bonthoux, Nancy
Carez, Toul
Chénoux, Lunéville

Lyon:

Baritel
Barret
Cellier
Flandin
Jacquenod

Paris:

Barré
Barrois
Cugnet
Desauges
Lequay Morin
Prévost
Védrène

Colporteurs:

Blaisot
Gilles
Planquais
"Troisième"

Choppin, Bar-le-Duc
Dalancourt, Nancy
Gay, Lunéville
Gerlache, Metz
Henry, Nancy
L'Entretien, Lunéville
Matthieu, Nancy
Orbelin, Thionville
Sandré, Lunéville

Minor Dealers:

Boisserand, Roanne
Billault, Tours
Bonnard, Auxerre
Caldesaigues, Marseille
Cazin, Reims
Chevrier, Poitiers
Fontaine, Colmar
Habert, Bar-sur-Aube

Jarfaut, Melun
Lair, Blois
Laisney, Beauvais
Malassis, Nantes
Petit, Reims
Resplandy, Toulouse
Sens, Toulouse
Sombert, Châlons-sur-Marne
Waroquier, Soissons

MAJOR DEALERS

Bergeret, Bordeaux

Bergeret made 16 orders, from June 1773 to February 1784 (but especially in the period 1775–78). They included 40 illegal works, of which the following 12 were most in demand.

1. *An (l') 2440.* . . [Mercier]	74	(3)
2. *Tableau de Paris.* . . [Mercier]	63	(3)
3. *Histoire philosophique.* . . [Raynal]	42	(5)
4. *Observateur (l') anglais.* . . [Pidansat de Mairobert]	42	(3)
5. *Bibliothèque philosophique.* . . [Brissot de Warville]	36	(3)
6. *Journal historique* . . . *par M. de Maupeou* . . . [Pidansat de Mairobert and Moufle d'Angerville]	30	(1)
7. *Lettres chinoises, indiennes et tartares.* . . [Voltaire]	25	(1)
8. *Lettre philosophique.* . . Anon.	18	(2)
9. *Christianisme (le) dévoilé.* . . [d'Holbach]	16	(2)
10. *Vérité (de la).* . . [Brissot de Warville]	14	(2)
11. *Plus Secrets Mystères (les)* . . . *de la maçonnerie.* . . [Bérage, trans. by Koeppen]	13	(2)
12. *Traité de la nature et du gouvernement de l'Eglise.* [Tailhé]	13	(1)

Blouet, Rennes

Blouet made 11 orders, from October 1772 to September 1776. They included 120 illegal works, of which the following 21 were most in demand.

1. *Histoire critique de Jésus-Christ. . .* [d'Holbach]   190 (5)
2. *An (l') 2440. . .* [Mercier]   100 (3)
3. *Monarque (le) accompli. . .* [Lanjuinais]   75 (3)
4. *Maximes du droit public français. . .* [Mey]   75 (2)
5. *Arrétin (l').* [Du Laurens]   72 (3)
6. *Journal historique . . . par M. de Maupeou. . .*
   [Pidansat de Mairobert and Moufle d'Angerville]   66 (2)
7. *Bon-Sens (le). . .* [d'Holbach]   50 (1)
8. *Thérèse philosophe. . .* [d'Arles de Montigny? or
   d'Argens]   43 (4)
9. *Christianisme (le) dévoilé. . .* [d'Holbach]   40 (3)
10. *Théologie portative. . .* [d'Holbach]   28 (2)
11. *Mémoires de Mme la marquise de Pompadour. . .*
    Anon.   26 (2)
12. *Système de la nature. . .* [d'Holbach]   25 (1)
13. *Lettres chinoises, indiennes et tartares. . .* [Voltaire] 25 (1)
14. *Dictionnaire philosophique portatif. . .* [Voltaire]   22 (4)
15. *Gazetier (le) cuirassé. . .* [Théveneau de Morande]   18 (3)
16. *Pucelle (la) d'Orléans. . .* [Voltaire]   18 (3)
17. *Lettres iroquoises.* [Maubert de Gouvest]   18 (1)
18. *Contagion (la) sacrée. . .* [d'Holbach?]   16 (2)
19. *Esprit (l') du clergé. . .* [d'Holbach]   16 (1)
20. *Choses (les) utiles et agréables.* [Voltaire]   14 (3)
21. *Recueil philosophique, ou mélange de pièces sur la reli-
    gion et la morale. . .* [Naigeon, ed.]   14 (2)

Buchet, Nîmes

Buchet made 18 orders, from March 1774 to October 1788 (but mainly in 1774–78). They included 42 illegal works, of which the following 16 were most in demand.

1. *Antiquité (l') et perpétuité de la religion protestante. . .* [Renoult]   162 (2)
2. *Observateur (l') anglais. . .* [Pidansat de Mairobert]   65 (3)
3. *Journal historique . . . par M. de Maupeou. . .*
   [Pidansat de Mairobert and Moufle d'Angerville]   54 (1)
4. *Dictionnaire philosophique portatif. . .* [Voltaire]   52 (2)

5. *Christianisme (le) dévoilé* . . . [d'Holbach]   26 (2)
6. *Anecdotes sur Mme la comtesse du Barry.* [Pidansat
   de Mairobert? or Théveneau de Morande?]   26 (1)
7. *Cent Nouvelles Nouvelles (les).* [Antoine de la
   Salle?]   26 (1)
8. *Commentaire historique sur les oeuvres de l'auteur de
   la Henriade.* . . [Voltaire]   26 (1)
9. *Histoire de Jenni, ou le sage et l'athée.* . . [Voltaire]   26 (1)
10. *Histoire des diables modernes.* . . [Adolphus Joy]   26 (1)
11. *Lettres chinoises, indiennes et tartares.* . . [Voltaire]   26 (1)
12. *Mémoires de l'abbé Terray.* . . [Coquereau]   26 (1)
13. *Mémoires de Louis XV.* . . Anon.   26 (1)
14. *Putain (la) errante.* . . [Niccolò Franco?]   26 (1)
15. *Histoire philosophique.* . . [Raynal]   19 (2)
16. *Traité des délits et des peines.* . . [Beccaria, trans. by
    Morellet]   19 (2)

Charmet, Besançon

Charmet made 55 orders, from December 1771 to March 1785. They
included 97 illegal works, of which the following 19 were most in
demand.

1. *Lettre philosophique.* . . Anon.   150 (3)
2. *Arrétin (l').* [Du Laurens]   137 (4)
3. *Anecdotes sur Mme la comtesse du Barry.* [Pidansat
   de Mairobert? or Théveneau de Morande?]   107 (5)
4. *Lyre (la) gaillarde* . . . Anon.   105 (3)
5. *Vie privée de Louis XV.* . . [Moufle d'Angerville?
   or Laffrey?]   104 (4)
6. *Essai philosophique sur le monachisme.* . . [Linguet]   93 (5)
7. *Pucelle d'Orléans.* . . [Voltaire]   75 (3)
8. *Espion (l') dévalisé.* [Baudouin de Guémadeuc]   60 (1)
9. *Histoire philosophique.* . . [Raynal]   59 (7)
10. *An (l') 2440.* . . [Mercier]   57 (6)
11. *Confessions (les).* . . [Rousseau]   54 (2)
12. *Contes de Boccace.* (trans. from Boccaccio)   49 (3)
13. *Pièces heureusement échappées de la France.* . . Anon.   45 (2)
14. *Lettres (des) de cachet.* . . [comte de Mirabeau]   44 (3)
15. *Tableau de Paris.* . . [Mercier]   42 (3)
16. *Ma Conversion.* . . [comte de Mirabeau]   32 (2)
17. *Putain (la) errante.* . . [Niccolò Franco?]   31 (2)

18. *Journal historique . . . par M. de Maupeou . . .*
    [Pidansat de Mairobert and Moufle d'Angerville]   31 (2)
19. *Mémoires de Louis XV . . .* Anon.   28 (1)

Letourmy, Orléans

Letourmy made 11 orders, from January 1775 to November 1779. They included 87 illegal works, of which the following 23 were most in demand.

1. *Journal historique . . . par M. de Maupeou . . .*
   [Pidansat de Mairobert and Moufle d'Angerville]   75 (3)
2. *Ecole (l') des filles . . .* [Milot]   68 (4)
3. *Recueil de comédies et . . . chansons gaillardes . . .*
   Anon.   66 (6)
4. *Lettre philosophique . . .* Anon.   61 (5)
5. *Fille (la) de joie . . .* [trans. by Lambert? or Fougeret de Monbron?]   61 (4)
6. *Putain (la) errante . . .* [Niccolò Franco?]   56 (5)
7. *Anecdotes sur Mme la comtesse du Barry.* [Pidansat
   de Mairobert? or Théveneau de Morande?]   56 (3)
8. *Chandelle (la) d'Arras . . .* [Du Laurens]   49 (3)
9. *An (l') 2440 . . .* [Mercier]   34 (4)
10. *Fille (la) naturelle.* [Restif de la Bretonne]   31 (2)
11. *Ami (l') des lois.* [Martin de Marivaux.].   25 (1)
12. *Lettres profanes à l'abbé Baudeau.* (unidentified)   25 (1)
13. *Mémoires de Louis XV . . .* Anon.   25 (1)
14. *Requête au conseil du roi . . .* [Linguet]   25 (1)
15. *Dîner (le) du comte de Boulainvilliers . . .* [Voltaire] 24 (3)
16. *Mémoires turcs . . .* [Godard d'Aucourt]   22 (3)
17. *Lauriers (les) ecclésiastiques . . .* [Rochette de La
    Morlière]   18 (3)
18. *Bonheur (le) . . .* [Helvétius]   18 (2)
19. *Pucelle (la) d'Orléans . . .* [Voltaire]   17 (4)
20. *Cruauté (de la) religieuse.* [d'Holbach]   16 (3)
21. *Philosophie (de la) de la nature.* [Delisle de Sales] 14 (3)
22. *Questions sur l'Encyclopédie . . .* [Voltaire]   14 (2)
23. *Vénus dans le cloître, ou la religieuse en chemise.*
    [Barrin]   14 (2)

Malherbe, Loudun

Malherbe made 32 orders, from September 1772 to November 1779. They included 117 illegal works, of which the following 27 were most in demand.

1. *Anecdotes sur Mme la comtesse du Barry.* [Pidansat
   de Mairobert? or Théveneau de Morande?]   338 (7)
2. *Mémoires de l'abbé Terrai. . .* [Coquereau]   296 (8)
3. *Paysan (le) perverti. . .* [Restif de la Bretonne] 188 (4)
4. *Système de la nature. . .* [d'Holbach]   167 (7)
5. *Recueil de comédies et . . . chansons gaillardes. . .*
   Anon.   152 (4)
6. *Arrétin (l').* [Du Laurens]   110 (6)
7. *Pucelle (la) d'Orléans. . .* [Voltaire]   77 (3)
8. *Journal historique . . . par M. de Maupeou. . .*
   [Pidansat de Mairobert and Moufle d'Angerville]   76 (6)
9. *Dialogue entre un évêque et un curé sur les mariages
   des protestants.* [Guidi]   76 (2)
10. *Essai philosophique sur le monachisme. . .* [Linguet] 75 (2)
11. *Compère (le) Mathieu. . .* [Du Laurens]   65 (5)
12. *Fille (la) de joie. . .* [trans. by Lambert? or Foug-
    eret de Monbron?]   65 (2)
13. *Histoire philosophique. . .* [Raynal]   55 (2)
14. *Homme (de l'). . .* [Helvétius]   55 (2)
15. *Lettres chinoises. . .* [d'Argens]   54 (2)
16. *Christianisme (le) dévoilé. . .* [d'Holbach]   52 (3)
17. *Thérèse philosophe. . .* [d'Arles de Montigny? or
    d'Argens]   52 (1)
18. *Histoire de dom B. . . , portier des Chartreux. . .*
    [Gervaise de Latouche? or Nourry?]   52 (1)
19. *Académie (l') des dames. . .* [Nicolas]   52 (1)
20. *Contagion (la) sacrée. . .* [d'Holbach?]   51 (2)
21. *Lauriers (les) ecclésiastiques. . .* [Rochette de La
    Morlière]   50 (3)
22. *Œuvres posthumes de J.-J. Rousseau. . .*   50 (1)
23. *Cruauté (de la) religieuse.* [d'Holbach]   50 (1)
24. *Ecole (l') des filles. . .* [Milot]   50 (1)
25. *Questions sur l'Encyclopédie. . .* [Voltaire]   39 (7)
26. *L'Enfantement de Jupiter. . .* [Huerne de la Mothe] 33 (2)
27. *Histoire critique de Jésus-Christ. . .* [d'Holbach] 28 (3)

Manoury, Caen

Manoury made 17 orders, from October 1775 to February 1784. They included 65 illegal works, of which the following 18 were most in demand.

1. *An (l') 2440. . .* [Mercier]   151 (4)
2. *Tableau de Paris. . .* [Mercier]   150 (3)

217

3. *Requête au conseil du roi. . .* [Linguet]   149 (4)
4. *Observateur (l') anglais. . .* [Pidansat de Mairobert]   144 (8)
5. *Foutro-manie (la). . .* [Sénac de Meilhan? or Mercier de Compiègne?]   100 (1)
6. *Plaisirs (les) de tous les siècles et de tous les âges.* Anon.   100 (1)
7. *Gazette de Cythère. . .* [Bernard]   100 (1)
8. *Mémoires d'une reine infortunée. . .* [reine de Danemark?]   100 (1)
9. *Plus Secrets Mystères (les) . . . de la maçonnerie. . .* [Bérage, trans. by Koeppen]   92 (5)
10. *Lettre de Thrasibule à Leucippe. . .* [Fréret? or d'Holbach? or Naigeon?]   75 (3)
11. *Mémoires de Louis XV. . .* Anon.   75 (2)
12. *Histoire philosophique. . .* [Raynal]   70 (7)
13. *Mémoires secrets. . .* [Bauchaumont, et al.]   70 (6)
14. *Dictionnaire philosophique portatif. . .* [Voltaire]   50 (2)
15. *Bible (la) enfin expliquée. . .* [Voltaire]   37 (2)
16. *Anecdotes sur Mme la comtesse du Barry.* [Pidansat de Mairobert? or Théveneau de Morande?]   37 (2)
17. *Journal historique, ou fastes du règne de Louis XV. . .* [Lévy]   37 (2)
18. *Morale (la) universelle. . .* [d'Holbach]   31 (2)

Mauvelain, Troyes

Mauvelain made 26 orders, from January 1783 to March 1785. They included 137 illegal works, of which the following 16 were most in demand.

1. *Fastes (les) de Louis XV. . .* [Ange Goudar]   97 (12)
2. *Chronique (la) scandaleuse. . .* [Imbert de Bourdeaux]   52 (5)
3. *Papesse Jeanne (la). . .* [Borde?]   51 (6)
4. *Portefeuille (le) de madame Gourdan. . .* [Théveneau de Morande]   44 (5)
5. *Muses (les) du foyer de l'Opéra. . .* Anon.   40 (4)
6. *Entretiens (les) de l'autre monde. . .* Anon.   38 (4)
7. *Petit-fils (le) d'Hercule.* Anon.   38 (3)
8. *Théologie portative. . .* [d'Holbach]   36 (5)
9. *Observateur (l') anglais. . .* [Pidansat de Mairobert]   33 (8)
10. *Mémoires sur la Bastille. . .* [Linguet]   33 (7)
11. *Mémoires secrets. . .* [Bauchaumont, et al.]   32 (10)

12. *An (l') 2440. . .*[Mercier]   32 (5)
13. *Lettres de Julie à Eulalie. . .* Anon.   32 (3)
14. *Espion (l') dévalisé.* [Baudouin de Guémadeuc]   31 (9)
15. *Anecdotes du XVIIIe siècle.* [Imbert de Bourdeaux]   31 (4)
16. *Lettres (des) de cachet. . .* [comte de Mirabeau]   27 (6)

Mossy, Marseille

Mossy made 33 orders, from July 1773 to May 1784. They included 50 illegal works, of which the following 15 were most in demand.

1. *Tableau de Paris. . .* [Mercier]   118 (6)
2. *Histoire philosophique. . .* [Raynal]   100 (3)
3. *Plus Secrets Mystères (les) . . . de la maçonnerie. . .*
   [Bérage, trans. by Koeppen]   92 (4)
4. *Observateur (l') anglais. . .* [Pidansat de Mairobert]   50 (1)
5. *An (l') 2440. . .* [Mercier]   44 (3)
6. *Vérité (de la). . .* [Brissot de Warville]   38 (2)
7. *Mémoires pour servir à l'histoire de madame de Maintenon. . .* [La Beaumelle]   31 (2)
8. *Théorie des lois criminelles,* [Brissot de Warville]   31 (2)
9. *Journal historique . . . par M. de Maupeou. . .*
   [Pidansat de Mairobert and Moufle d'Angerville]   30 (6)
10. *Secrets (les) de l'ordre des francs-maçons dévoilés. . .*
    [Pérau]   27 (1)
11. *Essai philosophique sur le monachisme. . .* [Linguet]   26 (1)
12. *Législation (de la). . .* [Mably]   25 (2)
13. *Fille (la) naturelle.* [Restif de la Bretonne]   25 (2)
14. *Confidence philosophique.* [Vernes]   25 (1)
15. *Mémoires sur la Bastille. . .* [Linguet]   25 (1)

Pavie, La Rochelle

Pavie made 14 orders, from March 1772 to March 1784. They included 68 illegal works, of which the following 21 were most in demand.

1. *Anecdotes sur Mme la comtesse du Barry.* [Pidansat
   de Mairobert? or Théveneau de Morande?]   94 (9)
2. *Adoption (l') ou la maçonnerie des dames. . .* [Saint-
   Victor?]   69 (4)
3. *Histoire de la tourière des Carmélites. . .* [Meusnier
   de Querlon]   50 (1)
4. *Vie privée, ou apologie du . . . duc de Chartres*
   [Charles Théveneau de Morande]   50 (1)
5. *Catéchisme du citoyen. . .* [Saige]   48 (2)

 6. *Ami (l') des lois.* [Martin de Marivaux.] Paris,
    1775.   48 (2)
 7. *Putain (la) errante...* [Niccolò Franco?]   44 (4)
 8. *An (l') 2440...* [Mercier]   38 (2)
 9. *Essai sur le despotisme.* [comte de Mirabeau]   32 (2)
10. *Journal historique ... par M. de Maupeou...*
    [Pidansat de Mairobert and Moufle d'Angerville]   31 (2)
11. *Histoire de Mademoiselle Brion...* Anon.   30 (3)
12. *Mémoires de Louis XV...* Anon.   24 (2)
13. *Théologie portative...* [d'Holbach]   24 (1)
14. *Vénus dans le cloître, ou la religieuse en chemise.*
    [Barrin]   24 (1)
15. *Fille (la) de joie...* [trans. by Lambert? or Foug-
    eret de Monbron?]   20 (2)
16. *Monarque (le) accompli...* [Lanjuinais]   18 (2)
17. *Recueil de comédies et ... chansons gaillardes...*
    Anon.   18 (2)
18. *Lettre philosophique...* Anon.   16 (3)
19. *Système de la nature...* [d'Holbach]   16 (3)
20. *Militaire (le) philosophe...* [d'Holbach and
    Naigeon]   14 (2)
21. *Thérèse philosophe...* [d'Arles de Montigny? or
    d'Argens]   14 (2)

Rigaud, Pons, Montpellier

Rigaud, Pons made 64 orders, from April 1771 to July 1784. They
included 53 illegal works, of which the following 18 were most in
demand.

 1. *An (l') 2440...* [Mercier]   346 (16)
 2. *Lettre de M. Linguet à M. le comte de Vergennes...*
    [Linguet]   200 (2)
 3. *Correspondance secrète et familière de M. de
    Maupeou...* [Pidansat de Mairobert]   100 (1)
 4. *Questions sur l'Encyclopédie...* [Voltaire]   70 (4)
 5. *Lettre d'un théologien...* [Condorcet]   70 (3)
 6. *Anecdotes sur Mme la comtesse du Barry.* [Pidansat
    de Mairobert? or Théveneau de Morande?]   68 (2)
 7. *Dieu. Réponse au Système de la nature.* [Voltaire]   50 (1)
 8. *Requête au conseil du roi...* [Linguet]   48 (3)
 9. *Système de la nature...* [d'Holbach]   43 (3)

10. *Histoire philosophique*. . . [Raynal]   35 (4)
11. *Journal historique . . . par M. de Maupeou*. . .
    [Pidansat de Mairobert and Moufle d'Angerville]   25 (1)
12. *Recueil de pièces fugitives*. . . [Voltaire]   24 (2)
13. *Œuvres*. Rousseau   23 (5)
14. *Tableau de Paris*. . . [Mercier]   22 (3)
15. *Lettre philosophique*. . . Anon.   20 (1)
16. *Pièces échappées du portefeuille de M. de Voltaire*. . .
    Anon.   20 (1)
17. *Philosophie (de la) de la nature*. [Delisle de Sales]   17 (3)
18. *Plus Secrets Mystères (les)* . . . *de la maçonnerie*. . .
    [Bérage, trans. by Koeppen]   16 (4)

Robert et Gauthier, Bourg-en-Bresse

Robert et Gauthier made 17 orders, from October 1772 to November 1783. They included 77 illegal works, of which the following 16 were most in demand.

1. *Dissertation sur l'établissement de l'abbaye de St.
   Claude*. . . [Christin]   100 (1)
2. *Vie privée de Louis XV*. . . [Moufle d'Angerville?
   or Laffrey?]   50 (1)
3. *Fastes (les) de Louis XV*. . . [Ange Goudar]   39 (1)
4. *An (l') 2440*. . . [Mercier]   37 (4)
5. *Œuvres*. Rousseau   36 (5)
6. *Histoire de dom B*. . . , *portier des Chartreux*. . .
   [Gervaise de Latouche? or Nourry?]   36 (3)
7. *Tableau de Paris*. . . [Mercier]   28 (3)
8. *Anecdotes sur Mme la comtesse du Barry*. [Pidansat
   de Mairobert? or Théveneau de Morande?]   27 (2)
9. *Système de la nature*. . . [d'Holbach]   24 (2)
10. *Chandelle (la) d'Arras*. . . [Du Laurens]   24 (2)
11. *Lauriers (les) ecclésiastiques*. . . [Rochette de La
    Morlière]   22 (3)
12. *Académie (l') des dames*. . . [Nicolas]   20 (3)
13. *Epîtres, satires, contes, odes et pièces fugitives*. . . [Vol-
    taire]   18 (1)
14. *Fille (la) naturelle*. [Restif de la Bretonne]   18 (1)
15. *Militaire (le) philosophe*. . . [d'Holbach and
    Naigeon]   14 (2)
16. *Histoire philosophique*. . . [Raynal]   14 (2)

Lorraine

These statistics were compiled from the orders of the following booksellers: Babin, Bonthoux, Dalancourt, Henry, and Matthieu of Nancy; Audéart, Augé, Bergue, Bertrand, and Orbelin of Thionville; Bernard, Chénoux, Gay, L'Entretien, and Sandré of Lunéville; Carez of Toul; Gerlache of Metz; and Choppin of Bar-le-Duc.

1. *An (l') 2440...* [Mercier]	282	(31)
2. *Système de la nature...* [d'Holbach]	167	(33)
3. *Questions sur l'Encyclopédie...* [Voltaire]	154	(28)
4. *Lettre philosophique...* Anon.	78	(13)
Examen important de Milord Bolingbroke... [Voltaire]	78	(8)
5. *Thérèse philosophe...* [d'Arles de Montigny? or d'Argens]	70	(6)*
6. *Catéchumène (le)...* [Borde]	64	(8)
7. *Recherches philosophiques sur les Américains...* [de Pauw]	62	(6)†
Questions (les) de Zapata... [Voltaire]	62	(8)
8. *Histoire philosophique...* [Raynal]	57	(15)
9. *Histoire critique de Jésus-Christ...* [d'Holbach]	48	(13)
10. *Lauriers (les) ecclésiastiques...* [Rochette de La Morlière]	45	(5)
11. *Contes et nouvelles ... de M. de la Fontaine.* La Fontaine	42	(10)
12. *Œuvres.* Rousseau	41	(14)
13. *Œuvres.* Helvétius	40	(9)
Homme (de l')... [Helvétius]	40	(6)
14. *Gazetier (le) cuirassé...* [Théveneau de Morande]	39	(6)
Journal historique ... par M. de Maupeou... [Pidansat de Mairobert and Moufle d'Angerville]	39	(5)
Pucelle d'Orléans... [Voltaire]	39	(3)
15. *Système social...* [d'Holbach]	37	(10)
16. *Epîtres, satires, contes, odes et pièces fugitives...* [Voltaire]	36	(7)
Plus Secrets Mystères ... de la maçonnerie... [trans. by Bérage?, ed. by Koeppen]	36	(7)
Fille de joie... [trans. by Lambert? or Fougeret de Monbron?]	36	(5)

*Includes order of 50 (1) by Bergue.
†Includes order of 50 (1) by Chénoux.

Taureau blanc. . . [Voltaire]	36 (4)
17. *Putain (la) errante*. . . [Niccolò Franco?]	34 (7)
18. *Arrétin (l')*. [Du Laurens]	33 (5)

Lyon

These statistics were compiled from the orders of the following booksellers: Baritel, Barret, Cellier, Flandin, and Jacquenod.

1. *Système de la nature*. . . [d'Holbach]	69 (5)[1]
2. *An (l') 2440*. . . [Mercier]	53 (4)
3. *Epîtres, satires, contes, odes et pièces fugitives*. . . [Voltaire]	50 (2)
4. *Essai sur le despotisme*. [comte de Mirabeau]	31 (2)[2]
5. *Supplément au Roman comique*. . . [Monnet]	25 (1)*
6. *Esprit (de l')*. [Helvétius]	24 (1)*
7. *Œuvres*. La Mettrie	17 (2)
8. *A.B.C. (l'), dialogue curieux*. . . [Voltaire]	18 (2)
9. *Recueil de comédies et . . . chansons gaillardes*. . . Anon.	16 (2)
10. *Anecdotes sur Mme la comtesse du Barry*. [Pidansat de Mairobert? or Théveneau de Morande?]	12 (1)*
Arrétin (l'). [Du Laurens]	12 (1)*
Christianisme (le) dévoilé. . . [d'Holbach]	12 (1)*
Contagion sacrée. . . [d'Holbach]	12 (1)*
Histoire des diables modernes par M. A***. Anon.	12 (1)*
Recherches philosophiques sur les Américains. . . [de Pauw]	12 (1)*
Requête au conseil du roi. . . Linguet.	12 (1)*
Recueil des romans. . . [Voltaire]	12 (1)*
11. *Fille de joie*. . . [trans. by Lambert? or Fougeret de Monbron?]	8 (2)
Système social. . . [d'Holbach]	8 (2)

*Represents only one order.
[1] Includes orders by Barret of 61 (3).
[2] Includes order by Flandin of 30 (1).

Paris

These statistics were compiled from the orders of the following booksellers: Barré, Barrois, Cugnet, Desauges, Lequay Morin, Prévost, and Védrène.

1. *Tableau de Paris*. . . [Mercier]   163 (3)[1]
2. *Chrétien (un) contre six juifs*. [Voltaire]   128 (3)[2]
3. *Anecdotes sur Mme la comtesse du Barry*. [Pidansat
   de Mairobert? or Théveneau de Morande?]   114 (6)[3]
4. *Mémoires authentiques de Mme la comtesse du
   Barry*. . . Anon.   50 (1)*
5. *An (l') 2440*. . . [Mercier]   43 (5)
6. *Parnasse libertin*. . . Anon.   33 (4)
7. *Ecole des filles*. . . [Milot]   30 (3)
8. *Vrais Principes (les) du gouvernement français*. . .
   Gin   28 (2)[4]
9. *Belle Allemande (la)*. . . [Villaret? or Bret?]   27 (4)
   Traité des délits et des peines. . . (Beccaria, trans.
   by Morellet)   27 (4)
10. *Monialisme (le)*. . . Anon.   26 (5)
    *Vie (la) voluptueuse entre les Capucins et les non-
    nes*. . . Anon.   26 (3)
11. *Apologie de la Bastille*. . . [Servan]   25 (1)†
    Bon-Sens (le). . . [d'Holbach]   25 (1)†
    Gazetier (le) cuirassé. . . [Théveneau de Morande]   25 (1)†
    *Mémoires pour servir à l'histoire de madame de
    Maintenon*. . . [Angliviel de La Beaumelle]   25 (1)†
    Mémoires secrets [Petit de Bachaumont, and
    others]   25 (1)†
12. *Système de la nature*. . . [d'Holbach]   23 (4)
13. *Fille de joie*. . . [trans. by Lambert? or Fougeret
    de Monbron?]   22 (3)
    Vénus dans le cloître. . . [Barrin]   22 (3)
14. *Recueil de comédies et . . . chansons gaillardes*. . .
    Anon.   21 (3)
15. *Putain (la) errante*. . . [Niccolò Franco?]   20 (3)
16. *Œuvres*. Rousseau   19 (4)
17. *Devoirs (les), statuts ou règlements généraux des F∴
    M∴* . . . Anon.   18 (2)
    *Examen critique des apologistes de la religion chrét-
    ienne*. . . [Lévesque de Burigny?]   18 (4)

*Represents only one order by Védrène.
†Represents only one order by Desauges.
[1] Includes orders of 150 (2) by Desauges.
[2] Includes orders of 125 (2) by Lequay Morin.
[3] Includes orders of 100 (2) by Desauges.
[4] Includes order of 25 (1) by Barré.

18.	*Histoire philosophique.* . . [Raynal]	17 (3)
19.	*Lettres de Mme la marquise de Pompadour.* . . [Barbé-Marbois? or Crébillon, fils?]	15 (4)
	Traité des trois imposteurs. [Vroes?]	15 (3)
	Vie privée de Louis XV. . . [Moufle d'Angerville? or Laffrey?]	15 (2)
20.	*Lyre (la) gaillarde.* . . Anon.	14 (2)
	Observateur anglais. . . [Pidansat de Mairobert]	14 (2)
	Œuvres. Crébillon fils	14 (2)

Colporteurs (Peddlers)

These statistics were compiled from the orders of Blaisot, Gilles, Planquais, and an unnamed peddler ("Troisième") who placed his order through Malherbe of Loudun.

1.	*Mémoires de Louis XV.* . . Anon.	200 (1)*
2.	*Système de la nature.* . . [d'Holbach]	131 (7)[1]
3.	*Thérèse philosophe.* . . [d'Arles de Montigny? or d'Argens]	130 (5)[2]
4.	*Pucelle d'Orléans.* . . [Voltaire]	120 (6)[3]
5.	*Système social.* . . [d'Holbach]	112 (4)[3]
6.	*Fille de joie.* . . [trans. by Lambert? or Fougeret de Monbron?]	82 (5)[4]
7.	*Lettre philosophique.* . . Anon.	60 (4)[4]
8.	*Bon-Sens (le).* . . [d'Holbach]	52 (1)*
9.	*Compère Mathieu.* . . [Du Laurens]	51 (2)*
10.	*Journal historique* . . . *par M. de Maupeou.* . . [Pidansat de Mairobert and Moufle d'Angerville]	50 (2)*
11.	*An (l') 2440.* . . [Mercier]	40 (5)
12.	*Evangile du jour.* . . [Voltaire]	39 (3)*
13.	*Correspondance secrète et familière de M. de Maupeou.* . . [Pidansat de Mairobert]	37 (2)*
14.	*Académie des dames.* . . [Nicolas]	35 (3)
15.	*Parnasse libertin.* . . Anon.	32 (2)[5]
16.	*Bonheur (le).* . . Helvétius	31 (2)[6]

*Indicates orders made only by Gilles.
[1] Includes orders of 106 (3) by Gilles.
[2] Includes orders of 104 (2) by Gilles.
[3] Includes orders of 102 (2) by Gilles.
[4] Includes orders of 54 (2) by Gilles.
[5] Includes order of 26 (1) by Gilles.
[6] Includes order of 25 (1) by Gilles.

Homme (de l'). . . [Helvétius]	31	(2)[6]
17. *Œuvres*. Helvétius	30	(2)*
Politique naturelle. . . [d'Holbach?]	30	(2)*
18. *Histoire de dom B . . . , portier des Chartreux*. . . [Gervaise de Latouche? or Nourry?]	29	(2)*
19. *Anecdotes sur Mme la comtesse du Barry*. [Pidansat de Mairobert? or Théveneau de Morande?]	25	(1)*
Christianisme (le) dévoilé. . . [d'Holbach]	25	(1)*
Essai sur le despotisme. [comte de Mirabeau]	25	(1)*
Recherches philosophiques sur les Egyptiens et les Chinois [de Pauw]	25	(1)*
20. *Questions sur l'Encyclopédie*. . . [Voltaire]	22	(4)
21. *Questions (les) de Zapata*. . . [Voltaire]	20	(4)
22. *Œuvres*. Rousseau	19	(4)
23. *Colimaçons du Révérend Père l'Escarbotier*. . . [Voltaire]	18	(3)
Gazetier (le) cuirassé. . . [Théveneau de Morande]	18	(2)*
Mémoires de Mme la marquise de Pompadour. . . Anon.	18	(3)
Théologie portative. . . [d'Holbach]	18	(4)
24. *Militaire (le) philosophe*. . . [d'Holbach and Naigeon]	17	(4)

MINOR DEALERS

These statistics were compiled from the orders of the following booksellers: Boisserand of Roanne, Billault of Tours, Bonnard of Auxerre, Cazin of Reims, Chevrier of Poitiers, Fontaine of Colmar, Habert of Bar-sur-Aube, Jarfaut of Melun, Lair of Blois, Laisney of Beauvais, Malassis of Nantes, Petit of Reims, Resplandy of Toulouse, Sens of Toulouse, Sombert of Châlons-sur-Marne, Waroquier of Soissons, and Caldesaigues of Marseille.

1. *Essai philosophique sur le monachisme*. . . [Linguet]	128	(7)
2. *Anecdotes sur Mme la comtesse du Barry*. [Pidansat de Mairobert? or Théveneau de Morande?]	125	(10)
3. *Histoire philosophique*. . . [Raynal]	110	(19)
4. *Mémoires de l'abbé Terray*. . . [Coquereau]	107	(10)
5. *Œuvres*. Rousseau	102	(17)
6. *Commentaire historique sur les oeuvres de l'auteur de la Henriade*. . . [Voltaire]	93	(8)
7. *Questions sur l'Encyclopédie*. . . [Voltaire]	88	(9)
Arrétin (l'). [Du Laurens]	88	(4)

8. *Monarque (le) accompli.* . . [Lanjuinais]	86	(5)
9. *Putain (la) errante.* . . [Niccolò Franco?]	82	(9)
10. *Tableau de Paris.* . . [Mercier]	77	(7)
11. *Homme (de l').* . . [Helvétius]	69	(6)
12. *Système de la nature.* . . [d'Holbach]	68	(16)
13. *Pucelle d'Orléans.* . . [Voltaire]	67	(13)
14. *Fille de joie.* . . [trans. by Lambert? or Fougeret de Monbron?]	66	(6)
Requête au conseil du roi. . . Linguet.	66	(4)
15. *Lettre philosophique.* . . Anon.	59	(4)
16. *An (l') 2440.* . . [Mercier]	58	(16)
17. *Mémoires sur la Bastille.* . . Linguet	54	(4)
18. *Vénus dans le cloître.* . . [Barrin]	52	(6)
19. *Mémoires authentiques de Mme la comtesse du Barry.* . . Anon.	51	(3)
20. *Recherches philosophiques sur les Américains.* . . [de Pauw]	49	(10)
21. *Journal historique . . . par M. de Maupeou.* . . [Pidansat de Mairobert and Moufle d'Angerville]	46	(11)
22. *Traité des trois imposteurs.* [Vroes?]	45	(7)
Lyre (la) gaillarde. . . Anon.	45	(4)
23. *Bible enfin expliquée.* . . [Voltaire]	42	(4)
24. *Belle (la) Allemande.* . . [Villaret? or Bret?]	41	(5)
Recueil de comédies et . . . chansons gaillardes. . . Anon.	41	(4)
25. *Christianisme (le) dévoilé.* . . [d'Holbach]	39	(6)
Monialisme (le). . . Anon.	39	(5)

MAJOR DEALERS

These statistics represent totals combined from the orders of the twelve major dealers whose individual businesses are described above.

1. *An (l') 2440.* . . [Mercier]	1,336	(108)
2. *Anecdotes sur Mme la comtesse du Barry.* [Pidansat de Mairobert? or Théveneau de Morande?]	946	(42)
3. *Système de la nature.* . . [d'Holbach]	700	(80)
4. *Tableau de Paris.* . . [Mercier]	612	(33)
5. *Journal historique . . . par M. de Maupeou.* . . [Pidansat de Mairobert and Moufle d'Angerville]	515	(35)
6. *Histoire philosophique.* . . [Raynal]	510	(70)
7. *Lettre philosophique.* . . Anon.	437	(34)

8. *Arrétin (l').* [Du Laurens]   424 (25)
9. *Mémoires de Louis XV.* . . Anon.   419 (14)
10. *Observateur anglais.* . . [Pidansat de Mairobert]   388 (35)
11. *Mémoires de l'abbé Terray.* . . [Coquereau]   370 (14)
12. *Pucelle d'Orléans.* . . [Voltaire]   369 (26)
13. *Questions sur l'Encyclopédie.* . . [Voltaire]   338 (54)
14. *Thérèse philosophe.* . . [d'Arles de Montigny? or
    d'Argens]   331 (22)
15. *Histoire critique de Jésus-Christ.* . . [d'Holbach]   324 (34)
16. *Fille de joie.* . . [trans. by Lambert? or Fougeret de
    Monbron?]   306 (24)
    Recueil de comédies et . . . *chansons gaillardes.* . .
    Anon.   306 (23)
17. *Plus Secrets Mystères* . . . *de la maçonnerie.* . . [trans.
    by Bérage?, ed. by Koeppen]   290 (29)
18. *Requête au conseil du roi.* . . Linguet.   252 (13)
19. *Paysan perverti.* . . Restif de la Bretonne   233 (18)
20. *Christianisme (le) dévoilé.* . . [d'Holbach]   220 (25)
21. *Lettre de M. Linguet à M. le comte de Vergennes.* . .
    Linguet   216 (4)
22. *Essai philosophique sur le monachisme.* . . [Linguet]   207 (12)
23. *Vie privée de Louis XV.* . . [Moufle d'Angerville?
    or Laffrey?]   194 (16)
    Bon-Sens (le). . . [d'Holbach]   194 (11)
24. *Système social.* . . [d'Holbach]   193 (26)
25. *Dictionnaire philosophique portatif.* . . [Voltaire]   185 (20)
    Ecole des filles. . . [Milot]   185 (13)

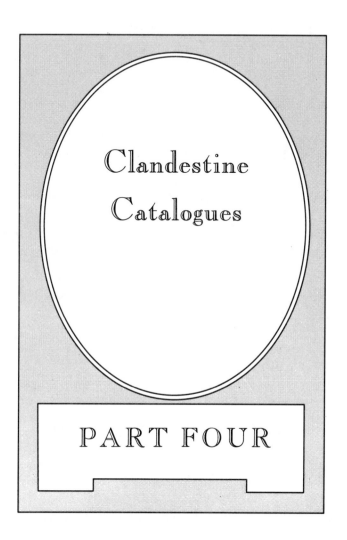

Clandestine
Catalogues

PART FOUR

Publishers in Geneva, Lausanne, and Bern

PUBLISHERS WHO DEALT extensively in forbidden books often issued special catalogues, which contained nothing but highly illegal works and circulated under the cloak like the books themselves. They might be printed or handwritten, relatively short or quite long, but they never contained any compromising information, such as the name of the publisher. Entitled *Livres philosophiques* or sometimes only *Note séparée,* the catalogues were used by publishers' sales representatives when they made the rounds of bookshops and by booksellers when they sent orders to their suppliers. Allied publishers also sent them to one another through the mail, so that they could refer to them when arranging exchanges. I have found five of them in the papers of the STN and one in the Bibliothèque Nationale of Paris. They were issued by the following Swiss publishers:

Gabriel Grasset, Geneva (letter to STN of April 25, 1774): 73 titles.

Gabriel Décombaz, Lausanne (letter to STN of January 8, 1776): 96 titles.

Jean-Samuel Cailler, Geneva (letter to STN of April 30, 1777); 26 titles.

Jean-Abram Nouffer, Geneva (letter to STN of February 4, 1778): 12 titles.

231

J.-L. Chappuis et J.-E. Didier, Geneva (letter to STN of November 1, 1780): 28 titles.

Société typographique de Berne, 1772 (Bibliothèque Nationale, ms. fr. 22101, folios 242–249): 170 titles.

The following calculations, drawn from these six catalogues, indicate the incidence of forbidden books in the stock of publishing houses other than the STN.

Distribution of Titles in Clandestine Catalogues

(GENEVA, LAUSANNE, AND BERN)

Five works appear in *five* of the catalogues:

Examen important de Milord Bolingbroke . . . [Voltaire]
  Grasset, Décombaz, Cailler, Chappuis et Didier, Bern
Histoire de dom B . . . [Gervaise de Latouche? or Nourry?]
  Grasset, Décombaz, Nouffer, Chappuis et Didier, Bern
Lettre philosophique . . . Anon.
  Grasset, Décombaz, Cailler, Nouffer, Chappuis et Didier
Pucelle (la) d'Orléans, poème héroï-comique. [Voltaire]
  Décombaz, Cailler, Nouffer, Chappuis et Didier, Bern
Théologie portative . . . [d'Holbach]
  Grasset, Décombaz, Cailler, Chappuis et Didier, Bern

Eight works appear in *four* of the catalogues:

Arrétin (l'). [Du Laurens]
  Grasset, Décombaz, Chappuis et Didier, Bern
Chandelle (la) d'Arras . . . [Du Laurens]
  Décombaz, Cailler, Chappuis et Didier, Bern
Fille (la) de joie . . . [Lambert? or Fougeret de Monbron?]
  Grasset, Décombaz, Cailler, Bern
Histoire critique de Jésus-Christ . . . [d'Holbach]
  Grasset, Décombaz, Chappuis et Didier, Bern
Homme (l') aux quarante écus. [Voltaire]
  Grasset, Décombaz, Cailler, Bern
Relation du bannissement des jésuites de la Chine . . . [Voltaire]
  Grasset, Décombaz, Cailler, Bern

Système de la nature . . . [d'Holbach]
   Grasset, Décombaz, Chappuis et Didier, Bern

Twenty-two works appear in *three* of the catalogues:

Académie (l') des dames . . . [Chorier]
   Décombaz, Chappuis et Didier, Bern
An (l') deux mille quatre cent quarante . . . [Mercier]
   Grasset, Décombaz, Bern
Christianisme (le) dévoilé . . . [d'Holbach]
   Grasset, Décombaz, Bern
Compère (le) Mathieu . . . [Du Laurens]
   Grasset, Décombaz, Bern
David, ou l'histoire de l'homme selon le coeur de Dieu . . .
[d'Holbach]
   Décombaz, Chappuis et Didier, Bern
Dictionnaire philosophique portatif. [Voltaire]
   Grasset, Décombaz, Bern
Droits (les) des hommes et les usurpations des autres . . . [Voltaire]
   Grasset, Décombaz, Bern
Espion (l') chinois . . . [Goudar]
   Grasset, Décombaz, Bern
Examen critique des apologistes . . . [Lévesque de Burigny?]
   Grasset, Décombaz, Bern
Ingénu (l'), histoire véritable . . . [Voltaire]
   Grasset, Cailler, Bern
Jésuites (les) de la maison professe de Paris en belle humeur . . .
   Grasset, Décombaz, Bern
Militaire (le) philosophe . . . [d'Holbach and Naigeon]
   Grasset, Décombaz, Bern
Philosophie (la) de l'histoire . . . [Voltaire]
   Grasset, Décombaz, Bern
Philosophe (le) ignorant. [Voltaire]
   Grasset, Décombaz, Bern
Profession (la) de foi des théistes . . . [Voltaire]
   Grasset, Décombaz, Bern
Questions sur l'Encyclopédie . . . [Voltaire]
   Grasset, Décombaz, Bern
Recherches sur l'origine du despotisme oriental . . . [Boulanger?,
ed. d'Holbach]

Grasset, Décombaz, Bern
Système social . . . [d'Holbach]
Grasset, Décombaz, Bern
Thérèse philosophe . . . [d'Arles de Montigny? or d'Argens?]
Grasset, Décombaz, Bern
Traité des trois imposteurs. [Vroes?]
Grasset, Chappuis et Didier, Bern
Traité sur la tolérance. [Voltaire]
Grasset, Décombaz, Bern
Vénus dans le cloître . . . [Barrin]
Cailler, Chappuis et Didier, Bern

Fifty-six works appear in *two* of the catalogues, and the rest—176 works—appear in only *one* of the catalogues.

A Clandestine
Catalogue of
the STN

THE STN DREW UP several clandestine catalogues of its own, which can be found in its papers in a dossier labeled "Société typographique de Neuchâtel." The following, a handwritten list entitled *Livres Philosophiques,* is the most extensive of them. It includes 110 titles, of which the first 81 appear in rough alphabetical order, no doubt because they composed the STN's stock at some point in 1775, when one of its clerks drew up the list. The other 29 works probably were added in the order of their arrival in Neuchâtel as the STN procured new books by means of exchanges with other publishers. The titles are given as they appear in the manuscript, followed by a correct version, based on standard bibliographical sources, in brackets.

Livres Philosophiques

Analyse de Bayle 12°. 8 Vol.
   [*Analyse raisonnée de Bayle, ou abrégé méthodique de ses ouvrages, particulièrement de son Dictionnaire historique et critique dont les remarques ont été fondues dans le texte pour former un corps agréable et instructif de lectures suivies.* 8 vols. [François-Marie de Marsy (vols. 1–4) and Jean-Baptiste-René Robinet (vols. 5–8).] London, 1755–70.]
Le Colporteur, histoire morale par Monsr. de Chevrier.

[*Colporteur (le), histoire morale et critique, par M. de Chevrier.* François-Antoine Chevrier. London, "L'An de la vérité" (c. 1761, according to Cioranescu).]

L'An 2440. Rêve S'il en fut jamais.

[*An (l') deux mille quatre cent quarante, rêve s'il en fût jamais.* [Louis-Sébastien Mercier.] Amsterdam, 1771 (actually 1770, according to Martin-Mylne-Frautschi).]

Angola, histoire Indienne.

[*Angola, histoire indienne, ouvrage sans vraisemblance.* 2 vols. [Charles-Jacques-Louis-Auguste Rochette de La Morlière?] Agra, 1746.]

L'Arétin Moderne. 12°. 2 Vol.

[*Arrétin (l').* 2 vols. [Henri-Joseph Du Laurens.] Rome, 1763. Later editions also published under the titles *L'Arétin, ou la débauche de l'esprit en fait de bon sens* and *L'Arrétin moderne.*]

La Belle Allemande, ou les galanteries de Thérèse. 1774.

[*Belle (la) Allemande, ou les galanteries de Thérèse.* [Claude Villaret?, or Antoine Bret?] Amsterdam, 1745. Also as *Les Galanteries de Thérèse.*]

Le Bon Sens, ou idées naturelles, opposées aux Idées surnaturelles.

[*Bon-Sens (le), ou idées naturelles opposées aux idées surnaturelles.* [Paul-Henri-Dietrich Thiry, baron d'Holbach.] London, 1772.]

Brunus Redivius, ou traitté des Erreurs populaires. 3 parties. 12°.

[*Brunus redivivus, ou traité des erreurs populaires, ouvrage critique, historique, et philosophique imité de Pompance.* n.p., n.d. (Also reprinted in *Pièces philosophiques.*)]

La Chandelle d'Aras, poème héroïcomique. 12°. 1774.

[*Chandelle (la) d'Arras, poème héroï-comique en XVIII chants.* [Henri-Joseph Du Laurens.] Berne, 1765. Also as *Etrennes aux gens d'église ou la Chandelle. . .*]

Le Christianisme dévoilé. 12°. 1774.

[*Christianisme (le) dévoilé, ou examen des principes et des effets de la religion chrétienne, par feu M. Boulanger.* [Paul-Henri-Dietrich Thiry, baron d'Holbach.] London, 1756.]

Commentaire sur le Livre des Délits & des peines.

[*Commentaire sur le livre "Des Délits et des peines," par un avocat de province.* [François-Marie Arouet de Voltaire.] n.p., 1766.]

Les Confidences réciproques. 12°. 1774.

[*Confidences (les) réciproques, ou anecdotes de la société de la comtesse de B . . .* 3 vols. [Anne-Claude Philippe de Tubières de Grimoard de Pestels de Lévy, comte de Caylus?] London, 1774.]

Contract Social par Jean Jaqˢ. Rousseau. 12°.

[*Contrat (du) social, ou principes du droit politique.* Jean-Jacques Rousseau. Amsterdam, 1762.]

Correspondance Secrette & les Oeufs Rouges. 12°.

[*Correspondance secrète et familière de M. de Maupeou avec M. de Sor***, conseiller du nouveau parlement.* 3 vols. [Matthieu-François-Pidansat de Mairobert.] n.p., 1771. Also as *Maupeouana, ou correspondance. . .*]

[*Oeufs rouges. Première partie. Sorhouet mourant à M. de Maupeou, chancelier de France.* [J.-M. Augéard?, or Matthieu-François Pidansat de Mairobert?] n.p., 1772].

Le Cousin de Mahomet. 12°. 2 Vol. fig.

[*Cousin (le) de Mahomet, et la folie salutaire, histoire plus que galante.* 2 vols. [Nicolas Fromaget.] Leyden, 1742.]

David, ou histoire de lhomme selon le Coeur de Dieu.

[*David, ou l'histoire de l'homme selon le coeur de Dieu. Ouvrage traduit de l'anglois.* [trans. by Paul-Henri-Dietrich Thiry, baron d'Holbach.] (trans. from *The History of the Man after God's own Heart* [1756] by Peter Annet?) London, 1768.]

Dieu & les hommes, oeuvre théologique, mais raisonnable. 8°.

[*Dieu et les hommes. Oeuvre théologique, mais raisonnable, par le Dr Obern. Traduit par Jacques Aimon.* [François-Marie Arouet de Voltaire.] Berlin, 1769.]

Le Diner au Comte de Boulainvilliers. 12°.

[*Dîner (le) du comte de Boulainvilliers, par M. St.-Hiacinte* (sic). [François-Marie Arouet de Voltaire.] n.p., 1728 (actually 1767, according to Bengesco and Cioranescu).]

Discours de l'Empereur Julien contre les Chrétiens. 12°.

[*Discours de l'empereur Julien contre les chrétiens, traduit par M. le marquis d'Argens. Avec de nouvelles notes de divers auteurs.* [ed. by François-Marie Arouet de Voltaire.] Berlin, 1708 (actually 1769, according to Cioranescu).]

——— sur l'Etat actuel de la Polit. & de la Science Milit. en Europe. 12°.

[*Discours sur l'état actuel de la politique et de la science militaire en Europe avec le plan d'un ouvrage intitulé "la France politique et militaire."* [Jacques-Antoine, Hippolyte de Guilbert.] Geneva, 1773.]

Doutes sur la Réligion par Boulainvilliers. 12°.

[*Doutes sur la religion, suivis de l'Analyse du traité théologi-politique de Spinosa.* [*Doutes* by Henri, comte de Boulainvilliers?; *Analyse* by Gayot de Pitaval.] London, 1767.]

Les Egaremens de Julie. 12°.

[*Egarements (les) de Julie.* [Jacques-Antoine-René Perrin?, or Claude-Joseph Dorat?] London and Paris, 1755.]

L'Espion Chinois. 12°. 6 Vol.

[*Espion (l') chinois, ou l'envoyé secret de la cour de Pékin pour examiner l'état présent de l'Europe, traduit du chinois.* 6 vols. [Ange Goudar.] Cologne, 1764.]

De L'Esprit par Helvétius. 12°. 2 Vol.

[*Esprit (de l').* [Claude-Adrien Helvétius.] Paris, 1758.]

Esprit du Judaïsme. 12°. 1770.

[*Esprit (l') du judaïsme, ou examen raisonné de la loi de Moyse et de son influence sur la religion chrétienne.* [trans. by Paul-Henri-Dietrich Thiry, baron d'Holbach.] London, 1770. (trans. from *A Discourse of the Grounds and Reasons of the Christian Religion* [1724] by Anthony Collins.)]

Essai sur le mérite & Sur la vertu par Schafftsbury. 8°.

[*Principes de la philosophie morale, ou essai de M.S*** sur le mérite et la vertu, avec des réflexions.* [trans. by Denis Diderot.] (trans. from *An Inquiry Concerning Virtue, or Merit* [1711] by Anthony Ashley Cooper, 3rd Earl of Shaftesbury.) Amsterdam, 1745.]

Evangile de la Raison.

[*Evangile (l') de la raison. Ouvrage posthume de M. D. M . . . Y.* [ed. by François-Marie Arouet de Voltaire.] n.p., n.d. (1764, according to Cioranescu and Bengesco).]

Examen Critique de St. Paul par Boulanger. 12°.

[*Examen critique de la vie et des ouvrages de Saint Paul. Avec un dissertation sur Saint Pierre, par feu M. Boulanger.* [trans. by Paul-Henri-Dietrich Thiry, baron d'Holbach.] (trans. from *The History and Character of St. Paul Examined* [1742?] by Peter Annet.) London, 1770.]

———— Impartial des principales religions du Monde. 8°.

[*Examen impartial des principales religions du monde.* Paris, n.d. (Condemned by Parlement of Paris in 1770, according to Peignot.)]

———— Important de Milord Bolingbrocke. 8°.

[*Examen important de Milord Bolingbroke, écrit sur la fin de 1736.* [François-Marie Arouet de Voltaire.] n.p., 1767 (First appeared in *Recueil nécessaire*, 1765, according to Cioranescu and Bengesco.)]

Fausseté des Miracles.

[*Fausseté (la) des miracles des deux testamens, prouvée par le parallèle avec de semblables prodiges opérés dans diverses sectes, ouvrage traduit du manuscrit latin intitulé "Theophrastus redivivus."* London, 1775.]

La Fille de Joye. 8°. fig.

[*Fille (la) de joye, ouvrage quintessencié de l'anglois de John Cleland.* "Lampsaque," 1751. [trans. by Lambert? or Charles-Louis Fougeret de Monbron?] (trans. from *Memoirs of a Woman of Pleasure,* 1748–49, by John Cleland.)]

Fragmens des instructions au Prince de Prusse.

Fragment des instructions pour le prince royal de ***. [François-Marie Arouet de Voltaire.] Berlin, 1766.

Guerre civile de Genêve. Poëme héroïque.

[*Guerre (la) civile de Genève, ou les amours de Robert Covelle. Poème héroïque avec des notes instructives.* [François-Marie Arouet de Voltaire.] Geneva, 1768.]

Histoire de Mlle Cronel, ditte Frekillon. 4 parties.

[*Histoire de la vie et moeurs de Mademoiselle Cronel, dite Frétillon, écrite par elle-même, actrice de la comédie de Rouen.* [Pierre-Alexandre Gaillard, dit de la Bataille?, or Anne-Claude-Philippe de Tubières de Grimoard de Pestels de Lévy, comte de Caylus?] The Hague, 1739.]

———— de La vie de l'Aretin. fig.

[*Putain (la) errante, ou dialogue de Madeleine et de Julie, par P. Arétin, fidèlement traduit en français par N.* "Lampsaque," 1760. (trans. from *La Puttane errante* [1540] by Niccolò Franco?.) Also as *Le Cabinet d'amour et de Vénus* and as *Histoire et vie de l'Arétin ou entretiens de Magdelon et de Julie.*]

———— Critique de J: Ch: 8°.

[*Histoire critique de Jésus-Christ, ou, analyse raisonnée des Evangiles.* [Paul-Henri-Dietrich Thiry, baron d'Holbach.] n.p., n.d. (1770, according to Vercruysse)]

———— Philosoph. & Polit. des Etablissemens des Européens. 12°. avec Cartes fig. 7 Vol.

[*Histoire philosophique et politique des établissements et du commerce des Européens dans les deux Indes.* 6 vols. [Guillaume-Thomas-François Raynal.] Amsterdam, 1770.]

L'homme aux 40 Ecus.

[*Homme (l') aux quarante écus.* [François-Marie Arouet de Voltaire.] n.p., 1768.]

De L'homme de ses facultes &c. p Helvétius. 2 Vol. 12°. 1775.

[*Homme (de l'), de ses facultés intellectuelles et de son éducation. Ouvrage posthume de M. Helvétius.* 2 vols. [Claude-Adrien Helvétius.] London, 1773.

Journal historique des révolutions opérées en France p M. Maupeou. 3 Vol. 8°.

[*Journal historique de la révolution opérée dans la constitution de la monarchie française par M. de Maupeou, chancelier de France.* 7 vols. [Matthieu-François Pidansat de Mairobert and Barthélemy-François-Joseph Moufle d'Angerville.] London, 1774–76.]

Lettres sur les Aveugles, les Sourds, & les muets par Diderot. 12° fig.

[*Lettre sur les aveugles à l'usage de ceux qui voyent.* [Denis Diderot.] London, 1749.]

[*Lettre sur les sourds et muets, à l'usage de ceux qui entendent et qui parlent, adressée à M***.* [Denis Diderot.] n.p., 1751.]

———— Cherakiessiennes par J: J: Rufus Sauvage Européen.

[*Lettres iroquoises.* 2 vols. [Jean-Henri Maubert de Gouvest.] "Irocopolis," 1752. Also as *Lettres cherakéesiennes, mises en français, de la traduction italienne. Par J.-J. Rufus, sauvage européen.* This collections contains 37 of the 43 "lettres."]

———— a Eugenie contre les préjugés. 12°. 2 Vol.

[*Lettres à Eugénie, ou préservatif contre les préjugés.* [Paul-Henri-Dietrich Thiry, baron d'Holbach.] 2 vols. London, 1768.]

———— Philosophiques de Voltaire.

[*Lettres philosophiques par M. de V. . . .* [François-Marie Arouet de Voltaire.] Amsterdam, 1734. Also as *Lettres écrites de Londres sur les Anglais et autres sujets.*]

———— de l'Abbé Terray a M^r. Turgot.

[*Lettre de M. Terray, ex-contrôleur général à M. Turgot, pour servir de supplément à la Correspondance entre le Sieur Sorhouet et M. de Maupeou.* [Matthieu-François Pidansat de Mairobert?] n.p., n.d.]

Margot La Ravaudeuse. 12°. fig.

[*Margot la ravaudeuse, par M. de M***.* [Charles-Louis Fougeret de Monbron.] n.p., 1750. (Cioranescu cites a suppressed 1748 edition.)]

Matinées du Roy de Prusse. 12°.

[*Matinées (les) du roi de Prusse, écrites par lui-même.* [Baron Benoît Patono?, or comte de Schwerin?] Berlin, 1766.]

Méditations Philosophiques Sur Dieu le Monde & l'homme.

[*Méditations philosophiques sur Dieu, le monde et l'homme.* [Théodore-Louis Lau.] Königsberg, 1770.]

Mémoires Autentique de M^e La Comtesse du Barry. 1775.

[*Mémoires authentiques de Mme la comtesse du Barry par le chevalier Fr. N . . .* London, 1772.]

Le Moyen de parvenir. 12°. 1773.

[*Moyen (le) de parvenir, oeuvre contenant la raison de tout ce qui a été, est, et sera: avec démonstrations certaines et nécessaires, selon la rencontre des effets de vertu.* [François Brouart, dit Béroalde de Verville?] n.p., 1610.]

De la nature humaine par Hobbes. 8°. 1772.

[*Nature (de la) humaine, ou exposition des facultés, des actions et des passions de l'âme et de leurs causes, déduites d'après des principes qui ne sont communément ni reçus ni connus. Par Thomas Hobbes: ouvrage traduit de l'anglois.* [trans. by Paul-Henri-Dietrich Thiry, baron d'Holbach.] London, 1772. (trans. from *Humane Nature: Or the Fundamental Elements of Policie* [1650] by Thomas Hobbes.)]

Oeuvres Philosophiques de La Mettrie. 12°. 3 Vol. 1775.

[*Œuvres philosophiques de M. de La Mettrie.* Julien Offray de La Mettrie. London, 1751, and subsequent editions with varying numbers of volumes.]

———— de Jean Jacques Rousseau. 8°. 11 Vol. fig. 1775.

[*Œuvres diverses de M. J.-J. Rousseau.* 2 vols. Jean-Jacques Rousseau. Paris, 1756, and subsequent editions with varying numbers of volumes.]

Opinions des Anciens sur les Juifs par Mirabeau & Reflex: impartiales sur l'Ev:

[*Opinions des anciens sur les Juifs. Réflexions impartiales sur l'Evangile, par feu M. de Mirabaud.* [Jean-Baptiste Mirabaud?, or Paul-Henri-Dietrich Thiry, baron d'Holbach?, pub. by Jacques-André Naigeon.] London, 1769. *Réflexions* also reprinted as *Examen critique du Nouveau Testament, par M. Fréret,* 1777.]

Le Parnasse Libertin. 8°.

[*Parnasse libertin, ou recueil de poésies libres.* Amsterdam, 1769.]

Le Philosophe ignorant. fig.

[*Philosophe (le) ignorant.* [François-Marie Arouet de Voltaire.] n.p., 1766.]

Philosophie de l'histoire par l'abé Bazin. 8°.

[*Philosophie (la) de l'histoire, par feu M. l'abbé Bazin.* [François-Marie Arouet de Voltaire.] Amsterdam, 1765.]

Pièces détachées, Relatives au Clergé Séculier & Régulier. 8°. 3 Vol. 1773.

[*Pièces détachées, relatives au clergé séculier et régulier.* 3 vols. [ed. by François-Jacques-Maxmilien de Chastenet, marquis de Puységur.] Amsterdam, 1771.]

Politique naturelle ou discours sur les vray principes du gouvernement. 8°.

[*Politique (la) naturelle. Ou discours sur les vrais principes du gouvernement par un ancien magistrat.* 2 vols. [Paul-Henri-Dietrich, baron d'Holbach?.] London, 1773.]

Le Porte feuille d'un Philosophe. 8°. 6 Vol.

[*Portefeuille (le) d'un philosophe, ou mélange de pièces philosophiques, politiques, critiques, satiriques et galantes.* 6 vols. [Henri-Joseph Du Laurens.] Cologne, 1770.]

Le Portier des Chartreux. 12°. 2 Vol. fig. 1775.

[*Histoire de dom B . . . , portier des Chartreux, écrite par lui-même.* [Jacques-Charles Gervaise de Latouche? or Charles Nourry?] Rome, n.d. (c. 1745, according to Martin-Mylne-Frautschi). Also as *Le Portier des Chartreux, Histoire de Gouberdom,* and *Mémoires de Saturin.*]

Profession de Foy des Théistes.

[*Profession (la) de foi des théistes, par le comte Da. . . au R. D. Traduit de l'allemand.* [François-Marie Arouet de Voltaire.] n.p., n.d. (1768, according to Bengesco).]

La Pucelle d'Orléans en 18 Chantes. 24.

——— en 21 Chantes. 8°.

[*Pucelle (la) d'Orléans, poème héroï-comique.* François-Marie Arouet de Voltaire. Louvain, 1755.]

Questions sur l'Encyclopédie. 8°. 9 Vol.

[*Questions sur l'Encyclopédie par des amateurs.* 9 vols. [François-Marie Arouet de Voltaire.] n.p., 1770–72.]

Receuil de Comedies & Chansons Gailliardes.

[*Recueil de comédies et de quelques chansons gaillardes. Imprimé pour ce monde.* n.p., 1775.]

Relation de la mort du Chevallier de La Barre.

[*Relation de la mort du chevalier de La Barre, par M. Cass***, avocat au Conseil du Roi, à M. le marquis de Beccaria, écrite en 1766.* [François-Marie Arouet de Voltaire.] n.p., 1766.]

Romans & Contes Philosophiques de Voltaire.

[*Romans et contes philosophiques par M. de Voltaire.* 2 vols. [François-Marie Arouet de Voltaire.] London, 1775 (actually 1772, according to Bengesco)]

Systême de la nature. 8°. 2 Vol. 1775 trés belle Ed.

[*Système de la nature, ou des lois du monde physique et du monde moral, par M. Mirabaud.* 2 vols. [Paul-Henri-Dietrich Thiry, baron d'Holbach? and/or Denis Diderot?] London, 1770.]

Systême Social. 8°. 3 Vol. 1775.

[*Système social. Ou principes naturels de la morale et de la politique, avec un examen de l'influence du gouvernement sur les moeurs.* 3 vols. [Paul-Henri-Dietrich Thiry, baron d'Holbach.] London, 1773.]

Tableau Philosop. du genre humain, depuis l'origine du monde jusqu'à Constantin. 8°.

[*Tableau philosophique du genre humain depuis l'origine du monde jusqu'à Constantin. Traduit de l'anglois.* [Charles Borde.] 3 vols. London, 1767.]

Tableau des Saintes. 8°. 2 Vol.

[*Tableau des saints, ou examen de l'esprit, de la conduite, des maximes et du mérite des personnages que le christianisme révère et propose pour modèles.* 2 vols. [Paul-Henri-Dietrich Thiry, baron d'Holbach.] London, 1770.]

Le Taureau Blanc p M. de Voltaire. 8°.

[*Taureau (le) blanc. Traduit du syriaque par Mamaki.* (also as . . . *par Dom Calmet.*) [François-Marie Arouet de Voltaire.] "Memphis," 1774.]

Théologie Portative. 8°.

[*Théologie portative ou dictionnaire abrégé de la religion chrétienne. Par M. l'abbé Bernier, licencié en théologie.* [Paul-Henri-Dietrich Thiry, baron d'Holbach.] London, 1768.]

De La Tolérance dans la Religion. 8°.

[*Tolérance (de la) dans la religion ou de la liberté de conscience. Par Crellius. L'intolérance convaincue de crime et de folie. Ouvrage tra-*

duit de l'anglais. [Paul-Henri-Dietrich Thiry, baron d'Holbach.] London, 1769.]

Traitté sur la Tolérance par Voltaire.

[*Traité sur la tolérance.* [François-Marie Arouet de Voltaire.] n.p., 1763.]

——— des trois Imposteurs.

Traité des trois imposteurs. [Vroes?] Yverdon, 1768. Also as *La Vie et l'esprit de M. Benoît Spinoza,* rev. by Jean Amyon and Jean Rousset.]

Venus dans le Cloître, ou la religieuse en Chemise. fig.

[*Vénus dans le cloître, ou la religieuse en chemise.* [Jean Barrin.] Cologne, 1683 (c. 1682, according to Gay). Also as *Les Délices du cloître ou la religieuse éclairée, La Religieuse en chemise ou la nonne éclairée,* and *La Nonne éclairée ou les délices du cloître.*]

Voyage & aventures de Jaques Macé 2 Vol.

[*Voyages et aventure de Jacques Massé.* [Simon Tyssot de Patot.] Bordeaux, 1710.]

Le Vray Sens du Systême de la nature. 8°.

[*Vrai (le) Sens du Système de la nature, ouvrage posthume de M. Helvétius.* [Claude-Adrien Helvétius?, or Paul-Henri-Dietrich Thiry, baron d'Holbach?] London, 1774.]

Singularités de la nature.

[*Singularités (les) de la nature, par un académicien de Londres, de Bologne, de Pétersbourg, de Berlin, etc.* [François-Marie Arouet de Voltaire.] Basel, 1768.]

Dictionnaire Philosophique. 12°. 2 Vol.

[*Dictionnaire philosophique portatif.* [François-Marie Arouet de Voltaire.] London 1764. Also as *La Raison par alphabet.*]

Evangile de la raison.

[*Evangile (l') de la raison. Ouvrage posthume de M. D. M. . . .Y.* [ed. by François-Marie Arouet de Voltaire.] n.p., n.d. (1764, according to Cioranescu and Bengesco).]

Examen critique de Freret.

[*Examen critique des apologistes de la religion chrétienne, par M. Fréret.* [Jean Lévesque de Burigny?] n.p., 1766.]

L'Epitre aux Romains.

[*Epître (l') aux Romains, par le comte Passeran. Traduit de l'italien.* [François-Marie Arouet de Voltaire.] n.p., n.d. (1768, according to Cioranescu and Bengesco).]

Le Cathécumêne.

[*Catéchumène (le), traduit du chinois.* [Charles Borde.] Amsterdam, 1768. Also as *L'Américain sensé par hazard en Europe, et fait chrétien par complaisance.*]

Le Militaire Philosophe.

[*Militaire (le) philosophe ou difficultés sur la religion proposées au R. P. Malebranche, prêtre de l'Oratoire. Par un ancien officier.* [Paul-Henri-Dietrich Thiry, baron d'Holbach, and Jacques-André Naigeon.] London, 1768.]

Le Compère Matthieux.

[*Compère (le) Matthieu, ou les bigarrures de l'esprit humain.* 3 vols. [Henri-Joseph Du Laurens.] London, 1766.]

Les Choses utiles & agreables.

[*Choses (les) utiles et agréables.* 3 vols. [François-Marie Arouet de Voltaire.] Berlin, 1769–70.]

Les Questions de Zapata.

[*Questions (les) de Zapata, traduites par le sieur Tamponet, docteur de Sorbonne.* [François-Marie Arouet de Voltaire.] Leipzig, 1766.]

Les Droits des hommes & leurs usurpations.

[*Droits (les) des hommes et les usurpations des autres. Traduit de l'italien.* [François-Marie Arouet de Voltaire.] Amsterdam, 1768.]

Le Collimaçons

[*Colimaçons (les) du Révérend Père L'Escarbotier, par la grâce de Dieu capucin indigne, prédicateur ordinaire et cuisinier du grand couvent de la ville de Clermont en Auvergne au Révérend Père Elie, carme chaussé, docteur en théologie.* [François-Marie Arouet de Voltaire.] n.p., 1768.]

Les trois Epitres.

[*Trois (les) Epîtres.* [François-Marie Arouet de Voltaire.] n.p., n.d. (Contains *L'Epître à Boileau* (1769), *L'Epître à l'auteur du nouveau livre des trois imposteurs* (1769), *L'Epître à Saint-Lambert* (1769).)]

Poesies gaillardes. 2 Vol.

[*Poésies (les) gaillardes, galantes et amoureuses de ce temps.* 2 vols. [ed. by Guillaume Colletet?.] n.p., n.d. (c. 1650, according to Gay).]

Saül, Tragédie.

[*Saül, tragédie tirée de l'Ecriture Sainte par M. de V. . .* [François-Marie Arouet de Voltaire.] n.p., 1755 (actually 1763, according to Bengesco).]

Thérèse Philosophe.

[*Thérèse philosophe, ou mémoires pour servir à l'histoire du P. Dirrag et de Mlle Eradice.* 2 vols. [X. d'Arles de Montigny? or Jean-Baptiste de Boyer, marquis d'Argens?] n.p., n.d. (1748, according to Martin-Mylne-Frautschi).]

Academie des Dames ou l'Aloysia. n: Ed: revue & augm: 8° 2 Vol. fig.

[*Académie (l') des dames, ou les entretiens galants d'Aloysia.* 2 vols. trans. by Nicolas Chorier, n.p., 1730. (trans. from *Joanis Meursii elegantiae latini sermonis* by Nicolas Chorier, 1680.) Also as *Le Meursius français ou l'Académie.* . .]

Bijoux indiscrets par Diderot. 8° fig.

[*Bijoux (les) indiscrets.* 2 vols. [Denis Diderot.] "Monomotapa," 1748.]

Le Bonheur Poëme par Helvétius.

[*Bonheur (le), poème, en six chants. Avec des fragments de quelques épîtres, ouvrages posthumes de M. Helvétius.* Claude-Adrien Helvétius. London, 1772.]

Fragmens sur l'Inde par Voltaire. 8°.

[*Fragments sur l'Inde et sur le général Lalli.* [François-Marie Arouet de Voltaire.] n.p., 1773.] Also as *Fragments sur quelques révolutions de l'Inde et sur la mort du comte de Lally.*]

Le Jeune Philosophe, ou Lettres de Florival a Sophie. 12°.

[*Jeune (le) philosophe, ou lettres amoureuses de Florival et de Sophie.* n.p., 1774.]

Les Lauriers Ecclésiastiques. 12°.

[*Lauriers (les) ecclésiastiques, ou campagnes de l'abbé de T. . .* [Charles-Jacques-Louise-Auguste Rochette de La Morlière.] "Luxuropolis," 1748. First edition as *Les Campagnes de l'abbé T****, 1747.)]

La tourière des Carmelites. 8°.

[*Histoire galante de la tourière des Carmélites. Ouvrage fait pour servir de pendant au Portier des Chartreux.* [Anne-Gabriel Meusnier de Querlon.] Paris, 1770 (actually 1743, according to Martin-Mylne-Frautschi). Also as *La Tourière des Carmélites.*]

Les Guêbres ou la Tolérance tragédie.

[*Guèbres (les), ou la tolérance, tragédie par M. D*** M***.* [François-Marie Arouet de Voltaire.] n.p., 1769. At least 2 other editions by 1777.]

L'humanité. Poeme nouveau en 6 Chantes.

[*Humanité (l'), poème en six chants.* [B. Voiron.] n.p., n.d.]

République des Incrédules. 12°. 5 Vol.

[Possibly *La République des philosophes, ou histoire des Ajaciens, ouvrage posthume de M. de Fontenelle.* Bernard Le Bouvier de Fontenelle. Geneva, 1968.]

Histoire des Diables modernes. 12°.

[*Histoire des diables modernes par M. A***.* [Adolphus Joy.] London, 1763. Also as . . . *par Mr. Adolphus, Juif anglais, docteur en médicine, troisième édition.*]

Dissertation sur l'abaye de S^r. Claude, & pièces p les main mortables.

[*Dissertation sur l'établissement de l'abbaye de St. Claude, ses chroniques, ses légendes, ses chartes, ses usurpations, et sur les droits des habitants de cette terre.* [Charles-Gabriel-Frédéric Christin.] Neuchâtel, 1772.]

Le Theïsme.

[*Théisme (le), essai philosophique.* 2 vols. [Charles Elie, marquis de Ferrières.] London, 1773.]

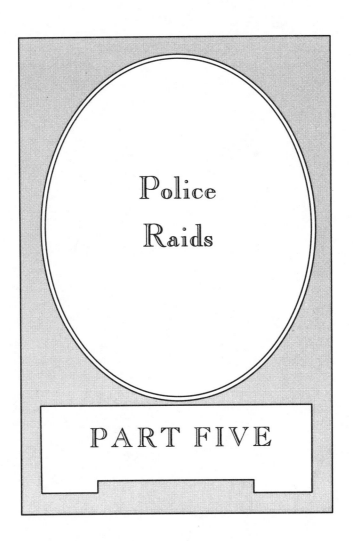

Police
Raids

PART FIVE

SPECIAL AGENTS OF THE POLICE *(inspecteurs de la librairie)* were charged with repressing the illegal book trade in Paris and the provinces. They often raided bookstores; and when they confiscated large numbers of forbidden works, they drew up inventories. Many of these inventories offer little help in the attempt to identify the illegal literature that actually circulated in pre-revolutionary France, because they contain an admixture of legal works or they are too sloppy to be trustworthy. But others provide a revealing glimpse of the literature that was sold under the counter. I have compiled titles from nine of them, and I have also drawn on an inventory of the *pilon* (pulping room) of the Bastille, where confiscated books were often sent. The material comes from the Bibliothèque de l'Arsenal in Paris, ms. 10305. It includes 300 titles from the following inventories of raids made between 1773 and 1783.

Dealer or Source	Date	Place	Number of Titles
Stockdorf	1773	Strasbourg and Paris	112
Pilon	1774(?)	Undetermined	110
Manoury	1775	Caen	18
Jouy, et al.	1777	Paris	21
Moureau	1777	Paris	14
Prot	1777	Paris and Saint-Germain-en-Laye	169

Dealer or Source	Date	Place	Number of Titles
Desauges	1780	Paris	30
Unidentified	1782	Lyon	7
Unidentified	1783	Paris	60
Unidentified	1783	Versailles	17

The following lists show which books appear most often in the ten sources concerning confiscations and raids on bookstores.

I. Six instances:

Academie (l') des dames. . . (Chorier)
  [Pilon, Manoury, Moureau, Prot, Paris, Versailles]
Arrétin (l'). (Du Laurens)
  [Stockdorf, Pilon, Moureau, Prot, Paris, Versailles]
Balai (le), poème héroï-comique en XVIII chants. (Du Laurens)
  [Stockdorf, Pilon, Prot, Desauges, Paris, Versailles]
Compère (le) Mathieu. . . (Du Laurens)
  [Stockdorf, Pilon, Manoury, Prot, Desauges, Versailles]
Thérèse philosophe. . . (d'Arles de Montigny? or d'Argens?)
  [Stockdorf, Pilon, Manoury, Prot, Paris, Versailles]

II. Five instances:

Espion (l') chinois. . . (Goudar)
  [Pilon, Moureau, Prot, Desauges, Paris]
Histoire de dom B. . . (Latouche? or Nourry?)
  [Stockdorf, Pilon, Manoury, Prot, Paris]
Histoire du parlement de Paris. . . (Voltaire)
  [Stockdorf, Moureau, Prot, Desauges, Paris]
Histoire de Mademoiselle Brion. . .
  [Stockdorf, Manoury, Prot, Lyon, Paris]
Pucelle (la) d'Orléans. . . (Voltaire)
  [Stockdorf, Moureau, Prot, Paris, Versailles]
Recherches philosophiques sur les Américains. . . (de Pauw)
  [Stockdorf, Pilon, Jouy, et al., Prot, Desauges]

III. Four instances:

An (l') deux mille quatre cent quarante... (Mercier)
[Stockdorf, Moureau, Prot, Paris]
Chandelle (la) d'Arras... (Du Laurens)
[Prot, Desauges, Paris, Versailles]
Christianisme (le) dévoilé... (d'Holbach)
[Pilon, Prot, Desauges, Paris]
Correspondance secrète et familière de M. de Maupeou... (Pidan-
sat de Mairobert)
[Stockdorf, Pilon, Moureau, Desauges]
David, ou l'histoire de l'homme selon le coeur de Dieu... (trans.
by d'Holbach from Annet?)
[Stockdorf, Pilon, Prot, Desauges]
Fille (la) de joie... (trans. by Lambert? or Fougeret de Mon-
bron?)
[Moureau, Prot, Lyon, Paris]
Gazetier (le) cuirassé... (Théveneau de Morande)
[Stockdorf, Pilon, Prot, Versailles]
Histoire philosophique et politique... (Raynal)
[Stockdorf, Pilon, Jouy, et al., Prot]
Homme (de l')... (Helvétius)
[Pilon, Jouy, et al., Prot, Desauges]
Imirce, ou la fille de la nature. (Du Laurens)
[Stockdorf, Pilon, Prot, Paris]
Lettre philosophique... Anon.
[Stockdorf, Manoury, Prot, Paris]
Nouveaux Mélanges philosophiques... (Voltaire)
[Stockdorf, Pilon, Prot, Paris]
Recherches philosophiques sur les Egyptiens... (de Pauw)
[Pilon, Jouy, et al., Prot, Desauges]
Système social... (d'Holbach)
[Stockdorf, Pilon, Prot, Desauges]
Vie de Madame la comtesse du Barry... Anon.
[Manoury, Pilon, Prot, Lyon]

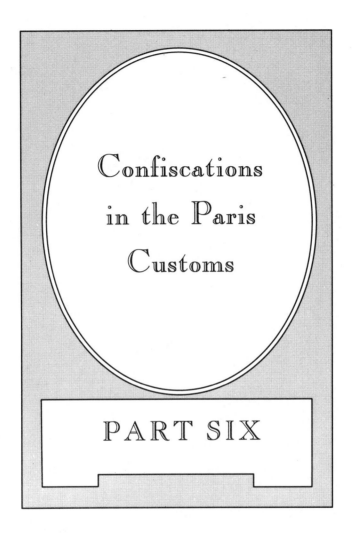

Confiscations
in the Paris
Customs

PART SIX

ALL BOOKS SHIPPED TO PARIS had to be cleared through the Parisian Customs and inspected by officers of the Parisian guild of booksellers and printers accompanied by a police agent. Suspicious works were "suspended" or stored in the guildhall pending further examination. On every Tuesday and Friday, the officials sorted through the suspended works to determine whether they were prohibited, pirated, or merely "not permitted" *(non permis)*, a category that covered a wide variety of illegal but inoffensive publications (for example, a book published legally abroad but imported without prior permission from the authorities). Prohibited works were to be confiscated and destroyed, but the others could be released or returned to their point of origin.

This sorting-out process had gone on since the seventeenth century; but it cannot be analyzed in detail until the last eighteen years of the Old Regime, because the early records do not provide much information about why books were "suspended." On January 4, 1771, the officials began to fill in printed forms, which imposed some systematic order on their record keeping, and included a column where they entered the reason for the confiscation of the books. From that date until the outbreak of the Revolution, one can identify every book that was seized as "prohibited." The prohibited books usually constituted between a quarter and a half of all the "suspended" works, although their proportion dropped drastically after 1779, and there were very few of them between

June 1786 and September 1789, when the system finally collapsed.

The registers—two handsome volumes in the Bibliothèque Nationale, ms. fr. 21933–21934—contain the titles of 280 works noted as prohibited. Remarkable as it is, however, this source has several deficiencies. The officials were inconsistent in their behavior. On some occasions they sent a book to the Bastille for pulping, and on others they released it as "not permitted" (i.e., inoffensive). They tended to be severe in the 1770s and sloppy in the 1780s. And they did not confiscate particular works often enough for one to make surmises about which books circulated most heavily. No doubt the condemnation of Raynal's *Histoire philosophique* in 1781 predisposed the officials of the guild to seize all the copies of it that came through the customs. But why should it have been confiscated forty-five times and d'Holbach's *Système de la nature* only eight? In fact, most forbidden books were seized in the customs only once or twice. The great bulk of the illegal literature was handled by professionals, who did not try to slip it through the customs. They found it safer to store the shipments in warehouses outside the city and to smuggle them into Paris in small packages hidden in coaches or their clothing. For those reasons, the customs registers provide a good indication of the forbidden literature that was sent to Paris by non-professionals, but not of the books that arrived regularly and in large quantities through the underground channels of the trade.

All of the prohibited books confiscated in the customs have been entered in the preceding bibliography. The ones confiscated most often appear in the following table:

Books Most Frequently Confiscated
in the Paris Customs
January 4, 1771, to September 22, 1789

	Number of Times Confiscated
Histoire philosophique. . . [Raynal]	45
Œuvres. Voltaire	41
Questions sur l'Encyclopédie. . . [Voltaire]	41
Nouveaux Mélanges philosophiques, historiques. . . [Voltaire]	18
Pucelle (la) d'Orléans. . . [Voltaire]	18

	Number of Times Confiscated
Emile, ou de l'éducation. Rousseau	12
Thérèse philosophe. . . [d'Arles de Montigny? or d'Argens?]	12
Analyse raisonnée de Bayle. . . [Marsy and Robinet]	11
Mémoires secrets. . . [Bauchaumont, et al.]	11
Œuvres. Rousseau	11
Recherches philosophiques sur les Américains. . . [de Pauw]	10
Tableau de Paris. [Mercier]	10
Antiquité (l') dévoilée. . . [Boulanger, ed. by d'Holbach]	9
Compère (le) Mathieu. . . [Du Laurens]	8
Système de la nature. . . [d'Holbach]	8
Bélisaire. . . Marmontel	7
Académie (l') des dames. . . [Chorier]	6
An (l') 2440. . . [Mercier]	6
Christianisme (le) dévoilé. . . [d'Holbach]	6
Histoire ecclésiastique, ancienne et moderne. . . Mosheim. [tr. Eidous]	6
Lettre philosophique. . . Anon.	6
Vie privée de Louis XV. . . [Moufle d'Angerville? or Laffrey?]	6
Colporteur (le). . . [Chevrier]	5
Contes et nouvelles en vers de M. de la Fontaine. [La Fontaine]	5
Commentaires sur les lois anglaises, par M. de Blackstone . . . (Blackstone, trans. by Gomicourt)	5
Dictionnaire philosophique portatif. [Voltaire]	5
Fille (la) de joie. . . [Cleland, trans. by Lambert? or Fougeret de Monbron?]	5
Lettres chinoises. . . [d'Argens]	5
Lettres de Mme la marquise de Pompadour. . . [Barbé-Marbois?, or Crébillon, fils?]	5
Observateur (l') anglais. . . [Pidansat de Mairobert]	5
Œuvres. Diderot	5
Recherches sur l'origine du despotisme oriental. . . [Boulanger?, ed. by d'Holbach]	5
Angola. . . [Rochette de la Morlière?]	4

	Number of Times Confiscated
Arrétin (l'). [Du Laurens]	4
Bijoux (les) indiscrets. [Diderot]	4
Bonheur (le). . . [Helvétius]	4
Candide, ou l'optimisme. . . [Voltaire]	4
Esprit (de l'). [Helvétius]	4
Gazetier cuirassé. . . [Théveneau de Morande]	4
Histoire de la tourière des Carmélites. . . (Meusnier de Querlon)	4
Mémoires justificatifs de la comtesse de Valois de la Mott. . . Anon.	4
Moyen (le) de parvenir. . . [Béroalde de Verville?]	4
Nature (de la). [Robinet]	4
Œuvres. Grécourt	4
Système social. . . [d'Holbach]	4